How to Market the Arts

How to Market the Arts

A Practical Approach for the 21st Century

ANTHONY RHINE AND JAY PENSION

OXFORD
UNIVERSITY PRESS

Oxford University Press is a department of the University of Oxford. It furthers
the University's objective of excellence in research, scholarship, and education
by publishing worldwide. Oxford is a registered trade mark of Oxford University
Press in the UK and certain other countries.

Published in the United States of America by Oxford University Press
198 Madison Avenue, New York, NY 10016, United States of America.

© Oxford University Press 2022

All rights reserved. No part of this publication may be reproduced, stored in
a retrieval system, or transmitted, in any form or by any means, without the
prior permission in writing of Oxford University Press, or as expressly permitted
by law, by license, or under terms agreed with the appropriate reproduction
rights organization. Inquiries concerning reproduction outside the scope of the
above should be sent to the Rights Department, Oxford University Press, at the
address above.

You must not circulate this work in any other form
and you must impose this same condition on any acquirer.

Library of Congress Cataloging-in-Publication Data
Names: Rhine, Anthony, author. | Pension, Jay, 1987– author.
Title: How to market the arts : a practical approach for the 21st century /
by Anthony Rhine and Jay Pension.
Description: New York : Oxford University Press, [2022] |
Includes bibliographical references and index.
Identifiers: LCCN 2022018872 (print) | LCCN 2022018873 (ebook) |
ISBN 9780197556085 (paperback) | ISBN 9780197556078 (hardback) |
ISBN 9780197556108 (epub) | ISBN 9780197556092 | ISBN 9780197556115
Subjects: LCSH: Arts—Marketing.
Classification: LCC NX634 .R485 2022 (print) | LCC NX634 (ebook) |
DDC 700.68/8—dc23/eng/20220623
LC record available at https://lccn.loc.gov/2022018872
LC ebook record available at https://lccn.loc.gov/2022018873

DOI: 10.1093/oso/9780197556078.001.0001

1 3 5 7 9 8 6 4 2

Paperback printed by Lakeside Book Company, United States of America
Hardback printed by Bridgeport National Bindery, Inc., United States of America

Contents

Preface vii

Introduction 1

PART I: MARKETING VERSUS ENGAGEMENT

1. Setting the Stage: A Shift from Traditional Marketing 7
2. Engagement 28

PART II: EDUCATION

3. Contrasting Frameworks: Promotion and Education 51
4. Promotion and the Arts 65
5. Education and the Arts 83

PART III: EXPERIENCE

6. Contrasting Frameworks: Product and Experience 109
7. Product and the Arts 125
8. Experience and the Arts 139

PART IV: ENVIRONMENT

9. Contrasting Frameworks: Place and Environment 159
10. Place and the Arts 171
11. Environment and the Arts 185

PART V: EASE OF ACCESS

12. Contrasting Frameworks: Price and Ease of Access 205

13. Price and the Arts	215
14. Ease of Access and the Arts	230
Conclusion: Piecing Everything Together	243
Notes	251
Index	265

Preface

Several years ago, a student asked this question: "If the marketing mix is so effective, why do so many nonprofit arts organizations struggle to keep their doors open?" It is a simple question, with answers so complex and convoluted that they can hardly be answered without an entire treatise on the topic. The first obvious answer was that all those nonprofit arts organizations are not following the marketing mix correctly. This is a simple answer and makes it easy to blame the arts organizations. The situation, however, is far more complex and intricate than the simple answer reveals. Many nonprofit arts organizations cannot precisely follow the basic tenets of the marketing mix because they are not designed to work with nonprofit arts organizations. It is a tricky situation that bore the thinking behind this book.

Though many books may be written in isolation, this one has not been. We have had such tremendous support from many people and are grateful to them all.

Though we originally intended to write an academic manuscript focused entirely on theory, our publisher saw the need in the marketplace of practitioners, so we revised our tone and structure and developed something that would provide nonprofit arts organizations a new approach to connecting with their communities. We would like to thank Norm Hirschy of Oxford University Press for his guidance, support, and kindness as we developed a way to communicate this new approach for nonprofit arts organizations.

Of particular note are those who helped keep the writing process going smoothly. Sam Stenecker provided detailing work for the manuscripts, helped us keep the flow moving nicely, and provided a third set of eyes when ours were growing bleary. Katelyn Woods provided some much-needed visuals, without which the engagement edge would be simply a collection of words.

We are particularly grateful to all those who provided interviews and information for the cases in the book. We felt it vitally important that we were able to demonstrate some examples of elements of the engagement edge in action. In some forms, many arts organizations are practicing it now. Whether cited by name or assigned a moniker for anonymity, those who participated in the case studies, have helped make this book work as intended.

Mary Beth Vanko has, as she has done many times, made this a book that is readable and worthwhile. She is more than an assistant and editor; she is a lover of the arts and their impact on our communities. Her passion for the arts coupled with her immense talent at making our words and concepts read appropriately, is unrivaled, and it shows in her work. We are both forever grateful for this enormous talent that she shares with us and with you.

We would also like to thank our colleagues at Florida State University: Pat Villeneuve, Antonio Cuyler, and Ann Rowson-Love, all of whom inspire us to be our best.

Jay would like to personally thank his family and Charlotte for their consistent support and encouragement both through the years and as he developed this book with Anthony. He would also like to thank the PhD Arts Administration and MFA Theatre Management programs at Florida State University.

Anthony would be remiss if he did not mention Joel Senft, who supports the process of book writing every time it is undertaken, with ease and aplomb. He is the perfect person to apply a little pressure when the writing schedule is getting slack, and just as good showing support when the schedule is tense.

To all these individuals, and the many, many others who have contributed to the process of getting this book published, we are grateful.

— Anthony and Jay

Introduction

This book stems from a collection of ideas we saw with increasing frequency in academic literature, international conferences, and trade publications. At the center was the idea of engagement. We also saw a renewed interest in the idea of experience. Relative, academic discourse included ideas connected to the concept of environment. These concepts all seemed to appear consistently, sometimes in conjunction with each other, and at other times, as new approaches to their function. There was no doubt that in the academic world of arts administration and cultural management, researchers in every niche, from marketing to social justice to fundraising to education, kept responding to the same themes. We felt that these disparate theories had to be cohesively told and placed against McCarthy's marketing mix developed in the 1950s.

When Ben Walmsley wrote that it was time for someone to consider an alternative for the Ps in marketing (product, price, place, and promotion), it was as if he had read our thoughts. We had been exploring this idea that the four Ps of the marketing mix did not fit the nonprofit arts well, if at all. We had no claim, however, on any academic approach that developed and plotted a new theory to replace marketing. We only knew that engagement, environment, and experience were all involved, and they all started with E.

So, we fretted, and still do, to some extent, that it will be argued that we have put forth an idea that allows the nonprofit arts to approach marketing differently for the world we live in, simply through semantic changes in the four Ps that make up the marketing mix.

This book is titled *How to Market the Arts: A Practical Approach for the 21st Century* because we have chosen to make it clear to the practitioner that this is not a replacement for marketing, but an **entirely different way to approach what marketing can mean by focusing on the construct centered in engagement.** In some ways, it might be as simple as saying that engagement is the new marketing, but we have intentionally chosen not to abandon or even suggest tinkering with the four Ps. What readers will find here is an approach to marketing that sits alongside the marketing mix (and its four Ps). In this book, the nonprofit arts will meet the engagement edge (and its four Es). The

How to Market the Arts. Anthony Rhine and Jay Pension, Oxford University Press. © Oxford University Press 2022.
DOI: 10.1093/oso/9780197556078.003.0001

engagement edge is a sibling of the marketing mix, and both are the children of marketing. The engagement edge adds a second strain of marketing that can be used to create engagement with more members of the community and transform the approach of nonprofit arts organizations.

In part I, we lay out the basic academic argument for how and why engagement is the appropriate construct for the nonprofit arts in the 21st century. **This does not mean abandoning the marketing mix but rather accepting its limitations in nonprofit arts and moving toward a model that is more sustainable and successful.**

In order to lay the groundwork for understanding the engagement edge, we begin with chapter 1. Bear with us, as it is a bit drier than the rest of the book. In it we discuss marketing, how and why we got to where we are, and where we see holes in that process.

In chapter 2 we explore the concept of engagement, the all-encompassing term for so many things, yet one that seems to defy a mutually acceptable definition. We lay the groundwork for what engagement is as we define it, and how we see it operate in the arts.

We then move into a more practical approach to looking at the engagement edge. Parts II–V of this book look at each of one of four sister constructs. Part II explores the notions of promotion and education. Part III takes a similar tack with the concepts of product and experience. In part IV, we look into the ideas of place and environment, and part V is an exploration of the notions of price and ease of access.

In each of these four parts of the book, three chapters are laid out in a similar fashion. In the first, common understandings and frameworks are explored for each of the Ps and Es, respectively. In the second chapter, titled for its marketing mix P, we look specifically at why that particular concept fails to function as intended for the nonprofit arts and deconstruct the function. In the third chapter, we explain the E and explore how it can be implemented to support an approach to engagement.

In the conclusion, we present how the four Es of the engagement edge may work together to vastly increase participation and attendance in the nonprofit arts.

Throughout the book are case study examples of situations where we can see the concepts at play. In cases related to the concepts of the marketing mix—product, price, place, and promotion—we have intentionally placed real situations into fictionalized contexts. We have done so because in these instances, we use the cases to demonstrate how the Ps in the marketing mix have failed, and we have chosen not to expose any real people or organizations. The cases are designed to allow you to see concepts in action and to use as a launching place for your own efforts in applying the engagement edge.

To use this book appropriately, an arts organization cannot simply hand the concepts to one marketing director and say, "do this." The theories and ideas presented here are meant to seep into the core of an arts organization because at their heart, these theories are based on the foundational principle that everyone involved in the goal of getting art offerings to the audience work collaboratively, and no one person is more or less important in that objective. The maker of the art is no more or less a part of the process of engagement than is the usher, and the result is not a creation of great art by artists but the creation of great art by a community of artists, audience members, and administrators. It allows for a new way of thinking about what marketing is and what it means. **Marketing does not have to be crass commercialism, but in fact, it is the means for connecting us to those who make art come alive: the audience.** This idea permeates this book, and we hope, as you drift through its pages, you will find yourself seeing arts marketing differently and with an eye for new tactics you can use to truly engage with your community.

PART I
MARKETING VERSUS ENGAGEMENT

In order to understand how the proposed engagement edge works, and why it works the way it does, one must begin with an understanding of the academic approaches that have brought us to the present day. The historic underpinnings of marketing, the development of the nonprofit arts, and their relationship are where we see the foundations of the engagement edge, and consequently, we begin there.

Chapter 1 focuses on the development of different marketing mix concepts and how they have never aligned appropriately with nonprofit arts organizations. The chapter starts with a discussion of the nonprofit arts, how they came into existence as we know them today, and how the challenges of our market economy affect them. The discussion then focuses on marketing concepts as they have developed from the industrial revolution to the present day and considers why certain adjustments became the various components of McCarthy's marketing mix. The chapter then moves toward an understanding of why the traditional and commercially minded marketing mix, which is the core of business marketing practices, in no way aligns with the work of the nonprofit arts.

Chapter 2 defines what engagement is for the arts. It follows the scholarly usage of the term as a means for interaction between organizations and audiences of the arts. The discussion begins by exploring the broad usage of the term in both perspective and concept, the latter specifically tied to engagement as a means for market connections. The exploration includes historical understandings, including psychological effects of engagement as well as aesthetic applications of engagement. The chapter uses these historical understandings to underpin the notion of arts as civic engagement and audience development. The chapter concludes with a concise argument as to

Marketing Mix
A for-profit framework

Engagement
A nonprofit arts framework

Promotion
Persuasive elements to convince consumers to purchase a product.

Education
Engages community members to make discoveries and determine for themselves what experiences they would like to participate in.

Product
Physical objects or services designed to sell in order to earn profits for a business.

Experience
What occurs inside of the community member as they interact with and arts organization, art, and the associated happenings.

Place
The distribution channels that bring a product from to final delivery to a consumer.

Environment
The aesthetics of the locations where community members interact with and arts organization, art and the associated happenings.

Price
Strategies designed to maximize profits to a corporation through the sale of products.

Ease of Access
The reduction or elimination of barriers to entry. It eases access to experiences for community members.

Figure PI.1 Visualizing the components of marketing next to the components of engagement.

how these scholarly approaches allow for a reshaping of the traditional marketing mix into the engagement edge.

In the opening of each part, we strive to introduce you to the chapters in that part, and then to present a case that demonstrates the theories and ideas embedded within the chapters. In this first part, however, the theories and foundational ideas do not and should not link nicely together into a single case. It behooves us, however, to introduce both the four Ps of the marketing mix formally, and to do so alongside the four Es of the engagement edge (figure PI.1). The four Ps constitute the main function of marketing, and are the items a marketing manager must consider and balance appropriately to maximize profit. The four Es, cousins to the four Ps, each likewise constitute what we see as the four main functions of engagement.

1
Setting the Stage
A Shift from Traditional Marketing

Ben Walmsley, a professor of cultural engagement at the University of Leeds, recently wrote,

> A paradigm shift in arts marketing has occurred over the past two decades, from an overriding focus on neoliberal processes of consumption towards a relational, humanistic approach, which aims to enrich audiences and interrogate the wider value and impact of their arts experiences. The logical conclusion to be derived from this paradigmatic shift is that arts marketing is increasingly becoming an outmoded misnomer. This suggests the need for a fundamental reassessment of the traditional arts marketing concept.[1]

Much has been said about the notion of engagement in the arts, including civic engagement,[2] economic engagement,[3] health and well-being engagement,[4] audience talk engagement,[5] and community engagement as a replacement for audience development.[6] These are just some of the hundreds of ways scholars have advocated for engagement in the arts.

The study of engagement is not unique to the arts. Researchers have conducted countless studies on the concept of engagement as the internet and its globalization of commerce and social life has burgeoned. These changes have seemingly affected every aspect of human life in the modernized world. Studies examining the impact of human-to-human engagement suggest that the internet does not impact the quality of engagement we have with one another. In fact, some evidence exists to support the notion that we are engaging more as our technological world expands.[7] Engagement is changing as our access to others morphs with technology and as the clarity of the definition of "engagement" begins to blur. Though these studies rarely include the arts, they strengthen the foundation upon which we have begun to understand the long-term impact of the arts on society and how we can make the connections between the two better.

The arts have been around since the beginning of recorded history, and in fact, are a way history has been recorded, starting with cave drawings detailing the activities and lives of our ancestors. Religious ceremonies that attempted to explain the unexplainable became a means for communicating to the masses and made way for the modern arts as we know them today. Artists have always used their mediums to express social policy. Consider Shakespeare and his frequent writings that questioned the status of a monarchy in society. The arts have traditionally not only entertained but also shared vital information and shaped social attitudes. This tradition endures today as the arts have continued to advance.

That advancement has been largely assisted by governmental interventions that have eased burdens often faced by for-profit forms of business. In the United States, the taxation code was modified in 1969, allowing nonprofits to operate for the benefit of society, both untaxed and with the untaxed donations of citizens partial to their cause. The vast majority of arts administrators now in the field were not working during this this fundamental shift. Societies in the United States and throughout the world have recognized that the traditional commercial model of operation was unsustainable for service organizations. These organizations, however, have continued operating under the paradigms of commercial functions developed, proposed, and tested to understand how for-profit business works and how its functions can be improved. The 1969 incorporation of the 501(c)3 designation in the United States Internal Revenue Service code was an essential moment for defining these types of service organizations as unique. **Little has been done to consider that the function of business, the marketing function that includes product development, is also unique for social services and perhaps all nonprofit organizations.** The arts, in particular, represent a different beast. Though the nonprofit arts have a mechanism for generating earned income, unlike many of their counterparts in social aid such as the American Red Cross, churches, and the American Heart Association, they have struggled to find a marketing paradigm suited to their unique proposition.

Lessons learned through practice and academics have been largely based in paradigms developed for commercially driven organizations. Though some of those paradigms have served arts organizations fairly well, the rise of a global economy, social connectedness, and changes in how we consume information have begun to hinder rather than guide arts organizations.[8]

Though the 1969 update to the 501(c)3 designation may seem a distant memory, fifty years is a brief moment when we consider the history of business in the world. It, therefore, seems appropriate now to reexamine the way we think about connecting nonprofit arts organizations with communities.

Arts Engagement Today

In 2012, Doug Borwick introduced the world to his view that engagement's function in the arts was not merely about participation but was meant to capitalize on the communal nature of the arts as a means for strengthening communities. In short, Borwick suggested that both the community and the arts organization would receive something of value if they were more closely engaged.[9] The root of the argument may have been that the access desired by 21st-century, community-based arts is rooted in the notion of engagement. Though the conceptual framework around arts engagement and its psychological value to the user has only begun,[10] it is along this precipice that the engagement edge begins to appear.

Arts Marketing from an Academic Perspective

Ben Walmsley, a professor of cultural engagement at the University of Leeds, has investigated the idea of arts marketing as a unique concept, distinct from traditional commercial marketing. Within this concept, he suggested that the "product" produced by artists and arts organizations is actually an "experience" rather than a product or service to be consumed.[11] This view is rooted in Dewey's *Art as Experience*, which took a holistic approach to the idea that an artistic aesthetic exists not because the art itself exists, but when and because it is appreciated as art.[12]

Walmsley went further to propose that a paradigm shift is occurring in the field of arts marketing. This change may be because we have begun to focus both conceptually and practically on engagement as a vital part of integrating the arts into society. Walmsley noted that in this period of enrichment, arts organizations are fundamentally shifting from traditional marketing concepts to a model that more accurately represents how the arts intersect with society.[13]

The paradigm Walmsley proposed goes even further in suggesting that each marketing mix component can stand up to scrutiny that may very well open a new chapter in arts marketing. Specifically, he mused that in addition to the artistic experience being part of the mix, so too are exchange, environment, and engagement, with the latter representing the concept of promotion in McCarthy's marketing mix.

The research model seems to support common sense. A traditional product is designed and sold to satisfy a consumer need. Most commerce is organized around a marketing proposition that considers demand-side inputs. As Francois Colbert noted, the arts are focused on a supply-side approach, where the artists and their messages are developed and then pushed onto the marketplace.[14]

Colbert has for years demonstrated that arts marketing has some conceptual distinctions from traditional marketing in his supply-side discussions.[15] Even as the arts explore concepts of co-creation, audience participation, interactivity, place-based art, and more, marketing concepts traditionally applied to the arts are finding less validity, perhaps as consumer demand makes its way slowly into the art itself.

In considering the shifting paradigms, changing approaches, and fast-paced scholarly explorations of arts marketing related to the concept of engagement, one may see a vast list of concepts that seem to have little resemblance to one another. The marketing mix, the arts as value-consideration for the consumer, and the changing ways we as humans interact have all contributed to a new approach to examining, disseminating, and incorporating the arts into our society. However, just like the traditional marketing mix, this process that is the primary function of arts management is not simply an instruction to be followed. Rather it is a cutting-edge approach where four conceptual frames meet that require different levels of input for each frame, based upon the individual needs and characteristics of the art, the community, the artists, the organization, and the consumer. This is the engagement edge. Unlike Walmsley's proposal that the arts must shift their intellectual discourse from the concept of "promotion" to the more advanced concept of "engagement," the edge considers marketing from a much larger perspective. This approach suggests that Walmsley's meta-analysis of the prevailing literature that guides his thinking regarding a paradigmatic shift from arts marketing to arts engagement is completely accurate. Though arts managers may need to consider the complex bundle of attributes of value they sell to consumers as indeed an experience, we expand further on his notion that the original hegemonic concept of promotion requires a shift to the academically popular concept of arts engagement. Instead, as Jerome McCarthy built upon Neil Borden's marketing mix, we see ourselves building upon Walmsley's vital discoveries. Although our research has occurred simultaneously with Walmsley's, our conclusions bear out his thinking entirely, though perhaps not his findings. We do not believe that engagement is a process in the arts by which we promote the experience. Instead, we find that engagement is the entirety of marketing the arts. The four components McCarthy developed for his marketing mix have a more suitable architecture for nonprofits along the engagement edge.

Applying the Marketing Mix to the Arts

For many years, researchers sought ways to define and improve the functions that connected a business with its consumers. At each successive approach to marketing, the process through which organizations made this connection, arts organizations and researchers have attempted to apply the prevailing theories to the arts. In 1997, for example, marketing expert Philip J. Kotler and his graduate student Joanne Scheff published *Standing Room Only*, a tome that attempted to translate the prevailing marketing paradigm at the time into an acceptable and functional version that was sustainable for the nonprofit arts.[16] Its success and successful implementation seemed strikingly important, but its popularity was short-lived, as the lessons learned seemed still to be ill-suited for smaller, socially impactful, charitable arts organizations.

Nevertheless, for decades, nonprofit arts administrators have worked to apply the marketing mix to their approach for connecting their social benefit to their communities. What exactly were they trying to apply, and where does it come from?

Neil Borden

In 1964, Neil Borden published *The Concept of the Marketing Mix*,[17] which described how he evaluated, detailed, and explained the market forces that affect a business. It was a summary of work Borden had done earlier in his career.[18] His insightful paradigm consolidated the myriad forces into twelve succinct areas management must consider to satisfy market wants and needs properly. He listed the following twelve areas:

1. Product/planning
2. Pricing
3. Branding
4. Channels of Distribution
5. Personal Selling
6. Advertising
7. Promotions
8. Packaging
9. Displays
10. Servicing
11. Physical Handling
12. Fact-Finding and Analysis.[19]

The approach was revolutionary for both its scientific basis and its simplicity. Borden equated the process for the manager as one akin to that of a chef in a kitchen. To create the most successful recipe, the chef must know exactly how much of each ingredient must be added to the mix to ensure optimal success. For the corporate manager, the twelve factors established by Borden were those ingredients. Based on what the organization was trying to create, they may shift the amount of each ingredient. If there is more flour, there must inherently be more yeast and salt. Too much liquid might cause failure, yet not enough would end in a similar result. Borden built his paradigm on studies of the cost of food ingredients as a foundation for marketing food products, so it is no wonder that he opens his argument by saying, "Marketing is still an art, and the marketing manager, as head chef, must creatively marshal all his marketing activities to advance the short and long-term interests of his firm."[20]

Modifying Borden

Borden made way for the modification of his theories, suggesting that his twelve factors might be altered to contain more or fewer factors, depending on circumstance and how they are bundled together. His bundling of attributes into these twelve factors was only his way of defining the marketing mix for his students. Borden felt it essential that students understand that any decision regarding one factor would inherently have a bearing on the other factors. Though his goal was to provide a scientific approach for making a connection between organization and consumer, he could not reduce the process to sheer numbers, leaving its supposition open for future nuance and more detailed investigation. That opening is precisely from where the engagement edge comes forth. We explore this new paradigm for the arts and other service industries by harkening back to Borden's words: "Marketing and the building of marketing mixes will largely lie in the realm of art." Though Borden was suggesting that marketing would, for the foreseeable future, remain only tangentially associated with scientific approaches, his words belie the reality of the world in the 21st century. Marketing is the realm of artists. Instead, many scholars have tried to apply it to the nonprofit arts as if the marketing mix, designed for profit, was provided through the guidance of scientists.

Function versus Management

Before Borden, marketing experts worked with two models of marketing that seemed to prevail side-by-side through the 1950s.[21] The first and longer-held approach to marketing consisted of the value-added approach, which considered that collecting inputs through a supply chain and distribution channel added value to the product through employees and intermediaries.[22] The focus on product and value-added had complications as it limited the ability of management to solve problems through the distribution channels, so researchers began exploring models that were less based on function and more on management.[23]

Managerial Approach

In 1960, Jerome McCarthy, who is recognized as one of the founders of current marketing techniques, published *Basic Marketing: A Managerial Approach*.[24] It became a staple among marketing textbooks for redefining the marketing theory and models established years earlier.[25] McCarthy had studied marketing and was particularly interested in mathematical models and how they could describe and influence marketing.[26]

In his approach, McCarthy took the framework of the marketing mix, developed by Neil Borden some years before, and structured it around the four marketing management functions of product, price, place (distribution), and promotion.[27] McCarthy expanded on the managerial function of each of the four Ps and included practical usage material for the reader. Instead of focusing on increasing value, the mix provided the manager with a systematic approach for solving problems and adjusting each of the four Ps in the manner most appropriate for the product and marketplace. This shift was a major improvement to existing marketing paradigms, as it took a strategic approach and began to incorporate psychology and sociology into marketing as a means for interpreting consumer behavior, including issues related to social status, class, rank, and other psychographic and demographic markers.[28] The idea followed the notion that researchers, to understand and better predict their world, should use quantitative research. McCarthy incorporated this scientific approach into his methodology.[29] His theory resonated in both the marketplace and in academia.[30]

Neil Borden had introduced the marketing mix, but his twelve-function design was complex and remained mired in the notion of product-centric value as the driving concern in marketing.[31] McCarthy provided a tool for management to determine target market interest, and then developed tactics for the four Ps (price, product, place, and promotion) to maximize marketing efficiency and effectiveness. The model itself fits noticeably well with consumer products, and though managers sometimes struggle with applications to service or high-end goods, the model has the distinct advantage of being somewhat adaptable.[32] It is in this window that the arts exist, as they do not match the consumer good for which McCarthy's four Ps serves so exceedingly well.

Adapting for the Arts Manager

Though some components of the four Ps may fit the arts (and other services) with modest adaptation, other components become somewhat insignificant and must be completely reinvented by the marketing manager to incorporate the model successfully. Other models have also been introduced to assist service organizations, government organizations, and others, adapting the four Ps model to their specific environment. No such model, however, currently exists that can assist arts organizations in their marketing approach. The engagement edge maintains the simplicity of the McCarthy model, has its foundations in consumer-centric marketing, and takes a managerial approach to problem-solving.

Ian Fillis

Researcher Ian Fillis at Liverpool John Moores University, who is one of the world's leading experts in issues related to marketing the arts, has explored that the notion of art is one that can only be accepted within the context of the artistic creation and aesthetic value of the art. It is created based upon the values of the creator (the first person in the product development cycle). In their book *Creative Marketing: An Extended Metaphor for Marketing in a New Age*, Fillis and Ruth Renstcheler argue that the creative marketing approach used by the arts is more freeing than the typically restrictive and formulaic processes that exist. They further find that creative marketing is a much more user-friendly way to look at marketing for small and medium-sized businesses. Though we do not suggest that the engagement edge will work beyond the boundaries of the nonprofit arts, there is certainly an opportunity to expand it to do so, and, in comparison with Fillis and Rentschler, an even clearer picture of how that works may come into play.

Understanding McCarthy's Four Ps

To understand how the engagement edge functions, it is vital to discuss McCarthy's original model by examining each of the four Ps. Parts II–V of this book address each in greater complexity, exploring the notions of their original underpinnings and why they do not fit the nonprofit arts, and how they can be reimagined to provide a more suitable equation for the nonprofit arts manager. Here we begin by clarifying the four Ps' long-understood definitions and briefly demonstrate why these definitions have proved impractical and ineffective for the nonprofit arts.

Product

The term *product* is used to define a tangible good, intangible service, or idea that satisfies the needs and wants of the consumer. The consumer need not demand or even know that a product is something they desire or require—it is incumbent upon the manager to research, analyze, and understand the consumer mindset regarding the product. In the case of the nonprofit arts, the creation of product remains almost entirely the domain of the artist.

Though the manager may position the artistic product as an artist's representation of society, each piece of art, whether a ballet, symphony, statue, painting, or concert, has a unique relationship to each consumer.[33] That relationship is marked by the consumer's experiences both before consuming the product and during consumption, where the connection is most vital in the arts.[34] The nonprofit arts most frequently do not tailor this product to the marketplace, so the analysis of the core product, the art, requires an understanding of the experience a consumer will be immersed in upon consuming the artistic product.

Price

Though *price* is the amount of money paid in exchange for a product, it actually has a far broader reach. Price is also a consideration of the cost a consumer is willing to invest in accessing the product, which are issues of relationship management.[35] Though the concept of price as a component of the four Ps is the only component related to revenue generation, for the nonprofit arts, price cannot stand alone, since unearned, donated revenue is an essential component. Additionally, nonprofit organizations frequently provide free services to the community. Because the marketing mix does not readily incorporate the vagaries of fundraising and fund development, the traditional approaches for applying pricing strategy are stymied by the unique nature of the nonprofit arts. Though such unearned revenue might be delicately wedged into the marketing mix in a way that could incorporate its value in easing the access for the paying consumer, the issues of earned and unearned revenue function together at an organizational level rather than at a consumer level. Without unearned revenue having a bearing at the consumer level, the marketing mix function of price is pushed back into a functional assessment as opposed to a managerial strategy.

The concept of price goes beyond the actual monetary cost of access and stretches into the realm of intangible contributions the consumer makes for the access, such as time and effort. Because of this, for the nonprofit arts manager who must make revenue decisions based on both potential revenue earning and potential contributed revenue (a separate but distinct function of access that benefits the consumer with a sense of goodwill), price is a flawed concept. The nonprofit arts manager must understand the barriers to access for community members and make strides to ease that access, not necessarily by altering the monetary cost of the access but by engaging with the community about their needs. Hence, price is a function of profit, and ease of access becomes a function of the nonprofit arts. Ease of access applies to both earned revenue for access to the artistic experience and unearned revenue, donations given by community members for which they receive intrinsic rewards.

Place

The concept of place has to do with how and where the consumer will receive their product and how that product is distributed. In the nonprofit arts, this is typically the location where the art is presented: a theatre or gallery, for example. In the industrial world, however, place is often a complex system of distribution where the creator of the product warehouses, transports, distributes, tracks, and catalogs order fulfillment. In the electronic age, place may refer to the digital process where a consumer initiates the sales process, and the product provider's system of shipping, handling, and delivery processes. In the commercial world, place is manifested in the steps required between completed deliverable product and the point at which it reaches the consumer's hands. Though the nonprofit arts have and continue to explore the possibilities of place as a modifiable location for art delivery, these decisions are most frequently made to explore the notion of the environment in which the artistry unfolds. Though ticketing processes and delivery services are also incorporated into the concept of place, they are more functional by nature and lend themselves more easily to ease of access, essentially making the marketing mix function of place a reference to the actual location in which the art is displayed. That environment through which the consumer passes during their usage of an artistic product does indeed have managerial implications. **We contend that environment is a more appropriate function for the nonprofit arts than place and one that can be seen along the edge between marketing and engagement.**

Promotion

The term *promotion* is often the most misunderstood in the marketing mix, as it is the foundation upon which McCarthy's scientific approach was built, advertising. In fact, promotion refers to the communications and communication methodology used to disseminate information about the product. Though it includes communication strategy, design, and delivery through various selected communication channels, its fundamental concept is to effectively persuade the consumer. The concept of promotion requires the commercial organization to understand the degrees to which consumers are acquainted with a product and adequately inform in a way that encourages action to purchase. In cases where products are new to the marketplace, promotion requires a great deal of consumer education to describe the reasons why the new product should be wanted or needed. In the nonprofit arts, the art itself is always new because it is frequently generated only while the consumer is present, such as in a play presentation where each performance is unique, and because the consumer's experience with the art is an essential part of the art itself.[36] Just like a new product in a commercial enterprise when the promotional mix requires a heavy focus on education, the arts require an even greater emphasis. Consequently, we posit that commercial promotional strategies, though sound and similar to those required by the nonprofit arts, require a fundamentally different approach that not only emphasizes, but is founded, built, and fleshed out through various methods of education for the potential consumer. As we discuss in chapter 5, education is a much lengthier process than promotion, requires a community-centric (as opposed to product-centric) approach, and occurs in both long-term and immediate-return processes.

Value, Ps, and the Mix

McCarthy's marketing mix was developed with the clear intention to maximize value to the consumer and the organization. Organizations take tangible and intangible inputs and combine them to create something that is of greater value to the consumer than the sum of the parts. The difference between cost and revenue is profit. Because the "mix" provided a managerial and scientific approach, managers could set targeted financial goals, plan and organize processes to achieve those financial goals, and achieve the desired financial rewards with greater accuracy. Nonprofit arts organizations struggle to do the same largely because the for-profit methodology of the marketing mix fails to satisfy the unique characteristics of these organizations. Though the marketing mix, has proven adaptable to our changing global and interconnected society, the nonprofit and community-based arts are being left further behind. **The engagement edge allows the nonprofit arts to chart a marketing course of their own that is unique to them.**

Community-Based Arts Are Different

Community-based art organizations often suffer from the challenges of small budgets incapable of sustaining the type of marketing operation often required by the marketing mix. International brands are developed with millions of dollars, while local brands often struggle to gain traction.[37] Community-based arts organizations are recognized by their governments for their ability to provide a social service to their communities. However, they continue to attempt to do so by using techniques developed by studying global corporations and then modifying those techniques with little success. Though the term "community" could refer to the global community, we define community-based arts as those that have identified their local or regional community as an entire market niche, often under the premise, appropriate or not, that the arts are for everyone.

Functionality

Borden noted in 1942, "The forces met by different firms vary widely. Accordingly, the programs fashioned differ widely." Certainly, his contention was that every business has a different set of circumstances upon which it must operate. His paradigm called for a way of understanding various elements that required consideration, and he labeled them in twelve factors. McCarthy then reorganized them into the modern marketing mix of the four factors of product, price, place, and promotion that we use today. The development of marketing mixes had begun before the current function of 501(c)3 nonprofit arts organizations existed. To our knowledge, no paradigm has ever been developed to attempt to put Borden's long-standing conceptual framework into a structure applicable to the modern nonprofit arts organizations, which began to spring into existence years later.

A Brief Discussion of the Marketing Function

What is clear is that the marketing function has been redefined as the primary and sometimes total function of business and its managers. The nonprofit arts tend to eschew this concept because it implies that managerial decision-making regarding the marketing mix, *including the development and creation of product*, be handled by management rather than line staff. In the nonprofit arts the line staff, the artists and their work, though guided by certain organizational principles defined by mission, vision, and values, is hindered as little as possible by market influences to allow their true and personal reflection of society to emerge.[38] By shifting the paradigm and its associated language away from marketing and into the realm of engagement, the nonprofit arts can work within a model that treats the artistic product as a vital, immutable part, but only a part, of what nonprofit arts organizations are mandated to do.

Nonprofit versus For-Profit

All organizations attempt to operate from the guiding principles of their mission, vision, and values. Of the four functions of management, planning, organizing, leading, and controlling, nonprofit organizations often struggle to align the control function. Commercial enterprises are guided by mission but evaluate success based upon market factors and profit. Nonprofit arts organizations, inherently, have no such benchmark for success. Instead, they must attempt to understand how effectively they serve the community through their mission, a difficult if not impossible measure as it is rarely quantifiable. **Engagement, though equally as difficult to measure, provides a slightly more concrete, yet subjective scale.**

Nonprofit Arts versus Other Nonprofits

A similar paradox occurs when lumping all nonprofit organizations together under the same marketplace paradigm. Consider, for example, charitable organizations that function for the greater good of society entirely upon donors' benefaction. Though the support of those donors has to do with a similar exchange involving intrinsic and emotional rewards, the cost of the exchange is left arbitrarily to the donor with little connection to any service provided by the organization as a return for said exchange. The nonprofit arts straddle the for-profit model of marketplace responsiveness and the nonprofit model of full internal reward gained by donors. The engagement edge fills this intermediate void. In this model, the donation becomes a secondary exchange in support of the first, which ends in the provision of an artistic product. For those who choose only to consume art, there is one exchange. **For those who choose to support the arts as a vital structure in society, the donation exchange is a secondary process.**

The "Wedging" of Marketing into the Arts and Services

When an organization uses the marketing mix to improve outcomes, the managerial decision-making must consider product development and creation as a commodity worth accessing to the consumer. This requirement leads to product iterations that are measured based on sales potential. Both Borden and McCarthy argued that the marketing mix functions in a way that requires each ingredient, including the product, to be added through appropriate managerial decision-making. **Removing this ability, as nonprofit organizations must do, causes the entire "recipe" to fail, just as bread dough lacking flour would fail.** Certainly, there are ways to modify a bread recipe to allow for different ingredients, but the end result would not be bread but something close to bread. By forcing nonprofit organizations to follow the marketing mix, the result becomes something close to a business but not a business. A model that allows the business to structure its market interactions around the art, including how the art and associated interactions affect an experience, allows the arts organization to function as a business both akin to, but totally unlike, commercial enterprises.

The Marketing Mix as Defining Paradigm

Most importantly, Borden, McCarthy, and the myriad scholars who have studied, adapted, and refined the marketing mix have not tried to create a new way of doing things. Instead, they have dismantled visible processes, attempted to understand their individual value and worth, and pieced them back together with clear definitions and operating procedures. These models do not create a way of interacting with the marketplace. Instead, they are means for defining and understanding the best and most successful practices. The marketing mix is not an instructional guide as much as it is an explanation. In the engagement edge, we seek to define best practices for nonprofit arts organizations as they interact and intersect within their localized context. The benchmarks for the edge are rooted in a desire to provide the greatest societal impact within a community, and as Borwick has argued, that occurs through engagement.

The Engagement Edge

For years, terms such as *community service, community engagement,* and *community outreach* have been used and abused as a means for interaction between arts, artists, and arts consumers. Those three terms have often been interchangeably disseminated to arts organizations with little description or definition. As we explore the engagement edge, we look to define engagement in a way that allows us to consider the structure that underlies the edge.

We see *community service* as a process by which an outside party controls the work a person or organization will do. The service provider does not determine the needs, work, or terms around which that work will be completed. Though community service may be provided voluntarily, it is defined by how the recipient of the service controls the process.[39] Further, we see the recipient obtain the primary benefit of the service. Though the process may create goodwill for the provider, the recipient has the largest gains in the process of service.

On the other end of the spectrum is *community outreach*. In the process of outreach, the provider of the work determines and controls the process. Though the term has often been used to reference some other relationship between provider and recipient, we consider arts outreach to be when an artist or arts organization goes into the community to present, provide, educate, nurture, or otherwise disseminate some service that has been planned, organized, and executed by the organization. Most often, the process of outreach is as akin to good public relations as it is to create positive change for the recipient.[40] The recipient does receive something of value in the process of outreach, but the provider gains something of even greater value, such as enhanced public relations or grant funding.

In the middle of this spectrum is *community engagement*.

The National Guild for Community Arts Education defines community engagement in a way that we find resonates with an exploration of marketing as a form of engagement in the nonprofit arts:

> What is community engagement? *Community* describes the people and organizations that are related to a community arts education provider's mission: students, parents, families, artists, partner organizations, schools, government agencies, and so on. *Engagement* describes an active, two-way process in which one party motivates another to get involved or take action—and both parties experience change. Mutual activity and involvement are the keys to community engagement. Sometimes organizations interpret community engagement as collaboration, marketing to diverse audiences, or developing programs for underserved groups. While those are all worthy and necessary activities, an engaged community arts education provider does more. It promotes consistent community interaction that is a step beyond conventional programmatic partnerships. Consistent community engagement is not program based; it is part of organizational culture.[41]

We see the process of engagement as one in which both parties mutually control the interaction and receive roughly equivalent benefits of value. Though one party may do more or less than the other, the process is not completely controlled by either party. In some sense, we view engagement as a combination of service and outreach. Hence, we place all three terms on a spectrum and do not distinguish exactly where any individual process may fall. The engagement edge falls roughly in the middle of this spectrum as its goal is to maximize benefits to both provider and recipient. This is where the engagement edge aligns perfectly with Walmsley's thinking on the topic. Our diversion from his paradigm is that we do not see engagement as a means for bringing others into the organization for the benefit of the organization. Instead, we see that as a process of education of the recipient by the provider and consider this education only one part of the quadrumvirate that makes up the engagement edge. In this, the early stages of redefining marketing for the arts, the distinctions may seem wholly semantic, as the practical applications will likely require years of industry acknowledgment and use. Semantic or not, Walmsley has opened a new line of inquiry regarding arts engagement just as we have developed the engagement edge.

The Paradigm as Definition

It is not surprising that arts organizations have struggled with the definition and process of engagement. The 501(c)3 designation was created to allow organizations to better provide a *service* to the community. Though secreted under the term is the notion that any 501(c)3 designated organization, or its equivalent throughout the world, was akin to any other service organization. In practice, that thinking is useless. In the 1960s, the United States tax code was revised to help create a better society, and similar processes were created in nations worldwide. The engagement edge may very well be the next chapter in this process. As our world has become technologically inundated, which has also allowed commercial interests to bury us in targeted commercial marketing, the notion of arts organizations simply providing service is a less effective system than it once was. The connections between the arts and their patrons have weakened and fractured for countless reasons. The reasons include productivity, arts education, public funding, changes in tax laws, social interconnectivity, and more.[42] We propose that the engagement edge is not an understanding of the changes that have occurred, affecting the connections between the arts and their consumers, but instead a way to move forward.

Arts Marketing

To that end, there has been, at least for several decades, a scholarly and then practical focus on arts marketing.[43] Arts administrators have taken the guidance of academics in marketing as a path for increasing the amount of service an organization might be able to provide. In essence, artists create their art and then have looked to administrators to use the tools of modern marketing theory to reach audiences. The process has never worked exceptionally well for nonprofit arts organizations. Perhaps this is because the marketing mix requires control of the product, but in the arts, it seems counterintuitive to have an executive determining what art the artist must create to satisfy market demand. Commercial arts—and in this case, we think specifically of commercial theatre, though concerts, tours, movies, television, and the like also apply—can devise their "products" in response to market research, while the nonprofit arts tend to push their art onto the market.

As we explore what the engagement edge looks like, we note that we are not looking to create something completely new. Rather, we identify the novel mix of things happening in nonprofit arts organizations and how they are often stymied by arts administrators thinking of their business through the lens of the traditional marketing mix and the four Ps. Conceptually, the engagement edge is a more holistic approach to the nonprofit arts and their relationship with their consumers. **It suggests that, although art can be created entirely from the mind's eye of the artist without market influence, the vital work of the artist is only a part of what an arts organization does. The function is to provide a societal service, and Cameron rightly notes that this occurs through social interaction between the organization and arts audience.**

Roots in Ben Cameron

American arts administrator Ben Cameron has on a number of occasions made statements regarding the function of the nonprofit arts. "Our mission is the orchestration of social interaction, in which the performance is a piece, but only a piece, of what we're called to do." This is the root of the engagement edge. The art itself is a piece of the nonprofit organization, but it is not the function, at least as defined by governmental entities. **The function is to provide a societal service, and Cameron rightly notes that this occurs through social interaction between the organization and arts audience**. Managerial decision-making is the guide for maximizing social impact. Cameron does not suggest that the art itself must be altered or tailored to the market but instead notes that a nonprofit arts organization is not in existence to serve the artists and their need to express themselves but to serve society. Inherently, the art is a part of that process, but all other processes of the organization require a calculative process that can multiply the societal effect of the art as it reaches into the market. This is not to suggest that the art is something isolated from all other organizational processes. Conversely, the art leads us along the rest of the edge for organizational success as measured by societal impact through consumer engagement.

Defining the Edge

The word *edge* can be misleading as it implies a precipice. We see the engagement edge as the place where the conceptual pillars buried within it meet. The engagement edge is a paradigm to help nonprofit arts organizations come to alignment with issues related to education, experience, environment, and ease of access. There is no single formula for success in marketing the arts any more than there is a single definition of what makes an organization successful. Instead, we see the engagement edge as an approach that is on the cutting edge of connecting consumers to the nonprofit arts. In the engagement edge, we see this definition play out in two ways: First, its goal is to balance the scales between provider and consumer. The consumers' needs and wants, as Borden referred to them, are equally important as the needs and wants of the artists who express their impression of life through their art. In this sense, the artists themselves are equivalent to the marketplace, as their work satisfies their own needs and wants, though they also function as line staff, developing and creating the core product: the art. Second, both the art and the other processes of the organization share the same edge of society. The engagement edge guides us to see the art as part of a bigger whole, a part that is not superior or inferior to the processes of fundraising, accounting, administration, and management. For the engagement edge to be effective, it is vital that all parts of the organization's system function together in the process. **Unlike marketing, which has been relegated to a department whose function is to promote the artists' work, engagement requires all parts of the organization to work simultaneously on an engagement plan.** This description makes perfect sense as the second definition of engagement describes a process whereby several factors must be taken into account to complete a process effectively. In our case, that process is the bringing together of art and society.

Borden used the word *mix* to imply a blending of marketing components. The use of the word *edge* implies a connecting space between four areas we propose are vital to arts marketing: Education, ease of access, environment, and experience. A focus on only one of these components will be less likely to achieve the desired market saturation levels. We propose, however, that approaching these aspects of the engagement edge by calculating their relative value and worth both to consumer and arts organization within any specific marketplace will lead to growth and strengthening of the arts in society. This is not to suggest that the engagement edge is a one-time-only solution that can be repeatedly applied. **Because the arts are forever changing and evolving, and because the market is always in a state of flux, the engagement edge will allow the arts professional an approach of examining and assessing the components that help connect a community with the arts.**

Each concept relies upon and affects the others, and finding the right pinnacle, or edge, will improve the drive toward audience engagement.

Es versus Ps

These areas we propose, the four Es, are built on McCarthy's four Ps and provide a clearer view of marketing in arts organizations. This clarity should allow the arts consumer to initially engage with the arts organization and allow them to become a part of the organization. Just an audience is required for art to achieve its aesthetic statement as defined by Dewey. Once consumers are involved, they participate in the engagement process and help shape how the organization and the community function in a symbiotic relationship where the value of each is considered in the process.

2
Engagement

The arguments raised in chapter 1 suggest that engagement is more closely associated with the nonprofit arts and their market exposure than aspects of the conventional marketing mix would suggest. We ask that you briefly set aside the traditional notion of marketing while reading this chapter. Throughout this book, we will compare the marketing mix developed in the 1950s with the engagement edge to illuminate why we believe the engagement edge functions better for the nonprofit arts.

This chapter broadly explores the concept of engagement, describes the confusion between the concepts of involvement and engagement, and discusses the impact a focus on engagement has had in school systems. Ultimately, the chapter discusses motivation, and why a paradigm shift in arts marketing to the four Es of the engagement edge will lead to a renewed energy in the arts.

What Is Engagement?

Frequently in the arts, the word engagement describes the audience plugging into an artistic experience. Artistic directors often vividly recount how "engaged" an audience was while listening to a symphony or watching a ballet. They also often use "engage" to mean "hire," for example: "let's engage Jessica to design the costumes." Though the word "engage" might be accurate in such circumstances, these usages fall short of our intentions when we say that the ultimate goal of an arts organization is engagement.

As stated in chapter 1, true engagement in the arts occurs when organizations and community members are actively involved with each other, and each receives near-equal benefits. In proposing this new paradigm, we believe that when each component of the engagement edge is realized, the result is engagement between the organization and the community, and engagement between individuals and the organization. **Although the steps** culminating in engagement are active for both parties, the actual state of being engaged is a result, not a process.

In contemplating engagement as a replacement for traditional marketing, consider that corporations designed marketing as a means to an end: good marketing leads to profits. We encouraged you to set aside your notions of traditional marketing for this reason. In for-profit companies, marketing is a means to earn profits; in nonprofit arts organizations, engagement is an end in itself. This is not just a theoretical construct but how the United States, and many nations worldwide, have established support for these mission-driven organizations. They benefit the community and so the government treats them with deference to that goal.

Broadening the Perspective

Many arts organizations work diligently to ensure that their consumer base is involved. As arts leaders, we reach out regularly to communicate with our patrons and audiences. We encourage them to donate as a form of participation. We invite them to lectures and talk-backs. We ask what sort of programming they would like to see. We bemoan the fact that younger people do not seem to be listening to all the communication we are doing to let them know that what we do is worthwhile for them. We think, if they know we listen to and respect their feedback, wants, and needs, they might be more involved. Yet, for all this consideration, the involvement of many in our communities remains minimal, if they are involved at all. In this line of thinking, we blend the terms *engagement* and *involvement*. This blending leads to our own confusion. We spend our energy communicating what we are doing, but we are left asking ourselves, "Why aren't they more engaged?" and "What is our future if younger people never attend?"

External Forces

We will begin with a question that nonprofit arts organizations have been asking for years: are audiences dying off? Numerous studies have addressed the connections between younger people and the arts.[1] We know that an appreciation for the arts developed and cultivated in youth is the most likely way to develop a desire to participate in the arts as either an audience member or an artist. We also know that those young adults who have that deep-seated interest may be too busy working and raising children to act on the interest. Other obligations strain their capacity for involvement. Once they are well established in their careers and their children are grown, they may start to act on their long-ignored love for the arts. When retirement rolls around, there is even more opportunity to capitalize on those long-held interests. What arts marketers have been doing is communicating with people who already have an interest and capturing their attention when they have the capacity for involvement. Life is a collection of interactions and involvements that create our personal and social capital. It then stands to reason that most people will focus on survival needs, including earning an income and raising a family, until personal satisfaction can again become a priority. Hence, we arrive at the notion that our audiences tend to skew older. Audiences, as a whole, are not dying. As some audience members leave, new ones reach the point in life where they are ready to be involved.

Despite the differences between these stages of life, new audience members don't seem to be replacing those who drop off at the same pace, so we see numbers dwindling. Our theory suggests drop-off correlates to a society that has shifted from wanting opportunities for involvement to a desire for engagement. That theory, at face value, may seem confusing. Isn't the act of being involved the same as being engaged? Don't both the organization and the individual benefit from being involved?

Engagement versus Involvement

We considered the many definitions of engagement in our attempt to explore how engagement can replace the traditional marketing concepts that nonprofit arts organizations have tried to apply. Dictionary definitions run the gamut and include several that are not applicable to the discussion herein. For our purposes, a distinguishing definition of the word *engagement* is required: Engagement as a form of participation, to occupy oneself with, play a role, share in, be a party to, and establish a meaningful connection with. On the other hand, *involvement*, is a fact or condition, a state or personal, emotional association—a *noun*. In contrast, engagement is a verb—an act of doing, the action of being engaged, taking part, and sharing in. Consider that one often-cited definition of *engage* is to come together and interlock. You can see that this is a concept that has multiple parties doing something together. A definition of *involve* includes the words enfold and envelop. This definition implies that involvement is the act of doing something *to* another party as opposed to doing something *with* another party. Though involvement can be the gateway to engagement, it is something different from engagement. **Engagement is a concept in which all parties feel their contributions to the mutual association are roughly equal.**

Donation lends itself to involvement, and patrons receive the intrinsic rewards of positive feelings such as personal gratification and happiness through social participation. They also reap the morally congruent benefits of prosocial behavior.[2] Although the donor and the nonprofit organization experience mutually beneficial effects, and the donation is a positive expression of the donor's interest and support for the organization, their involvement has not yet translated into engagement. Involvement is a step on the path to engagement. **Engagement requires involvement, but plenty of arts lovers are thrilled to be involved without being engaged. They are probably already attending your events.** We are not proposing an end to arts organizations' efforts to achieve involvement. We propose a second layer of effort, focusing on those who wish to engage. **Organizations desiring engagement from individuals tend to spend more time listening than promoting.**

The Importance of Listening

The focus is on developing partners. To do that, one has to listen.[3] Engagement requires real relationships, two-way communication that is objectively heard, a welcoming environment that supports all parties, and shared decision-making.

Much of the research on community engagement has been conducted in relation to schools. Most of that research suggests that when schools cultivate engagement with families, the results are better for the students, the families, the schools, and the entire community.[4]

Lessons from Engagement and Schools

Schools focusing on family engagement have learned that school employees need to reach out and meet families on their turf to be effective. It requires meetings in homes. These are individual meetings and require time. Imagine a community where the local arts organizations meet with community groups, churches, clubs, and even individual families to talk with them. For many, it would be the first time any organization ever bothered.

Those conversations focus on learning what families do together, what they appreciate, and how they enjoy and experience life. When this type of engagement occurs in schools, the results are incredibly positive.[5]

In the arts, we tend to be informed by our exposure to the world, and present experiences in line with that exposure. We then wonder why people with different lived experiences do not come rushing to see the artwork of *our* lived experiences. **Engagement is a process that allows us to explore all lived experiences in a way that allows the artwork to transcend the individual artist.**

Researchers found a fascinating impact in a Sacramento, California school district while studying its engagement program.[6] The school discovered that parents wanted to learn more about how the school operated. As a result, the school launched a Parent University, held monthly. They designed the curriculum to enlighten interested parents on school policies, school procedures, and school administration. It also informed them about pertinent issues such as high school graduation requirements, getting into college, and financial aid. Some classes dealt with immigration issues and were taught in multiple languages. The engagement shaped the way the community and the organization interacted. People told their stories, which were shared throughout the community. The group then came together to develop a vision for something that would be possible only if they did it together. **Rather than challenging individuals to act on information being fed to them through promotions, these people were challenged to act based on their desires.**

The lessons learned from schools leaping into an engagement approach are similar to those that guide nonprofit arts organizations in true engagement. In 1916, a West Virginia Supervisor of Public Schools named L. J. Hanifan wrote, "Tell the people what they ought to do, and they will say in effect, 'Mind your own business.' But help them to discover for themselves what ought to be done, and they will not be satisfied until it is done."[7]

Organization to Person Communication

If you think about how your arts organization communicates with its community, you may find that it is primarily through a one-way communication developed by a promoter. Arts organizations looking to develop involvement use promotion as their primary means of communication when seeking participants as donors or audience members and telling people how they can participate in activities.

Engagement occurs when communication is two-way. There is a conversation, a partnership, a developing sense of ownership in that connection. Arts organizations practicing engagement do more *with* their audiences than *for* their audiences. They listen more frequently than they talk; their conversations are two-way; and they envision a community where audiences and artists are partners, where the community and the arts organization are partners.

A Practical Consideration: The Talk-Back

Many theatres throughout the world use "talk-backs" as a means for involving an audience, but do talk-backs also engage? Organizations often hold talk-backs to provide further detail and depth of understanding of the art experience that has just been presented (or will soon be presented). Arts organizations allow patrons to ask questions about what they have witnessed to develop their overall sense of appreciation for the art. Talk-backs seem like a little gift of exploration for those inclined to take advantage of it, but is this a two-way communication?

Most talk-backs as we know them rely upon an assumption that the artists at the center of the discussion hold the answers. Talk-backs are an opportunity for the audience to have contact with the artists and learn from them. Most begin with a moderator introducing the artist and providing foundational questions for the artists to answer. The moderator (often a staff member at the presenting organization) sometimes also fields and filters questions from the audience on behalf of the artist. In this scenario, talk-backs are a one-way form of communication—even when questions from the audience are included. The idea of using talk-backs to provide the community access to an artist is predicated on the notion that artists and community are separated. This idea of separation is further substantiated by the moderator framing and controlling the communication. Often there is even a physical separation between the artist (frequently on a stage) and the audience. Though talk-backs may be excellent ways of distributing information, they are typically a form of involvement, not engagement.

We do not suggest that holding events to create involvement is in any way misguided. **We do suggest that a clear understanding of the difference between events that create involvement and those that create engagement is beneficial to arts leaders.** To create engagement, you should consider the following questions: How can we produce a two-way, co-led discussion about the intersection of community issues and the art with members of the community? How might we connect with all participants (artists, staff, and audience) to plan a way to create art together? In holding this event, are we trying to persuade our community to think a certain way, or does this event provide space for us to actively listen to community needs, concerns, and interests?

Lynne Conner

Lynne Conner, a researcher at Colby College, noted in her tome *Audience Engagement and the Role of Arts Talk in the Digital Era* that part of the arts experience is enmeshed with the very basic function of arts talk, or discussing the arts in any number of ways. Conner proposed that the talk is actually part of the overall artistic experience and requires some level of engagement as part of the overall process, because the interpretive meaning of the receiver of the art is actually part of the artistic experience itself. Though we could easily use Conner to argue both for the notion of education as a means for replacing promotion, as well as environment replacing place, since arts talk occurs within bounds that are other than the place of sale, we let her work stand as it informs the notion of experience replacing product. That means that the artistic experience actually begins when the arts talk begins.

Motivation

If you are familiar with Maslow's hierarchy of needs, figure 2.1, you may recall that the first layer focuses on physiological needs with extrinsic values: basic needs such as water, food, and shelter.[8] Humans then seek out

Figure 2.1 Maslow's hierarchy of needs.

a safe environment, employment, resources, and property. When humans lack any one of these things, they are *motivated* to secure them, typically in an order similar to that which Maslow theorized. Maslow went further and proposed that when a human feels sated with the necessary physiological and safety needs for their life, they begin to pursue more **intrinsic needs that create personal satisfaction**. The next needs Maslow recognized are love and belonging, which are built from personal relationships. Motivation in this part of Maslow's hierarchy is linked to engagement. In particular, we may focus on the notion of a "sense of belonging," as that concept is rooted in social interaction.

The arts often function with social interaction, from audiences in a large auditorium, to community members strolling through a gallery. Regardless of the type of interaction, it still exists in that an audience is physically present and shares similar experiences simultaneously (even an audience of two). The chapter returns to higher order needs and the sense of belonging when it explores factors for different life stages, but for the moment, it focuses on motivation as something derived from a need. Not having a job might threaten our safety, so we are motivated to find and keep one. If we have savings, the danger in quitting and finding a new job is decreased, and the motivation shifts from a need to want. This space is where engagement exists: We are engaged in that which we want to be engaged in.

Employee Engagement

Researchers have conducted scores of studies to determine how employees engage and what motivates them.[9] The research into what motivates art consumers has far less breadth than those studies that attempt to understand employee behavior in organizations. Existing research about employees helps us to understand the value of engagement and its relationship with motivation.

Employees are typically motivated to action by three primary objectives: Trust in those around them, sense of purpose and pride in what they are doing, and enjoying time with their co-workers.[10] The first of those can be considered a basic or safety need. If you follow those three from one to the next, you can see the shift from need to want. The presence of all three is the hallmark of the engaged employee.

When employees respond with high levels of engagement, companies see better business results, higher motivation and performance, less turnover, and organizational performance results that outperform the mean.[11] Though we are not considering art patrons to be "employees" per se, we concur with scholars who consider them part of the organization[12] and an integral part of the art.[13] For-profit businesses have taken huge strides and made a great effort toward developing an engaged workforce as a means for improving company performance. It should also come as no surprise that those same companies also realize the value in engaging with consumers.[14]

Organizations that are developing engagement plans may be focused solely on motivation rather than on creating engagement. Motivated employees work harder, smarter, more efficiently, and more effectively, which, typically, leads to improved bottom lines.[15] As noted, motivation and engagement are generally linked, meaning that they often rise and fall together in individuals.

Adapting for the Arts

What does this mean for an arts organization? Consider that the audience will need to trust that the organization will provide something of value to them that is roughly equal to the consumer's cost. On its own, this might seem impossible to accomplish, as the reward from witnessing art is almost entirely intrinsic and differs from consumer to consumer. Some studies demonstrate the motivators of attending the arts, and if we look to satisfy those motivators, we can work toward engagement.

Forms of Engagement and Motivation in the Arts

In exploring the idea of motivation leading to engagement in arts patrons, we first must recognize that researchers have not solidified an understanding of motivation, largely because it deals with behavior and emotion in ways we have yet to understand completely.[16] Nevertheless, researchers in arts administration and arts marketing have attempted to understand the motivating factors that cause people to become audience members.

When we look at how society is changing in response to technological advances that allow us to create easily, we can see a seismic shift heading for the arts. This shift may change the process of creating art and the relationship between art, artists, and audiences. The lines between these roles are already blurring in demand for greater involvement.

In a study produced for the James Irvine Foundations, Brown and Novak detailed the various levels of arts participation and how they are occurring and shifting.

> We are in the midst of a seismic shift in cultural production, moving from a "sit-back-and-be-told culture" to a "making-and-doing-culture." Active or participatory arts practices are emerging from the fringes of the Western cultural tradition to capture the collective imagination. Many forces have conspired to lead us to this point. The sustained economic downturn that began in 2008, rising ticket prices, the pervasiveness of social media, the proliferation of digital content and rising expectations for self-guided, on-demand, customized experiences have all contributed to a cultural environment primed for active arts practice. This shift calls for a new equilibrium in the arts ecology and a new generation of arts leaders ready to accept, integrate and celebrate all forms of cultural practice. This is, perhaps, the defining challenge of our time for artists, arts organizations and their supporters—to embrace a more holistic view of the cultural ecology and identify new possibilities for Americans to engage with the arts.[17]

Note that these researchers have identified the need to embrace and identify new ways to *engage* with the arts.

The researchers presented "The Audience Involvement Spectrum," a model that describes the progression of audience involvement and the relationship between art and audience. The spectrum ranges from one end, where the audience is fully receptive, to the other, where the audience is fully participating.[18]

As a "spectator," the audience is the receptor of the art performance or finished construct. Through responses such as laughter and applause, art attendees do have an experiential role for themselves and those around them.

The authors' next level of participation includes value-added benefits provided by the organization. These include activities such as lectures, talk-backs, discussions, or simple interaction of some sort. The artist or organization largely controls this participation, which is generally a mix of promotion and education designed to impact audience awareness and heighten the performance experience. Some level of involvement from the audience may be considered, such as taking a survey.

In the middle of this spectrum, and the first time we see participation, is a space Brown and Novak call "crowd-sourcing." Arts organizations use crowd-sourcing to explicitly mine the community for the content that inspires and creates the art. Crowd-sourcing involves events sponsored, orchestrated, and executed by professional artists. Examples include exhibitions showing work by local artists, painting, photo, or literary contests, community programs of cultural representations of art or artistic performance, dance or talent presentations, and the like. Exceptional examples include operas composed through tweets from the audience and theatrical works created with stories from the community. These fall into a growing place on the spectrum, where the audience is not on stage but have input toward the creation of the art offering.

Next is "co-creation" where art becomes the result of some direct effort on the part of the intended audience, such as plays that incorporate audience members into the production, community dance events where professional dancers are joined in public spaces by attendees, or in "participatory public art" projects where communities allow for the creation (and often climbing on) of works of art. Each place on this spectrum fulfills a different need and is motivated differently. The slight differences between crowd-sourcing and co-creation are reflected in the amount of interaction between the artists and the audience. Though crowd-sourcing includes works contributed to a planned, sponsored event, a co-created opportunity differs in that the audience interacts with the artists as they participate in an "artistic experience" at a live event.

On the far end of the spectrum are arts presentations that require participation of the "audience-as-artist" in ways that would not allow the art to exist otherwise. Many artists and organizations carefully design, plan, and organize them. From poetry slams to live arts competitions, art demonstrations, and dance events, to name a few. These experiences allow the audience to function as both spectator and participant if they so choose. The salient point in this, the most participatory stage, is that the audience essentially takes control of the experience. Here, although the experience is planned and designed by a professional, the creative outcome, the experience itself, is dependent on the participation and creative endeavors of the audience. The creation of the art is live; the creative process is the performance. It is the element of control and the process of creation that differentiates audience-as-artist from crowd-sourcing and co-creation. As the authors note, "This phenomenon is not limited to [arts] culture, but part of a larger 'participation economy' in which social connection eclipses consumption."[19]

Audience Development and Engagement

All this suggests that behavior related to consumption and creation is shifting. This shift appears fed by a greater desire for creation than consumption. Though not a new concept, it is now taking on greater importance, particularly for the arts. Brown and Novak described it this way:

> It is becoming more difficult to satisfy everyone with one experience. Audience development, therefore, is not just a marketing problem. Primarily, it is a programming issue. Attracting the next generation of audiences and visitors will require a transformation in programming, not just better marketing. Even then, when new audiences appear on the scene, they will be different. Fewer will want to sit still in uncomfortable seats, and more will demand a larger role in shaping their own experience.[20]

As we explore how to incorporate all this into an organizational approach that shifts the emphasis from marketing to engagement, we will show that the idea of a transformation in programming does not mean that arts organizations can only be effective in engagement if they change the art they create. **In fact, the programming as it currently exists may remain intact under the engagement edge; however, it becomes part of a larger contextual approach to the experience that unites art, artist, and audience members.**

Perhaps the most striking result we find in research is that studies suggest the primary motivators for attending the arts are not the ones most typically associated with showing up and watching. One good example of this is a study conducted in France that examined motivators of both audiences and practitioners of theater.[21] The process attempted to categorize different "types" of people based on their rationale for being motivated to attend theater. The researchers identified four main types of audience motivation, with each participant in the study falling into one of these four categories. Those motivator types were as follows: entertainment, educational elitism, life enrichment, and social hedonism. These researchers identified four distinct types of people who attend theater based on the bundle of motivators that most closely align with the present need in life. Note that the first two types are closely associated with those who attend the theater to absorb what is presented to them, while the latter two suggest a desire to be part of a larger experience.

Other studies have come to similar conclusions, while using slightly different terminology or models. Walmsley examined several studies about motivators in the arts and reached this conclusion:

> Bergadaà and Nyeck's (1995) work confirmed earlier research into consumer behaviour, which found that the most cited motivations for a leisure experience were pleasure and escapism. [...] This predominant focus on the escapist and entertainment value of the arts and leisure experience is [...] challenged by Rojek and Stebbins, who support the view that many people are increasingly seeking more challenging and socially engaged leisure activities. In the fields of Sociology and Leisure Studies, there is an increasing awareness of the importance of the arts to community and social engagement. For example, Nicholson and Pearce list "enhanced socialization" as a motivation behind cultural participation.[22]

Scholars have conducted a considerable amount of research to investigate the motivators behind attendance of the arts, and it appears that these motivators can be combined to categorize (roughly) the different types of people who attend the arts. Walmsley's observations are part of a study to illuminate this confusing yet important issue of motivation. He found delineations between study participants largely based on these criteria: the pursuit of emotional experiences and impact, including true and authentic performances; edutainment, or the advancement of one's intellect, and the acquisition of knowledge from the entertainment offering; escapism from the routine of day-to-day life; and engagement with the artists involved. Given the complexity of motivations, it may seem difficult to determine which audience members desire benefits that either do or do not require engagement. Given the substantial number of motivation combinations, an arts organization could theoretically (at great expense) create individualized engagement plans for each of their audience members. Walmsley noted the challenge of tracking individual motivation when he wrote,

> This perspective would regard motivation as inherently subjective and would ultimately culminate in personal motivation charts for every individual theatre-goer. This approach would also acknowledge that people often want to fulfill multiple motivations simultaneously. While this may strike terror into theatre marketers, it does reflect the move towards personal customisation, which is facilitated by increasingly sophisticated CRM software. But in the meantime, it may be more practicable to segment audiences by their dominant motivating driver.[23]

Though scholars have many different perspectives about motivation, discourse continues because of the value in understanding motivation. If we do not understand what motivates someone to participate, we will have difficulty engaging with them.

Arts Engagement Preferences and Age

The Doris Duke Charitable Foundations, Theatre Development Fund, and Theatre Bay Area launched a joint research project called "Triple Play" to determine how best to make those important connections referred to by Carr and Paul.[24] The researchers were particularly focused on learning how audiences connected to playwrights of new works. In this study, they questioned over seven thousand participants from across the United States through questionnaires and focus groups. Their findings are valuable for us to consider in this shift toward engagement. First, it may be no surprise that they found a difference between younger audiences and older audiences. The study found that younger audience members were far more interested in challenging topics, nonlinear narratives, risky or risqué concepts, and plays still in development than older audience members were. Younger audience members, however, were resistant to paying a high price for new plays.

It may seem counterintuitive that anyone would prefer less developed work. As the researchers pursued this line of inquiry, they discovered the consumer motivation for this apparent discrepancy. Younger audiences perceive their participation in a new work as taking a role as an active contributor to the development of a new play. The researchers found that the value exchange for young people is less about money and more about a contribution in terms of time, effort, interest, and participation in shaping the work and spreading information about it afterward. In effect, though they are not co-creating anything, their motivation is a desire to be involved in the creation of a work that could one day become established in the literature. It appears the younger audiences many of us bemoan for not attending are less interested in paying for our art and more interested in engaging in the process of creating the art.

The Triple Play findings also shone a light on another distinction among theater-goers to new works that align nicely with the differences between younger and older audiences. New works draw audiences that are more highly attuned to both involvement and engagement. These audiences are far more interested in all forms of interaction with the organization. This factor positions these audiences toward the engaged side of Bergadaà and Nyeck's spectrum rather than the spectator side. Audience members who were satisfied being spectators voiced a stronger-than-typical desire to reflect privately upon the work after seeing it. **This finding supports the idea that engagement is a concept that appropriately matches the nonprofit arts and that satisfying motivators more closely align an audience member with their desired level of engagement.** It also suggests that organizations that engage with their community do not negate the positive experience enjoyed by those who are more interested in self-actualization than engagement.

Psychological

A recent report in *The Gerontologist* presented more findings that support the theories we have presented about motivation in this chapter.[25] In that study, the authors determined how theatergoing affects an attendee's psychological state based on age differences. What seemed unlikely proved to be true: theater engages and stimulates younger audiences more than older audiences.

Through the lens of Maslow's hierarchy, we see that arts patrons who have moved through lower levels of the hierarchy attend the theater to satisfy higher needs: to enrich and fill their lives with more experiences. These tend to be older people. In contrast, younger audiences are more likely to feel a need to engage and see the arts as providing some engagement and attend to satisfy lower-order social needs.

Final Thoughts

People are motivated by different things at different stages in their life. As our basic needs that allow for human survival are met, we look for more social needs. Eventually, we begin to expand our collection of experiences. There may be a lifelong relationship with the arts that changes as we mature. First, we are exposed to the arts in our youth. As we develop into young adults, we have a desire for greater social connections. As we mature further and satisfy our lower-order needs, the arts provide an opportunity to expand our lived experiences, explore knowledge and beauty through art, and reflect on the nature of the art and what it means to us and the world.

This chapter has divided audience motivation into two main categories: one that is driven by absorbing the art as presented (a desire for involvement), and one that is driven by participating in a larger social experience around the creation of art that may even border on a desire to be a co-creator—what Walmsley defines as the highest form of engagement.[26] Regardless of the level of engagement available, many patrons want only to be spectators of the artistic experience. Many arts organizations provide exactly that, a space to experience the arts through involvement, but they are not yet creating a space for engagement.

What if our approach to arts marketing provided value to those who desired involvement and those who desire engagement? With the latter, some level of interaction that goes beyond simply selling a ticket and allowing the audience member to enjoy would be required.

Eugene Carr and Michelle Paul's *Breaking the Fifth Wall: Rethinking Arts Marketing for the 21st Century* gives a useful starting place by advising arts organizations to reconnect "with arts patrons in a meaningful way after they have left a performance venue—by creatively and regularly reminding them of everything the organization has to offer."[27] However, we posit that it is not an arts organization's function to simply keep reminding people of what they offer but to engage them in a discussion that will help shape what they offer and how they offer it. For the arts in the 21st century, that means being engaged somewhere on a spectrum where its strongest level of engagement is a co-creating process.

As noted, arts organizations can become engaged with those whose motivators closely align with engagement even if they do not change the nature of the art or how it is created. The chapters that follow share an approach for how to do that. If you are curious but hesitant about co-creation, you are not alone. One concern about co-creating with the community is that we must share our limited capacity to create the art we feel is most important. This thinking, however, imagines that there is a limited amount of art that can be made, or a limit to the number of creative ideas that can be implemented. Instead, we propose that by engaging with community members, the total capacity for creating art and implementing creative ideas is increased exponentially, and the possibilities become endless.

PART II
EDUCATION

The three chapters in part II communicate a key tenet of the engagement edge: shifting from promotion to education. Of the four pillars of the engagement edge, moving away from promotion may cause the most visceral response. Unlike in for-profit corporations, when we think about the marketing department of an arts organization, the primary factor we may consider is promotion. Since promotion is central to the way marketing departments market the arts, we discuss this shift first.

Chapter 3 describes the frameworks and conceptions of *promotion* and *education*. It reviews the history of promotion and key ideas from McCarthy through contemporary promotion. It also defines our perspective of education. The chapter lays important groundwork which attempts to ensure that our use of the words and your interpretation are congruent, so that you can follow our path into chapters 4 and 5.

In chapter 4 we present why we believe traditional promotion is a poor fit for the nonprofit arts. We use examples from key ideas in chapter 3, and a brief case study which exemplifies the challenges of *promoting* in the nonprofit arts.

Chapter 5 describes some similarities between education and promotion. It presents why we believe education is a better fit for nonprofit arts organizations than promotion is, and it describes practical steps an organization can take to engage through education. The chapter includes the case of a theater company that used education as a means of audience retention and development.

To begin the consideration of a shift from promotion to education, we have included a short case that we feel exemplifies some elements of a transition from promotion to education. The case is about Audrey Bergauer, who became the executive director of the California Symphony in 2014, and how she transformed the organization and more than doubled their community impact in four years.

The Case of Aubrey Bergauer and the California Symphony

In 1986, Barry Jekowsky founded the California Symphony Orchestra in Walnut Creek, California. Walnut Creek is located twenty-five miles outside of San Francisco. Through the 1990s the California Symphony was a small but growing nonprofit. Community members were thrilled to have an arts organization in their town. For the first time they could attend a professional orchestra concert of great caliber without making the trip to busy San Francisco. The geographic location and the price point of the California Symphony made orchestral music more accessible to their community. The organization developed a strong following and expanded their season to account for demand. After several years, they created a Young Composer in Residency program. The program allowed composers to workshop new material and have it performed by a full orchestra. Every few years the organization would accept a new composer to take over the residency. Some called this residency program a national model for other orchestras.[1] The orchestra grew in popularity through the early 2000s and was named the "Best Symphony Orchestra in America" by *Reader's Digest* in 2005. Over the following eight years, however, the organization lost audience members, reduced their number of performances, and found themselves on the brink of closing.

In 2014, the California Symphony was at a crossroads. The trajectory of the organization had been consistently downward for years. To make matters worse, their finances were unsustainable and showed no signs of improvement. Due to their dire situation, the board was seriously considering declaring bankruptcy. Despite their efforts to persuade people to buy tickets and to donate, it seemed that the community had lost interest.

In exploring their options, they met with Aubrey Bergauer. Bergauer had set her sights on managing a symphony orchestra from a young age. She had what many considered (and may still consider) a radical approach to revolutionizing how symphony orchestras interact with their community. After ample consideration, the board opted to keep the California Symphony open and to hire Bergauer as their executive director. Over the next five years, Bergauer's approach not only saved the California Symphony as an organization, but also it changed the way they served their community.

Jay met with Bergauer to discuss the California Symphony and her efforts to engage with their community through education rather than promotion.

As he explained the concept of education vs. promotion she jumped in with a resounding "Yes!" She went on, "I just cringe every time I see anything 'salesy,' gimmicky, or persuasive. People post, 'buy your tickets now' or 'concert this weekend, don't forget!'" She considers this type of promotion disconnected from reality. "That's not even human, people don't do that! Nobody is reading that thinking, 'Oh I almost forgot, I'd better get my tickets.'" Though we laughed about it, she identified a sad truth. We have grown so accustomed to this type of promotion that we hardly recognize how strange the syntax is. Instead, we mostly gloss over and ignore it. She shared that this type of promotion was the primary approach the California Symphony marketing team took before she arrived. They would tell their community to hurry and buy tickets before they sold out—then they would not sell out. The majority of this communication took place through posters, direct mail postcards, email, and newspaper ads. Each time they produced a new concert, the cycle would begin again.

At the root of Bergauer's approach is the idea that people want to learn and need interaction. By creating a space (physically and digitally) where people can interact with interesting information and the organization, she helped develop increased levels of engagement. Their first step in transitioning from communicating through promotions to engaging through education was the introduction of Spotify playlists. For every concert the California Symphony produced, they distributed a playlist for the community. This allowed people to familiarize themselves with the music and have a greater grasp on what was being offered. Their potential audience could listen to the playlist on their own time, for free, and in any order they liked. Rather than creating a promotion designed to get the community members to buy, they shared the material that would be presented so that people could opt in if it interested them or opt out if not.

The entire approach shifted from promotion to education by engaging the community through content marketing. As Bergauer phrased it, "we were able to engage the community with meaningful content, and that really did the selling for us. Suddenly, we didn't have to try to persuade people to come." They stopped using their marketing department for the purpose of making sales in favor of using that energy to engage with the community and let the community opt in or out and control their experience. For the arts administrator who is managing a nonprofit arts organization on the brink of financial collapse, asking their marketing department to stop focusing on sales, frankly, sounds absurd. Yet, the result at the California Symphony? They started selling out for the first time in years.

Because many arts organizations struggle financially, fiscal sustainability is often the central consideration for marketing departments. These departments are tasked with monetizing the artistic offering. This value exchange often drives the way we think. Bergauer believes arts organizations "can and should provide value to people before the ticket purchase ever happens. Too often in the performing arts, especially in orchestras, so much of the education happens after the purchase." There is a fear that providing value to the community through educational engagement without a financial exchange means that people will not attend when there is a financial exchange. Bergauer shared that the data would tell us just the opposite. "Connecting with the community through education not only serves them better, it becomes the gateway for a future ticket purchase." In 2016, the California Symphony became the first orchestra to stream a concert through Facebook Live so that anyone in their community could have some experience of what they provide, making them more informed community members.

Bergauer acknowledged that making such significant changes is a real challenge. Not everyone at the California Symphony was on board with her approach. She categorized the staff members into three different groups. Some were on board from the beginning and, as she put it, "saw the value of changing the way we communicated." Others were willing to go along if they were led. The last group was resistant to change and wanted to maintain the marketing approach that had been entrenched for years. She noted that there was no correlation to how long a person had been employed at the California Symphony, their age, or their amount of experience in indicating which of the three perspectives they held. People who advocate for change may see age as an indicator of change resistance, but Bergauer did not see it that way. The California Symphony's oldest employee, who was in her late seventies, was one of the strongest supporters of a shift away from traditional promotion.

The California Symphony has even made small steps toward engagement through co-creation. At a recent offering, each audience member was given a piece of sandpaper, a comb, and a pair of wine glasses. These were items that the composer used when creating a piece of music. The composer then worked with the audience, exploring ways to play them as instruments during the performance. This experience was the only element Bergauer recalled that bordered on co-creation, and yet through shifting from traditional promotion to education, the California Symphony produced the same artistic offerings but substantially changed their impact and reach in the community.

From 2014 to 2019, the California Symphony more than doubled the number of tickets sold in a year, and more than tripled the number of donor households. In Bergauer's first year as executive director, the symphony saw a 20% increase in attendance. Before Bergauer began, the California Symphony produced four concerts annually and each sold between 50% and 60% capacity. By 2019, the California Symphony was producing twelve concerts annually, and most were sold to capacity. Perhaps the most telling number of all is their first-time attendee return rate. The national average of people who attend an orchestral concert for the first time, and return within one year is 10%; under Berguaer's leadership the California Symphony reached over 30%.

3
Contrasting Frameworks
Promotion and Education

Every day, each of us is inundated with thousands of promotions. We are bombarded. If you look around at this very moment, you will probably see several examples: A branding element on a product, a label, or sticker. If your television is on, chances are you will catch a commercial. In just looking at a phone or computer, it is almost certain that someone will *push* a promotion on you. Push is an actual marketing term sellers use when targeting potential buyers; when they believe they have something you want, they use *push advertisements*. These are some of the most recognizable advertising and promotional means we encounter.

Before describing the challenges of applying the concept of promotion to the arts sector and explaining why education is a better fit, it is vital that each is defined. This chapter first describes the basic process of promotion as it has existed since the development of McCarthy's marketing mix was published in 1960. It then presents the intended meaning when we use the word *education*. Of the four Es, education may be the most easily misunderstood. The word *education* has held different meanings through different moments in time, and an individual's experience likewise shapes their understanding of education. Though it may be tempting to skip this chapter and presume a true sense of what we mean by education, to do so may lead to great confusion. One may even find that our use of the word *education* is the opposite of your perception or experience.

What is Promotion?

Most people have a sense of how to define the word *promotion*. When we think of the marketing teams in our nonprofit arts organizations, most of the time we think about promotion rather than the other functions of the traditional marketing mix (product, price, and place). In this way of thinking, we conflate the words *marketing* and *promotion*. The origin of the word *promotion* is Latin: *promotionem*, which means to move forward. Consider promotion in for-profit marketing. Promotion *moves an idea forward* into the minds of those in the target market to increase awareness, create brand loyalty, and ultimately persuade them to purchase the product. In the 1970s, Boone and Kurts identified the three functions of promotion: supplying information to the marketplace, increasing demand, and creating differentiation for the core product.[1] These objectives are obtained (the company hopes) through promotional tactics most often developed in a promotional plan. Like the marketing mix, promotion has a "promotion mix" that blends promotional methods to find the right balance for a company. Promotional tactics that make up the mix take numerous forms, but the historical bedrock for promotion is *advertising*.

Advertising

Advertising is a form of communication that typically uses media of some type (print, email, billboard, radio, digital graphics, social media, etc.) to *persuade* its audience to purchase a product or believe an idea.[2] Historically, advertisements have been easily identified as paid for by the company (or their partners) to sell a product. When arts organizations print posters and postcards or send eblasts, they are usually advertising to promote an exhibit, performance, or another offering. The design and distribution of advertising is often the primary function of arts organization's marketing departments. Unlike many arts organizations, large for-profit companies' marketing departments spend substantial sums on market research to develop precise metrics for how advertisements should be designed and distributed. This research is usually completed through observation, surveys, and focus groups to establish target consumers' habits and perspectives. Through these research efforts, marketing departments aim to mix advertisements of just the right style, placement, and amount into their promotional mix. Through this work, the company hopes to ensure that they receive the best possible return on investment.

Marketers design advertisements to work in multiple media forms at once. These advertisements work together to achieve advertising objectives. All advertising goals fall under three primary objectives: to inform, to persuade, and to remind. Though objectives can certainly be broken down further, this chapter limits exploration to these three broad objectives for the sake of time and space.

To Inform

Advertisements inform, introduce a brand, product, or product trait to the market. Informative advertisements are most often used by new companies or at the first release of a revolutionary product. Informative advertising can also introduce a new target audience to an existing product, either because a new audience has been identified within an existing region or because the product is newly available in the area. Recently, a new internet provider began providing service to our region in Tallahassee. Marketers inundated the community with informational advertisements in the months leading up to the service's availability. Though a major national internet provider, marketers saw the need to inform their new (geographic) target audience about the upcoming availability. These informative advertisements do not expect a response from the consumer. They are foundational in the process and lay the groundwork for what will eventually come: a call to act/buy.

To Persuade

Marketers transition to persuasive advertising once the product and brand are established for the target audience. All promotion shares a basis in persuasion to sell a product or idea, but this segment of advertising is specifically designed to persuade through an emphasis on consumer benefit, most often relayed to the buyer using a value-oriented, emotive tactic. Persuasive advertising is especially vital in markets where there is significant competition and for products that people do not consider necessities. There are many subcategories to persuasive advertising. Many companies emphasize the quality or craftsmanship of a product, environmental benefits, aesthetic qualities, or even how cool a product is. Marketers consider the right blend of logic and emotional appeal to convince their audience to purchase. As soon as the new internet provider in our area began service, a new stream of advertising, this time persuasive advertising, appeared in mailboxes across the county. It touted new hook-up options, high network speeds, and a new approach to customer service. This line of advertising was designed not just to persuade the market to buy but also to convince us to cancel our current service and switch to another. The materials presented their company as the new, cutting edge, and elite carrier to distinguish themselves and persuade consumers to sign on.

To Remind

The purpose of reminder advertising is exactly as it sounds—marketers remind consumers that their product exists. This form of advertising appears only once a brand and product are well established. In for-profit marketing, reminder advertising is especially necessary in markets with high competition. Reminders maintain the attention of the audience and help to prevent competitors from taking current or potential business. Reminder advertising is also referred to as *retention* advertising.[3]

Sometimes, marketers include persuasive elements in reminders. Six to eight months after the internet provider began service, they reminded us of their existence in a direct mail campaign. The postcards noted their speeds were still the fastest and also appealed to our emotions by telling us that we had been left behind and that we were not a part of the elite group of customers they were now serving in the community. Logos and other branding are a tool to provide consistent reminders to users about who makes the product and who they should trust.

Madison and Vine

Madison and Vine advertising has taken a greater hold in recent years. The name references both the iconic streetcorner of Hollywood and Vine that represents the Hollywood entertainment industry and Madison Avenue, which brings to mind the traditional notion of marketing. Madison and Vine advertising is a way for promotions to break through the noise and clamor by turning the promotion into entertainment. In this type of promotion, products are placed into plotlines for the consumer to follow. In some cases, treasure hunts, searches, or consumer participation in the entertainment is used to promote something. This type of *advertainment* not only successfully draws consumers but also draws consumers in a way that allows them to be a part of the process.

The insurance company Progressive developed one of the best *advertainment* campaigns. They promoted products and services through a series of brief stories, told in advertisements that focused on the invented characters, Progressive spokespeople Flo and Jamie. Competitor Geico also uses advertainment to entertain and capture consumers.

Product Placement

Sometimes promotions are built directly into commercial entertainment. Product placement became a common form of promotion in the 1970s, though its roots can be traced back to the late 1800s.[4] Companies can build recognition for their products by embedding branding elements in films or television.[5] Just the mention of a product on-screen can be sold. The product placement market is worth over $1 billion a year in US films alone.[6]

Famously, in 1982, Universal Pictures and the Hershey Company came to an agreement to feature Reece's Pieces in the film *E.T.* The initial script called for M&Ms, but Mars Inc. declined to be involved. The Hershey Company provided $1 million in advertising in exchange for product placement in the film, promoting both the film and the candy. As a result of the collaboration, sales for Reece's Pieces tripled.[7] Through the simple influence of consumer recognition, product placement persuades people to make purchases generating billions of dollars in annual sales for corporations.

Social Media Influencers

Since 2006, companies have used social media as a channel for promotion. As individual users on social media platforms gained followers, they also gained the power to influence their followers' behavior.[8] Companies recognized and sought to use this power to promote their products. They created a new type of endorsement market by hiring social media *influencers* to use and discuss their products. Formerly, paid endorsements were almost exclusively obtained by celebrities and sports stars. These influencers had the appearance of being just like other users on the platform, so companies could persuade the other users to buy their products without the content feeling like a traditional advertisement. Over time, greater regulation has been established so that influencers must disclose that they were paid or received products in exchange for their reviews.

Societal Marketing Concept

One fairly recent conceptual approach to marketing that has taken hold is the idea of *societal marketing*. In the societal marketing model, marketers concern themselves with consumer needs and expectations for the organization and making sales that benefit society's long-term needs. Though the approach is beginning to take root in commercial enterprises, this concept happens to be borrowed from the very structure of nonprofit organizations. Though arts organizations tend to lean toward making decisions that benefit the art primarily (or the artist primarily), with the consumer and the long-term societal benefits being secondary to those decisions, the concept of societal marketing may shift arts organizations' focus to serving the community first. The concept of societal marketing is closely tied to *corporate social responsibility*, *sustainable development*, and the *triple bottom line*.

Social Marketing

Another similar yet distinct type of marketing related to the kind of engagement we espouse for the arts is *social marketing*. Social marketing concerns itself with marketing decisions designed to influence behaviors that will change the social fabric of a community—*behavior* being the watchword in social marketing. Differing from societal marketing, which embraces the need to accept and merge *social responsibility* into marketing promotions, social marketing employs specific *social issues*. To utilize this strategy, organizations must recognize a willingness to change or the potential for change on the part of the consumer and know the issues most likely to be on-topic for society at large. It is behavior that the social marketing concept is designed to target.

Because the arts are designed to inform and reflect life, record history, and instigate social change, social marketing is a concept that not only appears to be borrowed from the arts but also may take greater hold as issues such as the challenges of global climate change continue to influence generations with greater and greater urgency.

Promotion and Education

Many marketing professionals would insist that a large portion of their work is educating the market on a company's product through promotion, thinking that *to inform* is a function of education. Yet, this type of education differs from how the engagement edge applies it.

When a company has a new concept or an innovative product, the market needs to be informed about the value the latest innovation can bring them. Anthony recalls that when flat-screen televisions were in development, savvy marketing managers conducted research and realized that consumers would not spend significantly more for a television just because it was flat. The challenge was getting consumers to value a *trait* of the product, in addition to the core product itself. Since televisions already existed, consumers did not need to be told what a television was or how to use it for enjoyment. Months and months before flat-screen televisions hit the market, one television company started running advertisements showing how people could take advantage of the flat screen. Consumers could move it easily, it took up less space in their home, and they could hang it on their wall to improve the aesthetic experience. People needed to see how hanging a television on a wall was useful, particularly in small places. These benefits became the main features of these advertisements. Typically, push marketing requires a higher degree of convincing before consumers are persuaded to try a new product. By the time flat-screen televisions hit the market, consumers had been told the value the flat screen could bring to them and were prepared to pay the increased price.

Final Thoughts in Defining Promotion

There is a common thread throughout this chapter: In each area above, the motive is persuasion to create sales. If a company's promotions are successful, the company has persuaded consumers to accept a certain idea or purchase a product, or both. Companies use promotions to change the behavior of consumers. The only reason US companies spend hundreds of billions of dollars every year on promotions is to change behavior so that people will purchase a product or service that they might otherwise not buy. The concept of behavior modification is also evident in the example given above about educating the market on the value of flat-screen televisions. The ultimate goal of educating the market through guided promotions is to persuade consumers to buy, increasing profits.

Many countries have established legal restrictions on advertisements directed at children.[9] This legislation stems from the recognition that children have no understanding that the advertiser's purpose is to change their beliefs or behavior. Traditional advertisements are easily identified as company funded, but advertament, product placement, and social media promotions often blur the distinctions between what is and is not promotional material. In analyzing the term *promotion* in the context of a marketing tool, there is no inference of any moral perspective or criticism. Promotion as a part of the marketing mix is greatly effective in persuading consumers to make purchases; it suits for-profit organizations perfectly and has become a vital part of the market.

What Is Education?

Education is a process that has gone through innumerable changes. It started by sharing stories, but nearly six hundred years ago, the printing press changed the process of education drastically. Books that recorded information no longer had to be hand copied, so they became more widely available, and teaching practices began to change.[10] Eventually, people established the read/lecture/test method of educating. Education was about memorization. In the 1960s, Friere challenged this notion of education in his book *Pedagogy of the Oppressed*.[11] He wrote that when a teacher presents students with a collection of facts to memorize, they begin the process of oppressing their students. Freire calls this the banking model of education, and it reduces the students' humanity to a receptacle for facts. In such a situation, the teacher increases their own power instead of encouraging and strengthening students. The banking model assumes that students are oblivious and that they cannot know anything without their teacher. It is oppressive because it ingrains this concept in the students. The model indoctrinates students to believe that banking is the only way to learn, while in reality, the students lose their ability to control their education as a result.

Constructivism is at the base of how nonprofit arts organizations can use education to engage with their communities. Constructivism is an epistemological approach often attributed to Paiget[12] and Vygotsky.[13] Both were psychologists focused on child development. Constructivists see the development of knowledge as uniquely constructed by every learner based on their past experiences and existing knowledge.[14] Learners build knowledge as they have new experiences and interpret new information through the lens of their perspectives and previously built knowledge. As a result, every person can construct different knowledge from the same experience. Unlike the oppressive approach of an educator telling the student what to do or think, constructivism encourages the educator to create opportunities and experiences that enable the learner to develop their own unique knowledge.

With constructivism as a growing learning theory, researchers and teachers began to shift instruction modes.[15] The focus is now becoming *learner-centered education* as an approach to teaching. Essentially, this means that the practical work done in the classroom is not performed by the teacher. Instead, learner-centered teaching focuses on the fact that people learn better when they actively engage in something.[16] Many teachers prepare classroom exercises, discussions, work, and then explain how the day will work, letting the students complete their given activities. The teacher is present to answer any questions that may arise or facilitate discussions and exercises. **Notice that the work is done in advance so that when the educator and the students meet, the students are the ones who work for an understanding.** The shift empowers them rather than oppresses them.

Subscribers to the learner-centered philosophy have found that students are much more adept at developing their ability to think critically about a topic when they have explored it in a learner-centered fashion. The bulk of the work for the teacher is done long in advance of the class meeting. This preparation typically includes designing class exercises and games that encourage students to make discoveries as they work through problems. Often, these problems become interactive between the students. For example, in a course for arts managers on business issues in the arts sector, each student works on one of two teams to complete a contract negotiation. One group represents union production workers, and the other a performing arts organization. Over the course of several class days (in and out of class), the students navigate the terms of the contract while the teacher observes and answers procedural questions. At the conclusion of the exercise, a representative from each group signs the agreement, and everyone participates in a discussion. Ultimately, the teacher reviews the contract, and provides feedback to both groups. Learner-centered activities allow the student to *engage* with the subject material, classmates, and the instructor. Rather than being a one-way dump of information, it becomes an exploration. Students learn not through the process of rote memorization but by being involved in digging into how a concept works, what other issues might be related to the concept, and possibly practicing the concept.[17]

Why is this important in promoting the arts? Because the fancy brochures arts organizations create, where we describe the plot of a play, the artist's biography, or the background of the cellist, are a form of lecturing to the marketplace. The Facebook advertisement with a ballet title and little else does not seem to stir audiences into rushing to attend. **Learner-centered teaching is a pedagogy of engagement that allows the development of a long-term curiosity about subjects (the arts).** It introduces learners (our future audience) to experiencing life (seeing art) in a way that satisfies their psychological and self-fulfillment needs (Maslow). Please note that the learner-centered approach does not tell people what to think. **Instead, it helps them discover pathways of thought and then lets them explore on their own.** Telling a potential audience member the plot points of *Romeo & Juliet* and the historical value of Shakespeare is mini-lecturing in an inefficient format; however, explaining that "two teenage lovers have died at their own hands rather than suffer the hate of rivaling wealth" allows the audience to explore (and feel, and think about) the story's core concept emotionally in their own way.

Education is not a means to teach what to think; it's a tool to open pathways for how to think. Traditional promotion as we know it tells its audience what to think about a product. That is the function of conventional promotion, and it works well in the for-profit sector to sell products. In the flat-screen television example, the company created the awareness of a benefit and inspired the consumer's imagination before moving into *push* promotions. Even when flat-screen television companies inform consumers in this way (what they might call education), they do not cross into the realm of engagement. Most promoters who insist that a part of their work is education approach the market by telling them what to think—not helping their community develop for themselves *how* to think. Education that creates engagement between the organization and the individual matches the nonprofit arts sector better than traditional promotion. As service organizations, rather than telling their audience *what* to think, nonprofit arts organizations can engage in dialogue with their community to help them develop for themselves *how* to think and feel about arts experiences.

Education and Arts Organizations

Dance, visual art, music, theater, and other forms of artistic creation are all included in *the arts*. It is recognized that each art form's benefits must be promoted as we offer it in the marketplace. It is, however, often assumed that communities do not need to discover the art's value. This assumption fails to see those who have not discovered the impact the arts can have. We instantly marginalize anyone who does require that information to make an informed decision about whether to attend or not. Like the arts organization that distributes a survey to their attendees to ask what they would like to see next, this approach fails to engage with those in the community who are not already participating. **Some of our communications should promote the idea of being able to enjoy the arts.** Purposeful communication and consistently engaging in a dialogue with community groups about their values and desires, and finding the appropriate matches within the arts organization, are of utmost importance. Determining what values community members share with your arts organization and how you can manage those shared values is an ongoing process as communities are constantly growing and changing.

In this context, education is not about an organization citing relevant research on the cognitive growth an arts consumer may experience. **The best education is based on discussing concepts and finding ways to inform an understanding of the arts, so that community members can determine for themselves how to value arts experiences.** The arts must explore the most efficient way organizations can conceptualize, design, and frame their offerings to respond to the community's needs, wants, and demands. In this way, education becomes a dialogue and moves into the realm of engagement. **In the arts, we cite policy statements about the importance of the arts to communities as an entity, but we rarely share how the arts can satisfy individual needs.**

Many arts organizations already consider some of their promotion to be education. We talk about the brilliance of the individual artists, explain the story, mention songs, and throw "laugh-out-loud funny" into the description. Insights are shared about the painter's tragic life, or we provide some other bits of historical information. The people who want the lecture, who would like to learn why those names are significant, and those who appreciate the historical relevance, seem to be coming to us using the processes we have already been using. As long as this strategy works to attract some audience members, those processes do not need to change. Yet, we know something is missing. We go through all that effort and wonder why new college graduates do not come rushing to our doors. The reason is relatively simple: **We never engage with them about what they are looking for in relation to what we provide.** We told them about the specific piece of art and attempted to impress them with some names they are unlikely to recognize, explained the plot, and even went as far as to tell them how we expect them to behave: laugh out loud. Yet, we never asked them what they wanted, we never taught them about how we offer what they want (because we often do), and we did not give them a chance to be a part of that process. Trying new ways of promotion to reach beyond the demographics of those who are already attending may seem futile. **Consumers are inundated with promotions. Instead, we must engage through education.**

The arts require some level of push marketing. Because the art itself is typically new, we have to provide education about each experience's unique value. **For the purpose of convincing consumers to buy, promotion is neither enough nor appropriate since the primary function of the nonprofit arts organization is service to the community.** The arts organization should be helping community members understand the value to them. How will they feel when they experience the art? What are the values they have that we will be satisfying?

The Purpose of Education

If the main objectives of advertising are to inform, remind, and persuade, how do those fit with the concepts of education and promotion? One of the functions of education is to inform, so there seem to be some parallels between the two concepts. Persuasion, however, is not a function of education. Likewise, though educators may sometimes remind students of lessons they have learned, reminders are not necessarily a primary function of education.

The primary function of education is not to fill students' heads with information maintained through rote memorization. Though it is important to retain information, meaningful learning such as learner-centered education instills the *transfer* of information. Mayer explained that "retention requires that students remember what they have learned, whereas transfer requires students not only to remember but also to make sense of and be able to use what they have learned."[18] In any educational setting, the main function of education is to train the brain to be able to process information for itself, to teach the individual to ask questions, seek answers, and to learn how to learn on their own.

Beyond the training of the brain, another important function of education is socialization. Through education we learn the values, norms, standards, and practices of our society and community. Those values often include individualism, respect for authority, punctuality, patriotism, competition, and similar ideals. We also learn how to interact and communicate with others.

In this realm, the function of education is *social integration*. Social norms are learned through how we interact with one another at various stages of our educational development. Through social integration, we develop a sense of being part of the social fabric.

The lesser-perceived function of education is social and cultural innovation. Education spurs learners to think of new ways of describing, defining, and understanding the world. Note that cultural innovation is also a part of this function. Artists develop their art based on their education in society and its social reflections, and they tell stories based on their understanding of that social experience.

These functions are all associated with socialization. These theories embolden the suggestion that education is much more than the often-used memorization model. Here is why that matters: In chapter 1, we mentioned the root of the engagement edge and suggested that arts administrator Ben Cameron had sounded the bell regarding that topic years ago with his oft-repeated quote, "Our mission is the orchestration of social interaction, in which the performance is a piece, but only a piece, of what we're called to do."[19] The function of the arts is social, primarily. Though we like to believe that the arts are meant to entertain or enlighten (a variation on to educate) , their primary function is a social one. We gather with other human beings to experience a reflection of society created by an artist or collection of artists. We hear the sounds others make, and we respond communally. When we hear laughter, applause, sobs, we are likely to laugh, applaud, or cry, respectively. We overhear comments on the art, and we enter into intellectual discourse with our friends about the quality or content of the art. It is a social experience. Though artists have experimented with art that does not have a social function for the community at large,[20] mainstream art continues to be primarily, as Ben Cameron put it, "a social interaction."

The concepts of art being a social experience and education working to help us learn to adapt to society, seem to be more precisely aligned than the concept of promotion and the work of nonprofit arts organizations, which may now appear to be almost in conflict.

Conclusion

This chapter reviewed the definition of "promotion" as outlined in McCarthy's marketing mix. Unfortunately, this term in the arts has become synonymous with the word *marketing* in general. Although the two are related, promotion is only one piece of the marketing mix. It is used by an organization to provide information about a product to the marketplace, convince consumers to want it, and differentiate it from other products on the market. Advertisements are at the core of promotion, and product placement through commercial entertainment as well as social media have become increasingly prevalent. The chapter also discussed the engagement edge's alternative to promotion: education. Learner-centered education, which places the teacher in the role of facilitator, builds curiosity. By applying this learner-centered approach to the arts, marketers will be more effective in attracting new consumers. Otherwise, non-profit arts professionals are doomed to push an endless stream of experiences on audiences that may not want or appreciate them. The next chapter will take a deeper look at the reasons why the current approach of persuading potential arts consumers through promotion is failing. This will be essential to understanding chapter 5, which explains why education should replace promotion for nonprofit arts organizations.

4
Promotion and the Arts

Every year, hundreds of billions of dollars are spent on advertising in the United States alone. That is an incredible sum of money dedicated to convincing us to make purchases. When for-profit corporations use promotional tactics, they work; so it makes sense that nonprofit arts organizations would desire to gather customers through traditional promotional channels. Though not all for-profit corporations that sell products turn a profit each year, the vast majority of those that do use promotion to persuade people to make a purchase.

Large corporations have an easier time advertising to large populations than small ones do because they can wield massive advertising budgets around the complex maze of media pathways to reach the consumer. Though small businesses may desire to push their advertisements onto the market, they frequently look around and think there is no point in attempting to compete. How could a small budget ever be impactful enough to break through the clutter of advertising in the world today? That approach is shortsighted. Small businesses have an advantage over larger corporations when it comes to building a customer base. Smaller companies are nimble; they can move and respond quickly. They can reach consumers at the micro or individual level and can often more effectively communicate directly with potential consumers face-to-face.

Imagine a local sandwich shop opening in a town of fifty thousand. To create their base, they may reach out by direct mail with discounts and coupons, submit an ad to the local newspaper, and put a sandwich board outside of their location advertising their sandwich of the day. If someone comes to their shop and asks them to take out an advertisement in the local school's yearbook or sponsor a local sports team, the owner can participate without passing the request through the corporate office or consulting a manual. By forming these types of relationships, the small business quickly embeds itself within the community.[1] It can then create meaningful connections that a large corporation never could.

Embedding their business within the community is exactly what most small nonprofit arts organizations want to do. There is, however, a stark difference in purpose between the sandwich shop's behavior and nonprofit arts organizations. The sandwich shop distributes coupons for discount sandwiches not to serve the community but to increase their sales. Any benefit to the community is a byproduct of that purpose. The sandwich shop purchases an ad in the yearbook to promote their shop and sell more sandwiches. Even if they say it is about supporting the community, that is a byproduct, not the purpose. Consider it this way: what if the same person went to the shop and said, "would your business donate $400 to the high school? No one will know the shop donated, the shop will not receive any recognition or promotion, but it would certainly help us out." Very few for-profit businesses would ever consider such an arrangement because the purpose of the business is profits.

In contrast to both large and small businesses, a nonprofit's primary purpose is to serve its community, not to generate profit for its owners.[2] As we noted in chapter 2, this is the only reason governments provide special tax benefits to nonprofits. It is the overarching issue with promotion for the nonprofit arts. Marketing experts designed promotion as a tool to persuade the recipient to make a purchase so that corporations can earn profits. **The purpose of nonprofits is service, not profits. Under promotion, nonprofit arts organizations would use persuasion on the very people they are supposed to be serving.**

Chapter 3 reviewed the foundational principles of promotion and several techniques for crafting promotional messaging. This chapter reviews them with an understanding of what they are, how they work, and describes why they are less effective for the nonprofit arts than for-profit corporations.

Promotional Messaging

One of the first lessons of promotion is that, typically, messaging must clearly define the product. For a utilitarian product, this means describing what the product does and its most valuable features. Communicating the product's strengths is vital to helping it stand out.[3] The sandwich shop might describe the quality of ingredients, how quickly they can make the sandwiches, or share quotes from customers. In the nonprofit arts, marketing departments often try to describe the art or who is performing. Part III of this book centers on exploring the idea of product in the arts. Shared is Dewey's notion that art is not the physical piece of art in a museum or a play that takes place on stage, but rather, the art is related to an internal occurrence that happens as the audience has an experience. Unlike a utilitarian product that is complete after it is manufactured, an art product is not complete until it is experienced. In creating promotional messaging, the arts organization producing a play six months from now cannot accurately describe their product's strengths because the product has yet to exist. When creating messaging about an art exhibit, the exhibit's strengths can only be assumed until audience members experience the art. **Knowing the strengths of an artistic product is impossible until a suitable number of audience members have rendered their opinions.**

Some organizations create videos of the audience sharing their experience after an event. In the videos, the audience usually describes their experience. These are often the first components arts organizations use to provide messaging about the product (experience) itself. These edited advertisements put a previous audience at the center of the communication to show what the experience could be like for the viewer. Though they may still function from a basis of persuasion and encourage them to make a purchase, this type of promotion can border on education since the former audience members function as models who have been positively rewarded from the arts experience.[4] For messaging in a promotion to work, the messages must be consistent and have time to circulate. Unfortunately, most nonprofit arts organizations house the same event or gallery exhibit for only a few weeks. By the time the audience has the experience, and such a video can be shot, edited, and distributed, the promotion barely has time to have a meaningful impact. Right from the beginning, the nature of many arts experiences limits the potential of traditional promotion messaging.

Creating Effective Messaging

When arts organizations describe a product through promotional messaging, they describe features they expect the audience to experience. This line of information-based communication can close sales with those who regularly attend what the arts organization offers. Arts organizations can simply say, "we are having an event," and some people from the community will attend. These existing customers already know what to expect. Most arts organizations' promotional messaging is aimed at frequent attendees. Their messaging often describes the distinguishing factors between different art products. That, however, does little to educate those who do not yet consistently attend.

Traditional promotional messaging also seeks to stimulate or provoke the consumer. It is this stimulation that ultimately leads to the sale. Marketers use color, font, typeface size, artwork, photos, and more to stimulate the consumer. In the arts, we mimic this process as well, matching the colors of our advertisements to the emotions expected to be elicited from patrons while consuming the art. We try to capture what the audience will feel. However, a colorful advertisement that is in a language different from one the consumer speaks is of little use. When a potential audience member who has not had the appropriate art education receives this advertisement, the communication falls as flat as if it had been disseminated in a foreign language. Telling someone who has never attended a play that the experience will make them feel sad for the protagonist is not likely to generate much in terms of sales.

The clever marketer also often incorporates a marketing hook into their promotional messaging. The hook aims to catch a consumer with something novel, special, or unique like a jingle or catch phrase that stays with them.[5] For example, the famed "Where's the beef?" from the 1980s is still recognized today by those who heard that promotion. Jingles were once the best marketing hook out there. Most people recognize Budweiser's "Whassup," from 1999–2000, KFC's "Finger lick'n good" slogan from the 1950s, and "Got milk" from 1993.

Often, marketers use a promotional campaign with a discount or free offer.[6] In the arts, we attempt to use discounts as a hook. We create subscriptions, which traditionally offer a discount for purchasing every offering available for the year. Subscription campaigns as a hook are a perk for those who already attend and choose the discounted price because of their existing participation. The Valencia Dance Ensemble case demonstrates this issue perfectly. For the person who attends infrequently, or for those who have never attended, this particular campaign is useless. Even a free offering may not entice audience members who do not feel welcome because of the collection of social rules they may feel are required to attend. They may see arts organizations as elitist, even when an arts organization says, "all are welcome."

Finally, savvy marketers use promotional messaging to give themselves credibility. When arts organizations try to do this, they most often detail what a critic has to say about the art. Like the promotional video of prior audiences sharing experiences, this messaging can only be distributed just after the event's opening since the critic needs to have a complete experience. When the critic writes, generally the central focus is on the exhibit or performance itself. When an arts organization shares the critic's review, those who frequently attend and those who regularly read that critic's writing can benefit from the communication. We posit, however, that for those who have not had many arts experiences, providing deep intellectual analysis by a critic, is akin to providing the chemical composition of toothpaste to consumers. It can make the experience seem inaccessible.

The vast majority of promotions from arts organizations are aimed at those who already attend. The promotional messages of arts organizations often do little to attract or build new audiences. Because it is easier and less expensive to maintain existing customers, communications are almost exclusively targeted to them. Then we question why new people are not attending. One way to build an audience is to **reach those who do not currently attend and engage with them around arts experiences—not for the sake of persuading them to attend but to provide value to the community through the interaction**. In the case of the Valencia Dance Ensemble, we present an arts organization that did just the opposite by following strict promotional methodology without developing depth in engagement through education.

Case of the Valencia Dance Ensemble

In 1992, Sophia Masterson founded the Valencia Dance Ensemble (VDE) in Valencia, Spain. At the time, it was the only company doing work of its kind in the geographic area. VDE produced dance performances inspired by local stories. In the early years, they began with three to four productions annually, with each production having five performances over one week. By 1997, they presented eight productions each year, with each production having between eight and twenty-four performances over periods ranging from one to three weeks. They maintained this rate of performance throughout the next ten years and had great success. Over that time, they welcomed more guest artists from around Spain and internationally and, as a result, relied less on local talent. Masterson shared that at the time, "the community support was outstanding. Every year we seemed to welcome more and more people and grew in our ability to bring world-class dance experiences into our neighborhood."

In 2008, as Masterson neared retirement, she noticed a concerning trend as they came to the end of their sixteenth year. Performances that were previously sold out frequently had available seats. In reviewing the data from the years 2005–2008, she noted that each year attendance had dropped between 3% and 5%. Though they had the data available, no one at the organization had been tracking annual attendance. The marketing director Tomas Vence had tracked the performance attendance from event to event. Audience members attended some productions more than others, so there was consistent fluctuation from production to production. The trends seemed consistent, but Vence had missed the larger trend that had occurred over time. Masterson noted, "we had spent our early years focused on building our audience. Once we had a consistent audience base, we worked to keep them buying tickets by enhancing the level of talent in our performances." She recognized that the implications of this consistent annual drop-off in attendance could have meant the end of the organization.

Before Materson had the opportunity to meet with Vence to discuss the downturn in attendance, a relative of Vence's passed away, leaving him with a significant inheritance. Vence announced that he would be going into early retirement and gave four weeks' notice along with a generous donation. Masterson's concern only grew, "it was a really challenging time. I was supposed to be retiring, and we lost our marketing director, and we had this downturn in attendance. I didn't know where to turn." Though Vence had two marketing associates, they were new to the organization and had limited marketing experience. One was a former dancer with the organization, and the other's background was in graphic design. Neither was equipped to take over the position. Masterson decided to use the situation to transition VDE's marketing department to new leadership rather than hiring from within. Masterson's son-in-law, Isaac Romero, had completed a master's degree in marketing several months before and had yet to find a corporate marketing position.

Masterson and Romero met to discuss VDE and the marketing director position. Masterson felt that Romero would be a perfect fit because of his promotions background. It didn't hurt that him filling the position would allow Masterson to remain more personally connected to the organization after she retired.

In their meeting, Romero laid out his perspective about the shift in attendance. He believed the issues stemmed from an issue with promotion.

He thought the pricing was not a problem, he didn't think anything should change about where they sold their tickets, and he certainly was not going to address the product and tell his mother-in-law how the dancers should move around the stage. Though he took no issue with Vence personally, Romero felt that the drop in attendance was due to a lack of knowledge and implementation of tried-and-true promotion methods. "By the end of the meeting," Masterson shared, "I was convinced that I had the right person to steer the marketing [department]."

VDE welcomed Romero as the new director of marketing, and he and Vence spent several weeks reviewing the existing promotional plans before Vence left the company. The company had long relied on posters and postcards with simple graphics to announce their upcoming performances and events. Vence also ran advertisements in several local newspapers and twice promoted through a radio station that broadcast arts news. He stopped the radio advertisements because they seemed to have no effect. VDE was also active in using their email list of previous buyers to, as Masterson phrased it, "promote the upcoming events and encourage patrons to buy tickets."

Romero began constructing a new promotional plan for the company with one primary objective: boost VDE's sales by recapturing the audience that had dropped off over the previous several years. Masterson remembers, "he came in with a real fire and passion to get the company back on track."

Though Masterson had the data about how many tickets were sold and that fewer had been sold each year, they did not have information about which audience members had stopped attending. It was possible that audience members hadn't dropped off entirely but were attending fewer events each year. Likewise, it was possible that some audience members were attending more frequently, and a larger number than projected had stopped attending. Romero proposed that the company create a bundled offering with a discounted price for their upcoming season of performances. He believed that this hook would encourage those who currently attend to purchase more and that the communication could recapture audience members who had dropped off over the previous years. He was especially drawn to this idea because this was a hook that could be shared with everyone on the organization's list and did not have to be specifically targeted to those who had stopped attending. This was the first time the organization had ever offered a package deal. The advertisement was simple: it included the dates and titles with a description of the discounted offer, and at the bottom of the ad was a sunburst with the words "call now" emblazoned in red.

Before the bundled offering went out, Romero approached Masterson with an idea. "He wanted to limit the amount of time our audience had to take advantage of a super early bird price," Masterson remembers. "The idea was that we could get them to buy immediately, because if they feared losing out on a steeper discount that they'd pull the trigger to get the tickets." Though Masterson felt a bit uneasy with such a hard sell, she recognized that what they had been doing was no longer working. Something needed to change, and that was why Romero was there, to create meaningful change. After the early bird, they would continue to use the bundled ticket price as a hook in communications until the first performance of the season. The hook and call to action went out, and recipients of the advertisement were given three weeks to respond to lock in the early bird price for the performance season.

The day the message went out, the ticket office was bombarded with calls. The organization had never experienced anything like it. Everyone in the organization shifted to support the ticket office to help make sales. Romero created a thermometer graph to track the sales progress and hung it prominently in the ticket office. His goal: sell at least 50% of the last season's annual sales by the first performance. In the following days, although the volume of calls decreased, the number of transactions still exceeded the two-person ticket office staff's capabilities. As the excitement of the increased sales subsided, staff members began to grumble that they should not continue to take ticket office calls. Though they had for years operated with only two ticket office staff members, Masterson decided that it was time to hire two additional ticket agents to help with the increased volume. It was a particularly exciting time, Masterson recalls, "there was a new energy in the organization, something we hadn't felt since the early days when we were just starting out." Over the next few weeks, tickets continued to sell fast—faster than ever before. Finally, the organization was on the right path toward meaningful change.

Though Romero's promotion had already resulted in the largest single-day and single-week sales records in the organization's history, he pressed on. He met with the marketing associate with a background in graphic design. Together they discussed the materials used to promote each production. In the past, the VDE's promotional materials were printed with a tan background. They included the VDE's logo and title art at the top, with dates, times, performance location, and the ticket information below. The art's primary use was in their central promotional channels: their website, email blasts, posters, postcards, and newspaper advertisements. Romero and the associate created a new plan to design specific art for each production. The design would be able to stand alone as a piece of art and communicate to the audience the feeling of the production using an image of some type in addition to the title art and pertinent attendance information. As the event drew closer, Romero planned to add a "buy now" call to action on the art.

Romero, Masterson, and the associate worked together over several weeks to develop the promotional art. Although many of the productions had not yet started being developed, Masterson was able to estimate each piece's feel so that Romero and the associate could create the promotional art. Masterson was thrilled, "I remember being so impressed by the eight pieces of art that we had them printed as 24x36 posters and hung them in the lobby. They were so beautiful. I still have several as art just in my house." Romero focused on using the new promotional art to promote the first production. Posters were hung around the city, postcards mailed, and an email was produced using the images and a reminder of the bundled discount as a hook.

The ticket office remained so busy in the month leading up to the first production that VDE hired two additional ticket agents to handle the demand, bringing the total count of agents to six. By opening night, the sales had exceeded Romero's ambitious goal and reached 64% of the previous season's total sales. The lobby was decorated with the new art for the season, and the ticket office was still busier than ever.

Over the three-week run of the performance, however, ticket sales began to slow. Though the bundle discount was set to run out at the end of the production, most of the tickets sold during the run were single ticket purchases rather than the bundle. Despite the downturn in sales volume, the first production was still more highly attended than the first production the previous year, and the VDE had ample funds in the bank because of the tremendous presale.

In the weeks after the first production closed, the ticket office made very few sales. Masterson had to lay off the two new ticket agents they had just hired two months before. "We simply didn't have the volume of calls to make it possible. It was a hard decision, but it was the right one," she said.

As the season moved forward, Romero moved from promoting one production to the next as each was presented. His primary methods remained the same as the first production: distributing posters, postcards, and emails with the new art. Ticket sales would occasionally increase then return to very low levels. By the end of the third production, although they were still better off financially than the previous year at that time, Masterson decided to lay off two more ticket agents, leaving only the first two who had been with the organization for some time.

Romero spent time in the ticket office and recognized that sales were far too slow—slower than the ticket agents could recall. To enhance the promotion, he started doing performer spotlights in which performers would be asked a series of questions, then the question-and-answer session would be shared in print and through an email blast. At the fourth and fifth productions, audience members remarked how much they enjoyed reading about the performers and how they felt more connected to the dancers on stage. Romero also arranged for critics from the newspaper to attend the opening of each production. When the reviews were printed in the paper two days later, he would pull quotes to send as email blasts and affix them to the poster boards outside of the building. By the end of the fifth production, the total season income was still slightly ahead of where they were the previous year at that time. Romero asked Masterson to increase his promotion budget to purchase a full-page advertisement in the arts section of the local newspaper. "I wasn't sure what to do," Masterson recalled, "we had never run such an expensive advertisement, but Romero thought it would boost our sales for our fifth production, which at the time was struggling." So, despite the expense, she agreed, and Romero ran the advertisement.

The day the advertisement ran, the ticket office was busy again. Not as busy as that first day when they launched the bundled discount, but busy enough that other staff members had to step in again to assist the ticket office. The next day they saw a significant downturn, but the ticket office was still busy, although two agents could handle all the calls. By the third day, volume had returned to very little. On the fourth day, they sold only four tickets. Despite the short bump in sales, the sixth production was selling worse than the previous five. Romero sent new content to the VDE's email list, but it seemed to have little impact on sales.

As the sixth production came to a close, Masterson recognized that they were in trouble. "I pulled the numbers for the season after the sixth show, and guess what . . . we were down 4% from the previous year in attendance." Though Romero had completely revamped the promotions and they appeared to work for a time, the attendance trend was unaltered at the end of the year. VDE experienced an even greater downturn in income. Rather than receiving 4% less income as might be expected since they saw 4% fewer audience members, they experienced a 28% loss of income over the previous year because they had provided discounts on close to 70% of the tickets sold. Worse yet, they had incurred added expenses with the additional ticket office staff and the new advertising costs. Following the sixth production, the ticket office began to receive calls from people asking when the early bird price would be available for the next season.

In the middle of the following year, Romero took another job, and the VDE welcomed a new marketing director. For Masterson, ultimately, she "had to delay retirement by three years to help the VDE catch up from that season." In those three years, the VDE reduced the number of productions they do each year to four and managed to gain greater stability, though they never returned to previous levels. Despite the challenges, Masterson does not blame Romero. "It was a moving target. We were all doing our best in a situation that was really unclear. Isaac is a good man, and he and my daughter have a terrific marriage." In 2016, the VDE closed its doors after twenty-four years.

Creating Advertising Objectives

In chapter 3, three advertising objectives commonly used in promotional campaigns were described: inform, persuade, and remind. Marketing experts designed these advertising objectives to work in tandem.[7] Each objective provides structural support to the other two. These objectives must find balance within a mix to be effective.

To communicate with the potential audience member who has never attended, balancing all three is a significant challenge for a nonprofit arts organization. Though most arts organizations do not present their art long enough to thoroughly move through all three objectives before the product no longer exists, a shadow of these components does often exist. Most arts organizations create a piece of promotion that functions to inform. The information advertisement provides a title, a description of the art, and perhaps information about the artists. Again, they cannot speak to the actual product because it cannot be fully defined until enough of the audience has experienced it. There may be a call to action in a move toward persuasion by adding "buy now!" or "tickets going fast!" to the poster. The call theoretically moves the first-time audience member to close the sale. Marketers often then move to reminder advertisements for those who have not yet purchased. These often include phrases like: "gallery opening this weekend, don't forget!" attached to the same informational advertisement they first sent.

For the audience member that regularly attends and for whom involvement is enough, the initial informational advertisement may be all that is required. They do not need to be persuaded to purchase their tickets because they have already discovered the value. The promotion tells them pertinent information about the offering (though it does nothing to engage). Purchasing paths differ for the new and existing customer, yet most arts organizations provide the same promotional material for both. The dividing line between these two types of customers is the engagement edge. The arts organization rarely has the necessary time to thoroughly mix all three advertising objectives for either the current attendee or potential new audience members.

Relationship Marketing

One approach to marketing that appears to be closely tied to education is *relationship marketing*. The primary function of relationship marketing is less about closing an immediate sale and more about developing a long-term relationship with consumers so that they continue to make purchases over time. The idea for relationship marketing began in the mid-1980s,[8] though in recent years, researchers such as Ruth Rentschler at Deakin University in Australia and others began to stress the existence and the value of relationship marketing in the arts.[9]

The concept of relationship marketing emerged from a study Berry conducted on the service sector.[10] The idea behind it is that both buyer and seller wish to engage in a more meaningful exchange that leads to a continuous relationship. In relationship marketing, the exchange is seen as a means for engaging with a consumer. Relationship marketing is very similar to the education component of the engagement edge. The notion of relationship marketing emphasizes customer satisfaction and minimizes the focus on the sale itself. That statement happens to intersect exactly with our premise that the function of education (as opposed to promotion) is to focus on the long-term development of arts patrons, not the individual sale. In both, sales are generated not by pushing to close a transaction but by developing relationships that lead to brand loyalty and continued patronage. Similar to our focus on education, relationship marketing focuses on individual consumers and not on advertising. There is a vitally important practical element to relationship marketing, in that the returning consumer is far less expensive to capture a sale from than the new consumer. In any business, acquiring a new customer is a costly proposition.

Relationship marketing focuses on maintaining close relationships with existing customers, while education works to develop a new customer base and maintain that base through consistent and quality education. Relationship marketing, like arts education, recognizes reciprocity. In the arts, reciprocity is vital, as art cannot exist without an audience.[11] Long-term customers are far less likely to change organizations or find different products or services to fulfill their needs. Relationship marketing and education leads to strong brand loyalty.

Additional Functions of Promotion/Advertising

The ultimate purpose of promotion is to persuade customers to make a purchase. With advertisements, the aim is to move the consumer directly into making that purchase. There are, however, other functions of promotion that indirectly lead to sales over time, but do not push the immediate sale of the product. For corporations in competitive markets, these functions of promotion are vital. This section explores eight promotional functions that step beyond a focus on making the sale. It explores whether those functions have been working for the nonprofit arts.

Brand Integration through Promotion

First, promotion **creates an image or brand** for the organization. The image can be one of low prices, prestige, or perhaps innovation. To return to the sandwich shop example, a sign with the word "LUNCH" provides a very different communication than a sign with the words "artisan sandwiches."

The branded design, however, is even more influential to interpretation than the words. A chalk sign on the sidewalk with "LUNCH" written in cursive may provide more of an "artisan sandwiches" feel than a yellow sign with red block letters that actually reads, "artisan sandwiches." The shop may provide the same product under both signs, but the experience of the brand is certainly different.

Most for-profit corporations change their offerings infrequently. As a result, their products and their brand are easily linked. Most nonprofit arts organizations have branding elements but spend most of their energy advertising each new offering. The branding elements become a byline of the offering they produce next. Many nonprofit arts organizations struggle with branding elements because they offer ever changing products which become the focus of all promotions.

Informative

Next, the promotion element **provides information** about the product or service and the various characteristics that make it up. The section about information advertising reviewed the challenge that the information provided by arts organizations is typically aimed at those who already appreciate the arts. Beyond this, the arts cannot be described in the way a utilitarian product can be, especially to those who do not currently attend. The benefits of an arts experience are intrinsic to the audience.

To accurately describe the information necessary to persuade a community member to purchase a ticket takes an enormous amount of information. It takes very little space to explain the quality of bread or sandwich ingredients. It would take significant space, however, to describe the intrinsic value of an arts experience to someone who has no baseline for why they should go to the symphony. Providing information about arts experiences simply takes up too much space to be an effective form of promotion.

Keeping Present

Third, promotion allows corporations to **preserve the popularity of the good or service** by keeping it in the public's mind.[12] This concept is especially critical for companies that produce products that last a long time before they must be replaced. Apple products are a prime example. Apple is known primarily for making computers, cell phones, and watches. Their customers may go years between making purchases of an Apple product. Yet, for many people, the core Apple products maintain a stronger presence in our minds than other products we purchase with greater frequency. Most nonprofit arts organizations rapidly shift their offerings in a way that is completely different from for-profit corporations. Imagine if Apple released a new cell phone with a vastly different aesthetic value every six weeks. Even a corporation of that size may struggle to maintain consumer awareness and popularity with such rapid changes. Because arts organizations rapidly change the art they present, keeping each art experience in the public's mind is a fairly useless endeavor.

Product Use

Fourth, promotions can be used to **change the way the consumer uses a product**. When promotions provide details about what a product is for, they can alter who their customers are and how their customers actually use the products. In the nineteenth century, Listerine was sold as a disinfectant for surgical operations, and in the early twentieth century, it was promoted as a floor cleaner before eventually finding its market niche as a mouthwash.[13] This same product was promoted in different ways to change consumer use. In the arts, audience members can experience the same art in different ways. They can develop their appreciation of the experience, but the promotion does not generally change how the audience uses the art. The next chapter discusses education, and the potential for education to help the audience shape their own experience.

Upselling

Fifth, many marketers design promotions to convince buyers to **move from a lower-priced product to a more expensive one**. In the arts, we try to move audience members from single tickets to a subscription or an advancement into the donor category. Although a subscription is more expensive than a single ticket purchase, the messaging around subscription sales is typically focused on the discount received through the bundled purchase. The audience member actually gets multiple offerings at a lesser price rather than a single product at a higher price. Even in a situation in which nonprofit arts organizations could use a promotion to persuade their audience to purchase a more expensive product, that function is inappropriate since their mission is not about profits but about serving the community.

Answering Questions

Sixth, promotions can be used to **answer consumers' questions** about the product. Explaining the features and workings of a product works particularly well for physical products. Promotions can highlight a car's specs, the size of a television screen, or the amount of water used in a washing machine. In answering the consumers' questions through promotion, corporations reduce the need for a communication loop in which the consumer asks a question, requiring the corporation to follow up. Nonprofit arts organizations primarily promote through informational advertisements. Since arts organizations are frequently offering a new art experience, it is rare for community members to have questions regarding the art itself. The closest arts organizations come to answering questions through promotion is providing information about the genre and the artists.

Public Relations

Next, a promotion may **provide favorable information** about a company. Some for-profit corporations base their branding and promotions on providing favorable information to the public.[14] In 2006, Blake Mycoskie founded Toms Shoes. The company's logo featured the phrase "one for one" directly under the corporation's name.[15] The phrase references the policy that Toms Shoes gives one pair of shoes to those in need for every pair of shoes purchased in their stores or online. The fact that they distribute shoes based on sales is a promotion to make them stand out among their competitors. It also serves to help the customer feel good about their purchase because they feel involved in providing shoes for people in need. Though it sounds charitable, Toms Shoes is a for-profit company, and providing this favorable information about the corporation is ultimately designed to increase sales and thus profits. If it were purely charitable, Toms Shoes would donate the shoes and not spend vast resources sharing their charitable work with the public and instead rededicate those resources to providing more shoes to those in need.

For nonprofit arts organizations, this type of communication is challenging. Nonprofit arts organizations have 501(c)(3) status because they provide art for the community and do not seek to distribute profits to shareholders. Members of the community, however, are the ones who support the organization partially through ticket sales. So, nonprofit arts organizations are charitably serving audience members who are purchasing tickets, often at great expense, to their offerings. Arts organizations do use promotions to provide favorable information about themselves in the fundraising process. Nonprofit fundraisers use facts and figures to tell the story of the reach and impact of the organization. The ultimate purpose is to persuade potential donors to support the work of the arts organization. Since this request is not a form of service from the nonprofit, unlike providing the actual arts experiences, this promotion element is appropriate for fundraising.

Enthusiasm

Finally, promotions can **create enthusiasm and curiosity** about a product or service within the market. This enthusiasm can inspire word of mouth that may increase the likelihood of sales. This function of promotion is one that nonprofit arts organizations do very well. In the nineteenth century, traveling and local arts events were much anticipated and served as a primary form of entertainment. Over time, competing factors have changed the way communities consider their entertainment options. Though community enthusiasm has shifted through time, arts organizations still benefit through word of mouth and the excitement created by a new gallery opening or a concert. Like many of the promotional elements explored in this chapter, however, the enthusiasm created may only serve to excite those who already appreciate the arts, though it may inspire curiosity for those who hear about the offering but are not familiar with the experience.

Promotion as Opinion

Promotion is ultimately a device used to persuade or convince someone to make a purchase. The idea behind promotion then is to shape an opinion about something. That is done by a corporation presenting ideas and visuals that will help to shape the undecided consumer's view. On the other hand, education focuses on engaging around ideas that create new connections and provide opportunities for the people receiving the education to explore their own ideas, develop their own opinions, and ultimately make an informed decision. Certainly, a promotion has an educational component, but its primary function is not to educate. A promotion's informational content is less about educating and more about persuading.

Because of the nature of producing art, and the way art is experienced, we believe that for nonprofit arts organizations, the role of promotion is inappropriate since it is based in persuasion. Since promotion focuses on convincing the recipient to make a purchase they might not otherwise make, it seems an improper fit for nonprofits, since exist to serve that very recipient they are trying to persuade.

5
Education and the Arts

In *Creative Arts Marketing*, we find a prescient quotation about arts participation that strikes a chord: "Participation in artistic activity is fundamental to the human spirit, enabling people to express who they are and tell their story. Yet, too often, cultural organizations and structures get in the way of this, through the codes we adopt, the jargon we use, the perpetuation of a myth that true art is for the few not for the many."[1]

Chapter 3 described our educational philosophy. The best educators do not use education as a tool to gain power, nor do they rely upon memorization of facts as their mode of teaching.[2] Instead, they set up scenarios in which students make the connections and discoveries.[3] Since information is readily available to people, the educator's role is to help learners develop how to discover, analyze, and synthesize information for themselves. This chapter describes how arts organizations can use these tenets to engage the community and create new relationships centered around artistic experiences. Not only does education allow an arts organization to engage with its community as never before, but it also enables an arts organization to serve the community in a new way. We can shift the effort and resources spent persuading potential audience members to attend, transforming that energy into something more valuable. **The move from promotion to education allows arts organizations to provide value to the community, even before a purchase occurs.**

Who Are We Trying to Reach?

Arts organizations almost exclusively use informational advertising with a persuasive element that asks consumers to "CALL!" We say: "We are holding an event," "concert," "performance," or "exhibit." We explain the plot, introduce the artists, and notify anyone who encounters the advertisement where and when the offering will take place. Each campaign's primary message begins and ends with the notion "We have an offering." One could argue that advertisements about each production or exhibit are reminder ads for the producing organization's brand. This statement may be a fair assessment, given that the audience who sees these advertising materials are often already familiar with the arts. Through this lens, arts organizations often lack informative advertisements designed to capture new audiences. This information void is where the crux of the issue manifests itself. Organizations communicate with the same materials to the same people and wonder why new people are not attending.

A vital component of communication is knowing who you are trying to reach, highlighting a need for research. If arts organizations understand the *demographics* and *psychographics* of those who already attend the arts, then they are more likely to find similar people, but this does not help the organization engage with people of different demographics. The former are people who have had enough of an arts education, either through formal education or through regular or multiple attendances, to appreciate what occurs while attending the arts. Knowing the demographics and psychographics of these current attendees does little to help locate those who do not have experience with, or an appreciation of, the arts but who would be eager to do so once they learn its value. Those who have had arts education, or a collection of arts experiences, are far more apt to appreciate the aesthetic value of the arts. Therefore, arts education must be targeted and resonate with those whom we seek to engage. Some arts organizations already implement this with their patrons (who have purchased tickets) but do little for those who lack arts education or experience. **The goal is not to create art critics, but to help our communities to discover for themselves what (if anything) they take from the arts experience.**

Aesthetics of Education

When we discuss *aesthetics*, we refer to a classification of the nature of beauty—frequently in the arts. *Aesthetic value* is a subjective concept, as each individual who appreciates the aesthetics of a work of art may find more or less value in that aesthetic than others.[4] Aesthetic value "is the value that an object possesses in virtue of its capacity to elicit pleasure (positive value) or displeasure (negative value) when appreciated or experienced aesthetically."[5] This is one of the primary reasons why it is believed that selling a "product" is insufficient in the nonprofit arts: the artistic product relies heavily upon its aesthetic to determine value, and that value can shift.

More than that, one might ask why education is more prescient than promotion when looking at the aesthetic *qualities* of a work of art. In order to discover the aesthetic qualities of art, which is a subjective determination, one must have some level of education to know how to interpret the use of particular principles within the art. Aesthetics are born out of core design conventions that elicit and define pleasing qualities within the art, qualities that evoke emotion. The factors relevant to visual aesthetics include those of balance, movement, pattern, shape and scale, color, and perceived weight. These same principles can be used in set design, backdrops, stage presence, costuming, and a myriad of other ways in all art forms. But the aesthetic experience is quite different and feels different for every person.

It is not suggested that art is only created for the educated. We often see, however, that the utilitarian function of art is only for those who are educated in how to appreciate and evaluate it. The latter concept is important because it is the voice of the audience that ultimately dictates the longevity of a work of art. Though highly trained and educated art critics may provide an important opinion on the art that an audience will see, it is the audience members themselves who make the final determination as to the art's perceived value.

Some argue that if educated audiences are required to evaluate art, this requirement must refer only to highly educated audiences, such as other artists and trained critics. Unlike science, however, where training is required to understand basic concepts, in the arts, value is also determined by the aesthetic experience, which is subjective to the individual making the evaluation.[6] Consequently, the education required is the one that allows the learner to know how to evaluate the aesthetic of art for themselves because the individual determines the art's value based on our emotional response to sensory input, a skill most often learned through repeated exposure to art. **If potential audience members have not repeatedly been exposed to art and developed an appreciation for it, then telling them to attend our events will do no good. We are left with only education as the key to engaging with these potential arts patrons.** The upcoming pages include the case of *Prospero*, where two distinct educational programs are created to engage with different segments of the population about the arts experience.

Coordinating with Artists

Some artists are taught to focus entirely on themselves (their process, their thoughts, and feelings as they create art) and to not consider the audience of the art. This is one way we see an audience neglected, because when the artist does not respect the audience as an integral part of the artistic experience, the audience is likely to respond in kind: by staying home. Certainly, for the artist to focus solely on the audience's desires is to commercialize the art. This is not suggested for the nonprofit arts, but barring a purely commercial approach, it appears we are left with only education as a clear solution to bridge the gap between commercialized and noncommercialized art. **The aesthetic value of everything we do is determined by those who experience the art.** This is not to recommend that arts organizations must now assume the burden of teaching every citizen about art and its qualities. **Fluency in artistic criticism is not the desired outcome of education for the director of engagement. Instead, this person should be seeking to develop some conversant level in the community which allows them to discover for themselves how and if they value what the arts organization provides.**

The Case of Prospero

In 1983, the Riverside Community College in Riverside, California agreed to allow one of their professors to start a professional theater company on their campus. Though in residence on the Riverside Community College campus, the company launched as a separate nonprofit entity whose mission included serving the Riverside community through theatre experiences. At the time of their launch, they presented three productions each year for an audience of about three thousand per production. By 1989, they produced a season of six productions annually. In a typical season, they had between ten thousand and twelve thousand attendees at their three largest musical productions and between three thousand and six thousand at their plays and lesser-known musicals.

The organization started as Danny Newman's book *Subscribe Now!* was taking hold as the primary marketing book for nonprofit theaters. Newman's tactics focused on burying a market with message after message, tracking potential consumers anywhere they could be found, and constantly promoting. In some ways, Newman was advocating an early model of the promotional mix, but it lacked the refinement and sophistication of modern marketing. Though it proved effective for a time, the pace slowed, and eventually, the success that Danny Newman devotees were accustomed to seeing stopped. The theater's marketing director, Jennifer Gelch, recognized the challenge early and aimed to enhance their single ticket sales.

Gelch noted that the theater had a growing crowd of eighteen-to-thirty-year-olds. They were primarily single ticket buyers (meaning they purchased tickets to individual productions rather than subscribing for a full season). Despite messages about the financial value of subscriptions, they continued to purchase tickets only for the most popular events. Of the ten thousand to twelve thousand attendees for the largest productions, this group made up about 17% of that audience. Though there were between 1,500 and 2,000 ticket buyers that matched this demographic at their large musicals, Gelch wanted to know more. At the time, the marketing department was only tracking audience information on their largest three events.

The marketing team then implemented the tracking of attendees at their smaller productions. Their tracking confirmed what Gelch had suspected, that the eighteen-to-thirty-year-olds that made up 17% of their audiences at the big musicals were significantly underrepresented at the three smaller productions. That spring, they produced Shakespeare's *A Midsummer Night's Dream*. Out of the 2,730 tickets sold, only twenty-four were sold to buyers aged eighteen to thirty. In reviewing ticket sales from previous seasons, Gelch noted that attendances had declined for the Shakespeare performance slots each year. The theater was at a programming crossroads. The Shakespeare performances were produced at a loss for the past three years and served fewer community members. Gelch strongly believed in the value of an arts organization serving their audience, but what did that mean for her and Riverside's community relative to their annual Shakespeare performances? If the Shakespeare performances were no longer what the community wanted, would the community be better served if they provided more big musicals instead? She was hesitant to suggest such a shift to the artistic director, and she was not sure it was the best solution. She recognized the need for more information.

She knew audience numbers for their Shakespeare performances were declining as a whole, and she knew that attendance in the eighteen-to-thirty-year-old group was essentially nonexistent. So, she set out to answer two questions. First, *why were audience members in the fifty-to-seventy-five age demographic slowly dropping off from the Shakespeare performances*? Second, *why were audience members in the eighteen-to-thirty age demographic not attending*? To answer these questions, she recognized she needed to understand the community members in those demographics better.

Gelch decided to start with the group she thought would be easiest to connect with: the fifty-to-seventy-five age demographic. They had already been attending, but many were slowly dropping off. She connected with a board member who offered to host a gathering at his house the next month. So, using their most recent data, she reached out to one hundred people in that demographic. She pulled fifty names from those who had attended a recent musical and fifty names from those who had attended the *A Midsummer Night's Dream* and asked if they would be interested in attending an event hosted by the board member to discuss the theater's performances. She was shocked at the response rate. Fifty-three people wrote back confirming their interest in attending. Each was invited with a guest, and she knew that over one hundred people would be far too large for the board member's home. After reaching out to him, they decided to host two separate events on different nights at his house.

Including guests, they met with thirty-seven the first night and forty-two the second. Each event included light drinks and appetizers, a memory board where attendees could share their favorite theater experiences, a brief trivia game with questions about contemporary and classic theater, and a discussion about the theater's performances. The discussion served as a rather large focus group (though not everyone chose to participate). The consensus was that interest in the Shakespeare performances was waning because the audience felt they knew what to expect and that they had seen it all. One component that surfaced in the discussion several times was that they thought the theater should continue producing Shakespeare so that younger audiences could experience it. Gelch saw the events as successful; it seemed that everyone had a good experience. She had the information she needed regarding the Shakespeare performances but was not yet ready to create a marketing plan. She first needed to connect with the demographic that had started her on this path, the eighteen-to-thirty-year-olds.

She reached out to a group of one hundred eighteen-to-thirty-year-olds who had attended their most recent musical to invite them to an event at a local restaurant. The restaurant committed to offering an appetizer from a select menu for each attendee. She heard back from nine who were interested, but only four confirmed. So, she reached out to another four hundred and ultimately coordinated with a group of thirty-eight for a one-night event. Like the event at the board member's house, the evening consisted of food, some trivia, and a discussion about the theater's performances. The participants held a perspective about Shakespeare that was very different from that of the fifty-to-seventy-five age group. They felt that it was boring and difficult to understand. Some shared that whenever they thought about Shakespeare, they thought about high school. They felt that musicals were more engaging and could deal with a wide variety of topics.

Gelch felt that she had been handed a gift. She had two demographics with disparate needs, but maybe they could enhance the value of Shakespeare to each other. The eighteen-to-thirty age group felt that Shakespeare was difficult to understand, and the fifty-to-seventy-five age group felt that Shakespeare was vitally important for the eighteen-to-thirty-year-olds. Gelch had heard of using education as a valuable method to increase arts attendance. Since the theater was already associated with the community college, she had access to classrooms and an English teacher who loved Shakespeare. She designed an offering: community members from both demographics would be invited to the community college for a night of Shakespeare. She created a buddy system that would pair someone from the fifty-to-seventy-five age group with a partner from the eighteen-to-thirty age group for the evening. Two actors would reprise their roles from *A Midsummer Night's Dream* and present two scenes, and the English instructor could share insights to help everyone understand the content. The buddies would then be given tickets to attend the next Shakespeare performance the following fall together.

Gelch believed this was a first step to giving everyone what they wanted. The fifty-to-seventy-five-year-olds could help the younger group come to appreciate Shakespeare, and the eighteen-to-thirty age group would finally understand it.

The result of Gelch's big plan? A disaster. Of the twenty eighteen-to-thirty-year-olds who agreed to come, only twelve actually attended the event at the community college, which meant most had more than one buddy. The buddies from the fifty-to-seventy-five-year-old group spent most of their time telling their buddy to like Shakespeare, and the English teacher provided a forty-minute lecture about the material, which to many of the eighteen-to-thirty-year-olds, was as baffling as the brief scenes themselves. On a post-event survey, none of the eighteen-to-thirty-year-olds who attended indicated they were more interested in Shakespeare, and only two of the twenty fifty-to-seventy-five-year-olds said that they would participate in such an event again.

Though discouraged, Gelch reconsidered what she had learned from the meetings. Again, many in the fifty-to-seventy-five-year-old group shared that they stopped attending because they knew what to expect and felt they had seen it all. This was valuable information. Perhaps the theater could design an educational campaign to engage this audience segment and help them discover new elements to Shakespeare and their biannual productions. With the fall Shakespeare production of *The Tempest* a few months away, Gelch worked with the director to gain a picture of what the theater experience would be.

From there, she invited four of the more vocal audience members from this demographic to lunch. They discussed the event at the board member's house and their thoughts about the Shakespeare play. Together, they created a plan to mail a package with a series of questions and activities that attendees from the same household could do together. The package came from the theater (with the theater's brand) but included a letter from the four audience members. The package's theme was *rediscovering Shakespeare*, and it challenged their established audience to engage with new ideas. The recipients were also encouraged to be creative with space to respond to a prompt with a poem, a joke, or a piece of visual art. The set designer had designed a set featuring hundreds of flowers, and as a final question in the package, the audience member was asked which of six flowers they felt most drawn to and why. The participants would then return the papers to the theater to enter a raffle for a gift certificate. Gelch planned to then feature the drawings, jokes, and poems in both the lobby and the program. As a final gesture, the participants who purchased tickets would find the flower they had selected on their seat along with a note from Gelch. She began implementing their plan as she considered her next steps with the eighteen-to-thirty-year-old group.

This demographic was much more challenging since many had negative feelings about Shakespeare's plays. Yet, they had provided some key information to Gelch. They felt his plays were difficult to understand, and they loved musicals. Gelch met with the artistic director and development director to discuss this eighteen-to-thirty-year-old group, and together they developed a plan. Given this group's love of musical theater, they decided to launch a new works program at the theater with a focus on musical theater. They had created a new musical several years before and had the staff to manage it. They met with the creative team they wanted to work with and pitched the idea, a new musical version of *The Tempest* called *Prospero*. Though the creative team would maintain artistic control, Gelch designed milestones over two years, where the eighteen-to-thirty-year-old group could witness, give feedback, and even participate in the creation process.

Audience members interested in joining the new works project would pick up an envelope containing information about Shakespeare, plot construction, iambic pentameter, and more. They could then fill out information based on what they recognized from seeing the fall production of *The Tempest*. Immediately following the performances, Gelch would hold information sessions for audience members interested in joining the new works project.

Gelch implemented both plans. Through the packets distributed to the fifty-to-seventy-five-year-old demographic, the theater saw audiences at Shakespeare performances return to previous levels. The initiation of the new works program brought a new audience of members in the eighteen-to-thirty age group to *The Tempest* who suddenly saw Shakespeare through a different lens. Gelch continued developing engagement materials for both groups for future productions with great success. Although the eighteen-to-thirty age group never quite reached the 17% of attendees they did for big musicals, they eventually accounted for close to 11% of Shakespeare performances. *Prospero* was developed over the course of two years. In those years, more community members came through the theater to witness and participate in the creation of the new musical than attended many of their smaller shows. Despite it being a new musical with no track record, the new work program created such buzz within the community that *Prospero* became one of their most attended productions of all time.

Promotive versus Education

Correlations between education and promotion exist in that they share similar narratives in the broad steps taken to engage with consumers. In the next three sections we examine the three major steps of promotion and the similarities between promotion and education for each.

Step 1: Identify Targets and Needs

In promotion, the first step is to *identify the target market*. This is the process by which we determine whom the promotion is designed to attract. This is not a step where we simply "decide" who we want our customer to be or make calculated guesses as to who will want the product offered. Identification requires research to learn about the potential consumers: Who needs or wants products we have to offer, and why?

Arts organizations need to know their community's desires and determine how best to reach them with the information we have about the arts. They must determine what types of educational processes would prove most effective in helping individuals learn to be comfortable with the arts, gain an all-important familiarity with and affinity for art. Numerous learning strategies are needed to facilitate connections with future patrons, as each individual would be at a different place in the process. Organizations could employ multiple educational options to see how people respond to determine how best to educate. It is trial-and-error, but it means working to develop a process that works for the learner (community member) not the instructor (marketer).

Every possible learning strategy must be assessed for its potential to meet the learning objective, which in our case is to help community members determine for themselves what value the arts could hold for them. Advanced research may require asking current audiences what they think about their experience (not the art itself) and develop strategies that work toward accomplishing similar responses in those who do not currently attend. The process can often begin by simply brainstorming what data we have about how our current patrons think. This step can lead to further inquiry and the completion of a detailed statement of active learning needs with our yet-to-patronize-the-arts audiences.

It is vital to identify the right location for providing education. Is it at a community center, a classroom, a church basement, a club meeting, a museum, theater or other entertainment venues, or perhaps even a mall? Determining what **environment** will best assist our learners is critically important. You'll note here that we intentionally use the term *environment* differently from how we introduced it in chapter 1. As we progress through the engagement edge, you'll often find the terms *environment, experience, ease of access,* and *education* intermingling. Later, we will discuss how they all relate to one another. For now, it is just important to consider how the environment might affect education in your community.

For current patrons, understanding what has worked to reach them in the past is vital. Are your current audiences actively interested in talkbacks? By considering what they attend, you can develop a sense of the type of environment in which your audience is most comfortable. An environment that is relaxed, yet conducive to learning, is key.

To create an educational approach to help community members gain experience with and an affinity for the arts, arts organizations should consider the needs of the community being served, and how to make art feel inclusive and approachable to all. **Education is provided for the attainment of knowledge, while promotion, particularly in the arts, often serves to maintain focus on the company and its products and offerings.**

Explaining to a consumer "what we do," is not an effective form of education. We cannot explain over and over what the art is. Instead, we have to educate as if the learner has asked: "what's in it for me?" **If a person doesn't know how to understand and appreciate those facets of the artistic experience derived from aesthetics, then they will not fully experience the intrinsic rewards of the arts, and so have little reason to attend.** Those who attend may answer the question, "what's in it for me?" differently from those who have yet to attend.

Step 2: Determine Objectives

Step 2 is devising an incentive that leads the consumer to interact with the organization, appealing to them through their desires, needs, and wants in a manner that frames the promotion as a benefit to them. It is the planning phase. When promoting a product, the need to *consider the features that will satisfy the needs and wants of the consumer* is of the utmost importance. First, evaluate the promotional campaign and the incentives offered.

For arts organizations, welcoming potential audience members begins with introducing the experiences others have had in the arts. By sharing how other people have experienced the product, we can put ourselves in their place and imagine ourselves taking advantage of the product as others have.[7] Of course, if a person has never stood in a museum, staring at a masterpiece, appreciating its depth and richness, then seeing an image of someone else doing so will have little bearing. We cannot see the connection between the person in the image and ourselves. Here is where personalized education is missing.

Knowing what their needs and wants are allows a message to be crafted that provides the consumer with a solution. If the consumer is unaware of the value to them, in other words, if the consumer has not discovered the need or want they might otherwise have, then they will not take advantage of the offer. For example, a consumer who knows how to enjoy football is more likely to act upon a promotional message about football than someone who does not know how football is played.

Step 3: Implementation

The first two steps have identified the promotional targets and devised incentives to capture the intended demographic and offered a beneficial solution that adheres to their desires, needs, and wants. In the last phase, it is time to define the goals, state specific objectives, and conceptualize the essential outcomes of the promotion. These considerations must be identified and thoroughly outlined in terms of cost, needed resources, any fundraising or donor contributions, staffing considerations, and practical needs such as the delivery of the promotion, social media campaigns, community outreach, and so on. A budget must be made to ensure that the promotion is viable, and that outcomes and objectives would warrant the promotion.

In education, we plan and design activities to assist in achieving outcomes by accomplishing objectives. These are our "solutions" to the problems we have identified; that is, there is a type or amount of knowledge the potential audience member may lack, and activities can help them make new discoveries. We then take our activities and develop them into a sequence of events through which learners construct their understanding. In this process, we may have to identify different steps toward a complete understanding and work on one step at a time. In other words, in education, if the goal is to learn how and why one may appreciate classical music, we might start with a foundational understanding of what classical music is and how it works. We might then move on to a deeper appreciation of how composers design specific music pieces to affect us. Then we might dig deeper into understanding the social system that occurs within a classical music performance and work on an activity designed to support that understanding. **This is never about telling the community member what to believe or how to think; it is about creating situations in which the community member makes their own discoveries.**

Learning Objectives

In education, we develop learning objectives and educational outcomes. A learning objective is something we expect the learner to do to move toward the successful achievement of an outcome. For example, a learning objective for arts patrons might be participating in an aloud reading of a new play. The outcome, however, tells us what is expected once the objectives have been completed. In our case, the learning outcome might be that the learner can demonstrate an ability to empathize with the characters in the play, or ultimately, that the learner becomes more involved with the arts program. For new consumers, a public art fair with a string quartet playing unassumingly at the event where the consumer can experience multiple forms of artistic endeavors at a single, casual venue may begin the process of acclimation to arts programs. In formal education, learning objectives and outcomes are included in a syllabus so that the learner understands the purpose of their participation. For arts organizations looking to use education to engage with audiences, it is vital that the learning objectives are shared and public.

Finally, in terms of promotional messaging and education, *we evaluate and assess our success based on the criteria we set forth*. For example, a business might plan to sell one million units of something as a goal. After their promotional process, they can easily assess whether they have achieved the goal of one million units sold. In commercial business, income, profit, and revenue are the sorts of outcomes we measure against since the ultimate goal is profit.

Many nonprofit arts organizations do not conduct formal evaluations against goals. Occasionally, arts organizations will evaluate their effectiveness based on the total revenue generated, net income over expenses (what would traditionally be referred to as profit), or other financial considerations such as total donations or total tickets sold. Since the arts organization was established for the public benefit and blessed with the moniker of "nonprofit," the better evaluative tool is its mission, which defines who the organization serves and how they are served. If the mission is clear, then the organization's work can be evaluated based on whether it meets its mission and how effectively. This can begin with a simple survey of current patrons.

Applying Engagement in the Learning Process

Collaborative learning, active learning, learner-centered teaching, and experiential learning are all theories which center on student activity.[8] Ultimately, the students do the work of learning rather than being spoon-fed information. Applying these theories of education can be complex or simple depending on three components: the target audience, the educational goals, and the arts organization's capacity. Regardless of how simple or complex the education, the arts organization must carefully design it based on each of those three components.

Let's examine what engagement in the learning process might look like practically. Consider the three steps we introduced earlier in the chapter that established the similarities between education and promotion. **Step 1: Identify Targets and Needs.** To begin, think about the patrons who currently attend your arts organization. (We use current patrons here so that no research is required as you imagine ways to engage through education.) If you have a wide variety of demographics, pick one demographic of your current attendees. We know that socialization is a significant factor—but beyond that, what topics specifically about your offering drive this demographic to attend your organization? Since they already attend, you know that they are likely drawn to what you offer. Though you have done little formal research, you probably have a fairly accurate picture based solely on your experiences with them, and knowing what you already provide.

Step 2: Determine Goals/Set Education Objectives. Now that you have established who you are providing the education for, consider an aspect related to what you currently offer. If you offer art that produces concerts of early music, an objective might be for learners to recognize essential differences between Renaissance and Baroque music. If you offer art that challenges social norms, an objective might be for students to question their beliefs or discover new perspectives. To engage through education with those who already attend, you can start by looking at what you do and build around it. Remember, the goal is not to sell a ticket; it is to engage through providing something of value to your community.

Step 3: Implementation. Once you have determined who you seek to engage through education and the learning objectives, you can move on to designing the activities. As noted, these activities can be simple or complex, but they should be designed specifically for your target audience and to complete the learning objective. You will need to consider your environment for the activities (something we will explore deeply in part IV). Depending on what you are doing, the activity could take place anywhere; try not to limit yourself to the confines of the space where your organization presents art.

With the example of the arts organization that aims for learners to recognize essential differences between Renaissance and Baroque music, they could create a game in which pieces of music from each period play, and through trial and error participants work to determine whether the piece is a Renaissance or a Baroque composition based on feedback to their answers. As the game evolves, participants could even select pieces of music from either period to try to stump the others. At the conclusion of games (whether online or in person), participants could share something they discovered, the organization could distribute prizes, there could be a short performance, there are many options. One wrong way to end a game would be to make a hard pitch for your upcoming event, or to say, "ticket sales only cover xx% of our operating expenses, please give us money!" **Trust that the participants are smart. They know who you are (if you have branded the education carefully) and will recognize that they have received something for free from a nonprofit service organization. If after the educational experiences, they choose to attend events there will be plenty of time to ask for a donation in the future.**

With the arts organization that aims for participants to challenge their beliefs or develop new perspectives, the organization could provide a series of questions or present an ethical problem that must be solved (that may have no clear answer). They could host a debate in which groups are assigned different perspectives to argue. Participants could even create and present a short piece of art based on a prompt that challenges their own predispositions.

The educational offerings an organization uses for engagement could be as simple as a crossword puzzle based on the art or a series of questions online about a piece of visual art; they can be as complex as a city-wide scavenger hunt or (if you dare) incorporating non-professional artists into your events. After reading this section, we hope you can feel the difference between telling people what to think through a lecture, and activities that are learner-centered in which the participants are active. Suddenly, a lens of education may not seem so oppressive when the education is designed to be empowering.

Learning What We Enjoy

Just as there are differences in the way each person perceives the world, there are differences in the way each person finds enjoyment. Enjoyment is tied to learning; when people enjoy the learning process, they gain more from it. In the arts, we always want our audience to enjoy the experience, but, depending on the content, they may not always have "fun." An arts experience may be dark, ugly, or emotionally painful, but when the audience leaves, they are changed. Some people enjoy the process of being changed by art.

When arts organizations provide education related to the specific pieces of art the audience will experience, they are preparing them for what to expect. The more an audience thinks about the arts experience they will have before they have it, the more they gain from it.[9]

Some people may be pleasantly surprised by an experience they did not expect to enjoy or when they discover something unexpected. After all, if people never did anything new, they would never make new discoveries. Arts organizations, however, should be wary of tricking an audience into attending something new. Instead, they should educate their community about what the experience is so that members of the community can opt-in or opt-out. The decision to try something new remains the purview of the community members the organization serves.

Brand Integration and Education

In replacing traditional promotion with education, arts organizations must be careful to strike a balance in their communications. People have become so accustomed to messages from organizations designed to sell us something that, when an offering is free, consumers question the purpose behind it. In offering education, we believe an arts organization will ultimately sell more tickets if the population has greater opportunity to discover the value of the arts and what the organization provides. In thinking about using education to replace promotion, however, the arts organization should not consider education a *form* of promotion in which the ultimate purpose is sales. To do so would only further substantiate the consumer's fear that the organization is providing something for free for an ulterior motive.

The aspect of sales is an element that sets nonprofit arts organizations apart from many other types of nonprofits. Because arts organizations receive a large portion of their operating expenses through ticket sales, members of your community may not see the organization as charitable—leading to the concern of the ulterior motives noted above. Consider the United Way, a nonprofit which focuses on community issues typically related to education and health.[10] When the United Way provides a free service, the community served does not question why because there is no sales pitch or ultimate sales goal. This type of nonprofit is seen as purely in service to the community when they provide something at no cost.

Now, imagine you are walking down the street on vacation, and someone at a booth stops you. They say, "I'd like to give you these two free passes for dinner at a local restaurant and a free pass for [insert tourist attraction name here], which is right around the corner. Come with me to my office, and we can set this up for you in about 20 or 30 minutes." In hearing that "free offer," most people recognize that it is likely a pitch for a timeshare. The free offering here is a persuasive tool to convince you to have a conversation or watch a presentation with the ultimate goal of persuading you to make a purchase.

Unlike the United Way, many nonprofit arts organizations charge a substantial price for their offerings. Unlike a company that sells timeshares, nonprofit arts organizations are in the business of service to their communities rather than profits. In providing education about how to enjoy the arts, arts organizations should aim to be closer to the approach of the United Way than to the timeshare company. To do this requires a careful balance of branding.

Those in the community that do not attend need to know who is providing the education, but the initial education must appear (and genuinely be) charitable in nature. This means introducing branding elements in such a way that the audience understands who the organization is but feels no pressure to make a purchase or to donate. If the communication pushes a sale, free educational offerings may be seen as a gimmick. Reducing branding elements so that the audience recognizes the organization that provides the benefit without assuming that the organization wants them to make a purchase requires a careful balance. **When considering branding elements in your educational pursuits, remember this: the purpose of the education is to provide value and knowledge to the community, not make a sale or have people discover your organization's brand.** Some people who receive the education will decide that they would like to experience the art once they better understand how to appreciate it, and others will decide that they have no interest. That is the ideal goal of education for the nonprofit arts organization; the sale of tickets and collection of donations is a byproduct of education.

The offerings from typical arts organizations come and go. Many performing arts companies produce events that only last for a weekend. If a nonprofit arts organization's goal is to grow its audience, its brand is more important than the individual events. Education provides a path to accomplish this. By integrating the brand into the education experience (carefully), the company can deliver consistent messaging over time, which will build brand awareness.

Audience Education and Artists

"When an arts organization's artistic offering sells out, we applaud the artist; when an arts organization's artistic offering bombs, we blame the marketing department." We cannot attribute this phrase to any single arts promoter because we have heard it from so many. The phrase presents two extremes; the truth is likely somewhere in the middle.

Artists and promoters sometimes find themselves at odds. Promoters may feel that they are given a product for which a consumer must be found (the reverse of typical marketing theory). Artists often feel that their art is being reduced to commercialized nuggets of information to get people in the door. Promoters may think that the final "product" is not ready early enough to promote it properly and that they must guess at what the experience will be so that they can advertise. Artists frequently resent feeling rushed through their process for the sake of promotions and come to despise the notion of commercialized art. The relationship between artist and marketer in many arts organizations is fractured. We do know, however, that when healthy collaboration occurs, that communication with the community improves.

A switch to a lens of education provides new opportunities for artists who want to connect with community members.

Like the balance of branding in education, arts organizations should carefully balance how artists participate in education. If the artist believes their involvement is about selling their art or their ideas, the education may feel like a sales pitch. However, when the arts organization, the artist, and the community all understand that the purpose is to educate (creating opportunities to make discoveries) and that no one in the room has all the answers, truly rich engagement can occur. This type of education has great potential as arts patrons are often unsure of their relationship with artists.[11]

Think about ways that the artist could lead an arts experience. What activities could all the participants do together? Could community members' stories or ideas be turned into art in front of them? What type of co-creation could exist? One way to balance the artist's involvement is to create learning objectives *with* the artist and *for* the artist so that everyone becomes engaged in the activity's benefits.

Ideally, the expectations of the artists are linked to their willingness to listen and respond to the community. Art is often created to challenge an idea, preconceptions, and highlight social issues—this is still a response to issues in the community and based on how the artist has listened to those issues, even if their approach is challenging hegemonic ideals. This completes the circle of education. When an artist creates art without listening to the community, they should *expect* nothing in return. Some artists have been incredibly successful in selling their art in this way though most are not. Instead, they are successful in creating art for themselves, and that is wonderful, but it does not serve the community through enlightenment since it is not actually created for them. When these artists create art for themselves, and expect everyone from the community to come running to buy a ticket and tell them their art is wonderful, they do a great disservice to themselves. Instead, by carefully listening to those the artist works to create art for, the artist may find themselves inspired with new creations based upon their community's interests and issues. Through careful communication, the artist is being educated by the community, and the artist is educating the community. In this way, there is a dialogue happening that we would call *engagement*. Ultimately, this is the path to engagement, and the creation of great art in communities. This is not to say that art cannot be created without community input as it certainly can, but the artist who fails to consider the community should expect nothing in return from the community.

Final Thoughts on Education

Education works to engage new audience members, patrons who regularly attend, and everyone in between. Education (like promotional materials) should be geared specifically to a target audience based on their needs and interests. Especially in the early phases of introducing the arts to community members who have never attended, this means expecting nothing. Within the engagement edge, education is one of the most challenging elements for arts organizations to introduce. Many leaders of arts organizations are stretched so thin that they barely have time to measure current impact, make significant changes, or even read a book like this. Compounding this factor is that many arts organizations struggle financially. The thought of a marketing department reducing their efforts to generate income, which is the opposite function of how most arts organizations view their marketing department, may seem impossible. Although transitioning fully from promotion to education may not be feasible in an instant, we believe that a transition (however slow) will enhance community benefit, be a more appropriate approach than traditional promotion, and ultimately increase the arts organization's bottom line.

PART III
EXPERIENCE

The three chapters in part III discuss one of the most vital components of the engagement edge: product versus experience. To define our meaning of art as an experience, we rely on McCarthy's framework of the marketing mix, and John Dewey's seminal work *Art as Experience*. Though the terms may seem interchangeable, the shift in thinking from product to experience is a shift that is more collaborative and beneficial to stakeholders.

Chapter 6 describes McCarthy's framework around product and several scholars' work on experience. It follows how McCarthy described product and looks at how the notion of products and services works within the marketing mix. It then reviews Dewey's definition of art and considers the various ramifications for a shift to experience.

Chapter 7 discusses not only how the notion of product was designed before the nonprofit arts as we know them existed but also how the application of product is a poor fit for the nonprofit arts. It compares and contrasts products and services, and evaluates why comparisons do not hold up to the notion of experience.

Chapter 8 then presents how the notion of experience is most appropriately suited to the arts. It explores both Dewey's work as well as Pine and Gilmore's notion of *The Experience Economy* and combines Pine and Gilmore's distinct arguments to differentiate nonprofit arts from other products and services. These differences are found in aesthetic issues, audience interaction, and experience required.

The Case of Moletedi One Ntseme explores the concept of art as an experience, rather than simply something to be consumed.

The Case of Moletedi One Ntseme and Arts Experiences in Botswana

In countries like Botswana, arts events are a more collaborative and interactive experience than many arts events in the United States. Though many people in the United States think of arts events as museum exhibits, theater performances, and concerts, arts events in Botswana include those and more. The concept of the arts extends to gatherings including funerals, weddings, and festivals. The differences in form and function of Botswana arts events make for events in which the audience members are regularly seen as participants rather than spectators in the experience. We met with Moletdi One Ntseme, a director and producer from Botswana, to gain his perspective about the arts as an experience, rather than a product.

The culture of Botswana is integrated in their arts events. "I come from a culture of people who do almost everything together. That culture is carried on in theatrical performances where people come to have an experience and can always join in and play a part if they want." That means that audience participation, including clapping, dancing, and singing is encouraged and expected during performances. Ntseme shared that it is common for audience members to leave their seats and join dancing actors onstage. "The actors, the stage, and guests are equal, as far as interaction is concerned. No one has more or less control over the experience, though some of it is rehearsed, it is rehearsed to allow for spontaneity as well."

In this culture, audiences do not simply "watch" a play, or "listen" to a concert. Instead, they come ready to have an uplifting and emotional experience where there are limits as to how the audience may use and appreciate the experience. It is involved, participatory, and engaged.

The collaborative and participatory nature of events transfers into the way news is spread about the event. Ntseme emphasized the value of "word of mouth" in the community. Community members are relied upon to share among themselves about upcoming experiences. Essentially, the success of selling out the next event depends on who is telling the story and how they are telling it. Ntseme noted that in Botswana, a significant component in the role of producers and directors is to bring a relatable and participatory experience to affected communities. "Our theatre is focused on building communities. We identify problems and address them through different forms of performance." Theater makers consider how to engage communities in the experience from the beginning. In Botswana, there is value in uplifting one another through art, and exposing community members to opportunities beyond their confined spaces.

An example of a Botswana arts experience that emphasizes community engagement is the Maitisong Festival. The festival is an annual event that runs through the month of April with preparations beginning in October. Artists and arts groups from around Botswana and surrounding countries gather to perform in the festival, and performances range from theater and dance to poetry and comedy. "It is an interactive form of cultural exchange." The vigorous engagement strategy includes artists going out into the community to connect with other community members. "We had to make sure that the people we approached knew more about the event than just words on a flier—we had to explain how we were choosing the right artists to share and attracting other community members." The presence of other community members is necessary to the success of the festival—and just as important as the performances at the festival. "It's not that the artists are preparing something for the community, it's that the artists prepare to create an experience with the community. Each community member leaves with a new internal perspective about art."

The Maitisong Festival is structured with multiple performances happening simultaneously, and after every performance, food and drinks are provided. During this social time, community members, performers, and crew spend time together. "We believe heavily on serving food at our events, and that's an important part of the experience: food included. That is part of our niche. So many great experiences happen over a gathering where food is served, and that is true for the arts in Botswana as well. The arts experience goes all the way through the meal." On his experience as a director at the festival, Ntseme recalls giving pre-show speeches about the production, the people the play is based on, and the social issues addressed in the play. "The speech had to clearly state the social issues being addressed, and be informative enough without giving away the contents of the show. The post-show conversations over food showed that audiences were interested in the experience and the concept behind it."

Although the Maitisong Festival has many elements of a local cultural event, they have formed a relationship with Western arts through a partnership with Juilliard. Ntseme explained that the Maitisong Company invited students from Juilliard each year to exchange cultural ideas about different kinds of theater. The workshop is free and ends with two large-scale performances where artists can show off their talent to the people in the audience (who are mostly friends, family, and loyal *Maitisong* audiences).

Although the performances in Botswana are more free flowing with audience and performers participating as one, arts competitions are frequent. Many drama and dance competitions in Botswana are judged based on the value of the narrative's impact on society. Competitions often travel from town to town to promote arts culture for a variety of communities. "Being in the productions as the one telling the story is another way of engaging people who are within the experiences. I was going through poverty when I told a story about poverty. Someone was going through the HIV/AIDS stigma and told the story about how this virus affects our way of living. The stories are ours, which makes them easier to tell and relate to the audiences."

In this setting, anyone who desires can be engaged in the making of the final product. The mission is to give people hope, belonging, and understanding of the issues they face in the community. Audiences make the decision to attend based on who is involved in the production and whether they relate to the narrative being told onstage. "It is important that as we travel around the country with our show, we find local artists who are recognized in their clans or communities." As visits to a particular town grow, so does community involvement. The production "transitions from being the actors and producers preparing, and becomes for the people, all of us together." Within the community the production is visiting, someone will offer to accommodate the actors and producers on their next visit, someone will offer to feed them, and some offer transportation. "The primary objective for theatre in Botswana is to elevate communities; there is ownership that arises from the people who are being elevated. It is a give and give situation."

This level of involvement often begins at the conceptual stage, where the art (theater) is planned using the stories that local people experience, further enhancing the theatrical experience because these are lived stories in their community. "When we have audiences involved, we create experiences they would not normally get except through the presence of a theatre production. This is the manifestation of theatre being for and by the people—a level of engagement that brings change and empowerment to struggling communities."

Ntseme brought up a theater organization in Botswana called *Enigma Theatre Productions*. When he first joined, his role was a guitarist for a recurring event called *Scars Project*. This arts experience began with actors performing a rehearsed scene that addressed a social issue. "It is a real scenario where the person/people whose stories are being told are sometimes in the audience. The purpose of the scene is to address social issues, like abuse, in a straightforward manner. These performances help to end the stigma surrounding speaking out about abuse and are especially important to people who may be afraid to speak out about their personal experiences with abuse or report their abusers." The scenes are written without complete endings, and the actors stop midway through the narrative to ask audience members how they would end the scenario, and for solutions to the presented problem. "Some audience members are confident enough to go up the stage and act out how they think the scene should end." The audience's desire to be involved in the performance, and the concept of sharing both thoughts and energies, stems from a culture of people who uplift one another and choose to experience life together. For the person whose story is being told, the performance is a platform to explore different options of how to handle the situation they are in. The person remains anonymous, but their story is told. Ntseme made clear that the person has the option to not watch the performance, but the ending scenarios can be reported back to them. "It is truly an experience grown from engagement: We hear the story, we rehearse the story, we tell the story and then we finish the story with our audience, our community. It is far more experiential than just watching a play. Ultimately, each person is having their own experience with the play inside themselves."

From festivals and plays to promotion and audience interaction, Botswana arts events are more than just a way to spend time. They are fully fledged experiences. Botswana artists are producing experiences that immerse the audience in the art. Ntseme, and other artists in Botswana, show how placing value on the audience experience makes for more meaningful arts events.

6
Contrasting Frameworks
Product and Experience

The art's core product is often thought of as a physical object or performance which the audience observes. As previously noted, Dewey's *Art as Experience* presented the idea that the product of art occurs within the audience as an experience.[1] This book encourages arts leaders to realign their thinking with Dewey's theory that the product of the art is experience. We have expanded the bounds to what the experience includes. Dewey's concept of "an experience" is the idea that experiences have a clearly defined beginning and end. **The engagement edge proposes that this beginning and end extend beyond the experiences of interacting with the physical piece of art or a performance.** Think of a typical visit to a museum. Visitors see individual pieces of art and can experience those pieces, but those pieces may make up an exhibit, which is also a defined experience. Likewise, the museum itself may be made up of multiple exhibits, and the museum visit as a whole, from the museum parking lot to leaving the museum grounds at the end, can be considered an experience.

Though we have conceptualized the experience as the product, Sinek encouraged companies to look beyond the product they create to get to the heart of their reason to do so. By focusing on the "why" an organization exists, they can more clearly define their offerings to match their core purpose or "mission" for the nonprofit organization.[2] By being mission-driven, nonprofit arts organizations are encouraged to consider why providing experiences in this way is valuable.

People discuss the aesthetic value of artistic products because the value that we find in beauty or art is a subjective concept since everyone approaches and appreciates beauty, and therefore art, differently from others. In fact, the aesthetic appraisal is why we believe that selling a "product' in the nonprofit arts is an ineffective approach, as art relies heavily on aesthetics to determine value, which causes value to shift constantly.

What Is McCarthy's Product?

McCarthy wrote extensively about product. Though he did emphasize both product and service, he did so by explaining that the product (or service) is not so much a thing as it is "the capacity to provide the satisfaction, use, or perhaps the profit desired by the consumer."[3] To demonstrate this, McCarthy discusses a washing machine: When people purchase a washing machine, they are not looking for a systematically put-together bundle of nuts, bolts, steel, and electronics with inlets for hoses and outlets for drains. When they purchase laundry detergent, they are not in need of so many chemicals mixed together in one package. Instead, they purchase a washing machine or laundry detergent because they desire to have clean clothes. People are uninterested in how the machine was created or how the chemicals work. The desire is for clean clothes, and the machine and detergent satisfy that desire.

McCarthy explained the product by saying, "it may not include a physical product at all! The product of a barber or hairstylist is the design, trimming, or styling of your hair. A medical doctor may simply look at you, neither taking away nor giving you anything tangible. Nevertheless, each satisfies needs and therefore provides a product in the sense that we use product."

What Is a Product?

The standard definition of a product is a thing or substance made or refined for sale. That working definition is how most think about the term. Products are things for sale. Beyond the *physical product*, consider the *extrinsic attributes*, including the brand, packaging, service, promises, and the like. To define the object or service for sale even further, consider the *total product* as a combination of the physical product, the extrinsic attributes, and the values, feelings, and associations consumers feel and attach to the product. In some ways, the latter, the personal appraisal and attachments made with the product, relates more closely to experience. Though one would be hard-pressed to refer to the acquisition of toothpaste as an experience worth any mention, one could consider it experience. Dewey, however, defines *an experience* as something that stands out as distinct from the humdrum of life.[4] Clearly, with toothpaste, the focus is on the physical and extrinsic attributes of the product, unlike the arts, where the focus seems to be more dominantly on the total product—or the aesthetic response to the physical product and its extrinsic attributes.

We define product as anything that can be sold to a consumer for attention, ownership, usage, or consumption, all of which must satisfy a need or want.

By definition, products are more than tangible items and can include services, people, events, organizations, ideas, locations, or any combination. Therefore, when we refer to a product, we refer to any of these possibilities.

Service and Intangibility

Sometimes products are referred to as "products and services," not because a service is not a product—it is—but because services hold a distinct and important role in marketing and are becoming more important in our globalized and information-laden world. Services are intangible, meaning there is nothing to be owned at the end of a transaction. Banks offer services, as do hotels, airlines, repairs, leases, and more. Note that leases appear in that list. Earlier in this book, we made reference to the fact that we could consider an arts marketer's role to be one of leasing space as their job is to fill seats or fill galleries. At the minutest level, the service is a lease made more and more valuable by adding things to it. For example, the time of day a lease is available will have a substantial effect on its value. A curtain of 8:00 p.m. certainly makes the 8:00 p.m. hour of the lease of a seat in the venue much more appealing than the one at 4:00 a.m. when nothing appears on stage. In fact, one might consider the 4:00 a.m. lease worthless or trash, as it is something no one will need or want.

For-Profit Experiences

At one end of the goods spectrum is the pure tangible good, which is something like the toothpaste that comes with no additional service, and at the other end of the spectrum are pure services such as a doctor or taxis. In the middle of the spectrum, there are all sorts of combinations of goods and services. In our current economy, businesses are beginning to see that simply offering their goods or services is ineffective and have begun to surround their products with buying experiences, giving rise to the experience economy. Disney theme parks have long been known for providing an experience to their guests, and they do so in much the same vein as arts organizations. Whole

Foods offers not just groceries but an entire grocery shopping experience with strategically laid aisles, lighting designed to induce pleasure, various offerings such as food and samples to encourage one to linger, a wine bar, a friendly and available customer service, and more. According to Kotler, one of the world's leading experts on marketing, "companies are moving to a new level in creating value for their customers. To differentiate their offers, beyond simply making products and delivering services, they create and manage customer experiences with their brands or companies."[5] The creation of experiences is nothing new in the arts. Ben Cameron has been saying for decades:

> Whichever kind of organization you sit in, I think it's worth entertaining at least three questions for the future. What if our role is no longer to produce artistic work, but our role is social orchestration? Orchestration in which the performance or the exhibit is a piece but only a piece of what we're called to do. What if our job is not merely to create products to be consumed but to provide experiences that serve as springboards to our audience's own creativity? What if we no longer think of ourselves as self-contained organizations and institutions but as platforms designed to aggregate creative energy?[6]

Cameron's discussion is important and one we will dig into further in chapter 8.

Product Levels

In business, product managers have to think about the creation of products or services in three different ways. Product managers must take a methodical approach to determine how best to serve and satisfy the consumer.

Core Customer Level

First, product managers approach the core product by thinking about what the buyer will purchase to satisfy a want or need. The core level only deals with wants or needs and does not add value beyond the original core product intent. Note that the initial connection is made between a want or need and satisfying that want or need.

Actual Product
The actual product considers all the features added to the product or service, such as the design, quality control, packaging, labeling, fonts, product parts, and all other attributes that provide value as part of the core product. This is the level where the actual product is developed or created, and the fine-tuning of the packaging and product occurs.

Augmented Product
The enhanced or augmented product is the version with value-added benefits through customer service and additional elements that provide the highest and best form of the customer's wants and needs in addition to all core benefits. It is this window where one would find a focus on consumer experience, which will be addressed in detail in chapter 7.

Consumers may not be aware of the various levels that product managers must address when considering a product, though it is important to know that products manifest the core customer value: the want or need for the product. The actual product itself is then given additional features to make it attractive and is then enhanced with external support features.

Product Types

Products and services are typically generalized under two categorizations. The first is *consumer products* which are products sold directly to the consumer for personal consumption. The second is *industrial products*, sold to businesses for further use toward conducting their businesses.

Convenience Products
Convenience products are designed for final consumption by the consumer almost immediately. These are typically low-priced and easily accessible at multiple locations. Convenience products are so named because they are designed for the consumer to readily purchase to fulfill a common, usual need, frequently bought with little decision-making. Convenience products might include toothpaste and other regular staples such as fast food, groceries, gasoline, and other basic needs.

Shopping Products

Shopping products are products that consumers purchase on a less frequent basis and are ones that they shop for more carefully, looking closely at things like quality, price, and suitability. With shopping products, consumers will take a greater amount of time making comparisons and looking for the right purchase for themselves. Shopping products are also differentiated by the fact that the business itself will have a decisive role in guiding the consumer's decision based on the business's reputation. Shopping products are typically sold at fewer locations than one might find convenience products. The prices are higher, but the products and services typically come with greater customer service, as there is a decision-making process that the consumer must enter into when purchasing a shopping product. Shopping products include things like clothing, hotels, and furniture.

Specialty Products

Consumer products and services with unique characteristics or brands that are highly recognizable and identifiable for their reputation are considered specialty products. Certain specialty products include high-end and luxury items, such as Tiffany jewelry or Louis Vuitton luggage. As you can imagine, in both those cases, consumers do not have to shop or compare retailers but go directly to the brand retailer they associate with the product they want to purchase. With specialty products, marketing managers do not need to entice the consumer to buy from them specifically.

Unsought Products

Unsought products and services are ones the consumer either is unaware of or is aware of but is not interested in purchasing. Many unsought products are innovative or new products that customers are unaware of until they have been told about them through promotional efforts. Other examples include items that are seen as rarely needed or used, such as reference books, fire extinguishers, and funeral services. Unsought products require a great deal of money and time to promote because the consumer needs to understand the product or service and how it is useful for them.

Industrial Products

Products purchased by a business for further processing or use in conducting the business are considered industrial products. The major distinction between a consumer product and an industrial product is the intention or need for the product purchased. Consider a cleaning person who purchases a broom for their own home. That's a consumer product. When that same cleaning person, however, purchases a broom to take with them to do work in another's home, it becomes an industrial product. Supplies and services are one type of industrial product that businesses use. Examples include repair and maintenance items and office supplies. Services include tax assistance, legal help, management consulting, computer repairs, and other such services. All these services are typically done under a contract with the service provider. Industrial products may also be capital items. *Capital items* add value to the company and generally are for long-term use. Their purchase is required to complete the business's work, such as buildings, factories, offices, copy machines, computer systems, office furniture, and the like. Industrial products can also include materials and parts, the raw materials used to create the product or service they will sell. Raw materials generally come out of the ground like wheat, rice, corn, cotton, or even oil, petroleum, and precious metals. One might also think of raw materials as animals or livestock, fruits or vegetables, and other things that are intentionally grown or harvested. *Created materials and parts* are usually component parts such as small motors, tires, or other items used in the production of a larger product. Price and service are more important when promoting materials and parts than is branding or advertising.

Ideas, Organizations, People, Places
Because tangible products and services are not the only types of things available for sale to consumers, marketing experts have expanded the definition of a product to include intangible products like people, ideas, organizations, and places.[7] Organizations also need to *sell* themselves when they fundraise and when they support charitable works. For example, the American Red Cross and the American Cancer Society are organizations that need to sell themselves. In the same way, nonprofit arts organizations may sell themselves to capitalize on donors. Sometimes the product is a person's skill in that a person, such as a lawyer, doctor, or celebrity, for example, has a skill to sell.

Product Attributes

Because marketing's function is to create value for the consumer, we look at the various attributes of a product to see what they provide. Let's start with quality. We think of *product quality* as the product's ability to satisfy the consumer needs with zero defects, problems, or challenges, but that may be too simple of a definition for the term quality.

Product Quality

Total quality management is the process by which all members of the company—employees, volunteers, and other stakeholders are primarily focused on providing a high-quality product to the consumer. Customer-driven quality is now the goal of most organizations, and is seen to increase the bottom line. However, as mentioned, simply having zero defects is too simple a definition. That is because there are actually two levels of quality the marketer can consider. The first level is *conformance quality*. In conformance quality, the product or service conforms perfectly to its intended goals, and it achieves value by providing zero defects. All organizations seek to deliver conformance quality in their products and services. The second level of product quality is *performance quality*. Companies ensure performance quality by realizing the highest and best performance out of their product or service. As a result, higher quality items are typically exclusive items such as higher-end vehicles: a Ferrari or Porsche, for example. Those cars provide higher performance quality than a typical Ford or Toyota due to the exaggerated focus on quality in their construction. Ford and Toyota may function just as well as the Ferrari or Porsche, but the quality experience is much higher for the latter two. Performance quality does not have to come from an exclusive manufacturer, however. Amazon, for example, provides outstanding performance quality by distributing its products in a very limited time window while providing superior customer service.

Product Features

Product features are another area of focus for marketing managers. *Product features* are those added to the core product to increase value and differentiate one product from another. Often, companies will survey current consumers to ask how they like a product, what features they do or do not like, and what features might make the product better. The marketing managers then use this information to create or improve their product with greater value to consumers versus the cost to the company by adding, eliminating, or improving features.

Style and Design

Another way marketing managers add value to a product or service is through style and design. *Style* refers to the appearance of a product. It may grab attention and be quite attractive, or it may be dull and unattractive. Regardless of how pleasing the aesthetics of the product or service, style does not cause the product or service to perform better. *Design*, however, is much more than appearance. Design has to do with the good looks, ease of use, and performance of the product or service. Good design doesn't happen by simply making fun decisions in a laboratory or a research and development center. Instead, good design starts with brainstorming ideas and then watching how customers use the product or service to improve on it and ensure the product or service is of the highest quality and has the greatest value to the consumer.

Final Notes Defining Product

This section has defined multiple ways marketing scholars think about the construct of product. A component of this section included the for-profit approach to experiences such as theme parks and experiential retail. These experiences are sold to fulfill consumer needs and have utilitarian purposes. This next section dives deeper into the notion of experience and the frameworks and theories that build the conception of experience for the engagement edge.

What Is Experience?

When people think of experiences, they tend to think of those moments that are unique, engaging, special, exciting, touching, endearing, upsetting, or some other form of hyper-emotion attached to an occurrence. Some may also define experience as something one gains after repeated practice at something or those who have scholarly and academic training. Of these ways of identifying experience, it is the first in which is vital for arts organizations.

Experience is the process through which a conscious organism perceives its surroundings. Though a broad statement, it encapsulates the notion of experience over product when looking at the arts. Experience is a perceptual process where people use sensory input to absorb those things in our immediate external environment. As these sensory inputs are enjoyed, our cognitive processes combine thoughts, feelings, perceptions, and memories to form overarching new memories as a complex combination of these sensations. So, though it is said that consumers experience a product, and in the purest sense that is true, the experience itself is something manifested both from the product and all the sensory input resulting from the product. In the case of a tube of toothpaste, there is little to appreciate and sort into new experiential memories. Though the experience of brushing one's teeth for the first time may take particular precedence in our memories and hold some philosophical sway over us, the routine procedure of daily toothbrushing may not classify as the higher-level "experience," to which we wish to attach appreciation for the arts.

Social experience has the closest relationship to the art product as experience because we experience art most frequently with other human beings. The presence of a subsection of society sharing an experience also assumes that we are also sharing norms, ethics, customs, values, traditions, and our roles in the process of a social experience. Although it is beyond the scope of this book to dive into the individual and cultural value of social experiences such as attending the arts, this is an important part of the engagement edge.

Philosopher Immanuel Kant once famously said, "Nothing, indeed, can be more harmful or more unworthy of the philosopher than the vulgar appeal to so-called experience. Such experience would never have existed at all, if at the proper time, institutions had been established in accordance with ideas."[8] In contrast, **the engagement edge asserts that education may help further inform an experience, but the experience itself is still made of emotions, memories, and perceptions in addition to intellectual thought.**

Customer Experience

According to *Forbes*, the customer experience is not just something that occurs at one or two points along the consumer's journey with the provider of the good or service. Customer experience is the culmination of all the touchpoints or critical moments that a consumer encounters or interacts with an organization. Those touchpoints and their cumulative impact on cognition, emotion, memory, and how we react to the overall experience (positively or negatively) is the central defining feature of a customer experience.[9]

The Experience Economy

In their work for the *Harvard Business Review* entitled "Welcome to the Experience Economy," B. Joseph Pine II and James H. Gilmore laid out exactly how society has come to shift its focus from sales to experience, and how we got here. They began with a simple but convincing example about making a cake:

> As a vestige of the agrarian economy, mothers made birthday cakes from scratch, mixing farm commodities (flour, sugar, butter, and eggs) that together cost mere dimes. As the goods-based industrial economy advanced, moms paid a dollar or two to Betty Crocker for premixed ingredients. Later, when the service economy took hold, busy parents ordered cakes from the bakery or grocery store, which, at $10 or $15, cost ten times as much as the packaged ingredients. Now, in the time-starved 1990s, parents neither make the birthday cake nor even throw the party. Instead, they spend $100 or more to "outsource" the entire event to Chuck E. Cheese's, the Discovery Zone, the Mining Company, or some other business that stages a memorable event for the kids and often throws in the cake for free. Welcome to the emerging *experience economy*.[10]

In 1998, Pine and Gilmore noted that, though considering experience was a relatively new way of looking at a developing situation, economists had, for some years, "lumped experiences in with services."[11] There are some important distinctions, and the value of the experience is now becoming clear.

Pine and Gilmore rightly argued that when the experience economy reached a mature stage, businesses would charge for the experience of engaging with a product or service that they can purchase. To charge a fee for an experience, however, the experience must be of value to the consumer and unique enough to encourage their return. Though it may be difficult for businesses to make a switch from service alone to experience, just as it was difficult to switch from an industrial economy to a service economy, those organizations that make the shift will be the ones to survive and thrive.

So how did Pine and Gilmore, two non-artist consumerism researchers, define an experience? They defined experience using terms borrowed from the theater: "An experience occurs when a company intentionally uses services as the stage, and goods as props, to engage customers in a way that creates a memorable event. Commodities are fungible, goods are tangible, services intangible, and experiences *memorable*."[12] Those who buy experiences are buying value that the company reveals over time. Each experience reveals a new facet of the organization's creativity.

Experiences are entirely personal and exist only within and for each consumer. Experiences persist in the mind, an amalgam of emotions, intellect, physical stimuli, and even spiritual understanding. Pine and Gilmore noted that experiences like those they expect to see at all business levels have long been at the heart of entertainment businesses, with the Walt Disney Company and its theme parks being prime examples. Those theme parks constantly improve, upgrade, and change their experiences to maintain a robust following. Themed restaurants like the Hard Rock Cafe and the Rainforest Cafe have likewise taken strides toward offering an experience, although they may struggle because they rarely update their offerings.

The paradigm shift that Pine and Gilmore see coming is a time when consumers pay an extra fee for the experience, above and beyond the purchase of a good or service. They described the story of IBM shifting from selling and manufacturing computers and providing free services, to paying for a consumer's equipment in order to charge for the service of it. IBM saw a shift from an industrial product offering to a service-based product and is proven by the fact that IBM now makes more profit from services than goods. A sign, then, of the experience economy's immaturity is that organizations that provide experiences are not yet charging exclusively for the experience. Charging for an experience does not mean that goods and services are no longer priced. Disney parks charge an admission fee for the experience and make plenty of profit from parking, food, merchandise sales, and more in the parks.

Organizations charging admission to sell goods or services is not a new concept, as seen in the arts, but the practice is becoming more commercialized. Consider, for example, renaissance festivals that charge for admission but are, in reality, large trade shows, where food, goods, and services are sold at a premium. Trade shows themselves are typically experiences where there is an admission fee for the opportunity to make a purchase once inside.

We think of experiences in distinct ways. One of those is customer participation. As we have mentioned, this ranges on a spectrum from fully active participation to passive participation.[13] In active participation, consumers are fully immersed in and can alter the experience. Active participants are doing something as part of the experience. Think of golfers in a tournament who pay to participate and are actively engaged in creating the experience for themselves, while observers of the golf tournament are passive. In passive participation, the consumer has no significant effect on the experience. Although even completely passive participation is active in the sense that a mere presence is enough to contribute to the touchpoints that make up a total experience.

John Dewey: Art as Experience

The second way we can look at experiences is through the notion of connection. Some consumers can be immersed in an experience, while others are absorbed in it. Watching a movie in a theater filled with vibrating seats, Dolby sound, popcorn smells, sticky floors, and dozens of other patrons surrounding you immerses you in the experience, whereas watching the same film at home on DVD allows you to absorb the experience.

Dewey noted a distinction.[14] To Dewey, experiences are constantly occurring in a fluid motion through life as we encounter anything outside of ourselves.[15] They have starts and stops, bumps, interferences, and interruptions. Life is a constant collection of experience. Dewey noted that for something to become *an* experience, however, it requires completion. An experience is something interactive with pieces outside of us that interact with us both externally and internally, and comes to a finale. Dewey saw this finale not as an end, but as an experiential completion, "so rounded out that its close is a consummation and not a cessation. Such an experience is a whole and carries with it its own individualizing quality and self-sufficiency. It is *an* experience."[16]

Pine and Gilmore used the two factors of connection and participation to create a grid of four dimensions to show where consumers will dwell within an experience.[17] For those who are passively participating and absorbing the experience are enjoying *entertainment*. *Educational* experiences are typically ones where consumers are actively involved in the experience but are still absorbing rather than being immersed in the experience. *Escapist* experiences are those where the consumer is immersed in the experience such as when an actor is playing a role in a play, or a hiker is exploring the California Redwood Forests. In these cases, the consumers are immersed and active. However, if the extent to which the consumer is participating is reduced to something passive, such as looking at the Redwood Forest or watching the play, escapist experiences become *aesthetic*, where the consumer is immersed but not actively shaping the experience.

Dewey noted that, upon consummation, these become real experiences after we use the phrase, "that was an experience."[18] We must designate them as experiences by using the adjective "that." In other words, an experience is achieved when it is named *that* play, *that* painting, *that* ballet, or *that* symphony. As we recall an experience, we can see that there are dominant and less dominant forces at play in creating what the experience was.

So how does one design an experience that is effective? Pine and Gilmore provided five pillars for doing just that.[19] Understanding these pillars will help managers design your experience in a consumer-focused way. The first is to **theme the experience**.

The theme for an experience need not be known to the consumer, but the theme is a means for pulling all the various pieces of an experience together in a unified fashion. Pine and Gilmore used the Forum Shops at Caesar's Palace to define the concept. The shops are themed like an outdoor Roman market, complete with a skyline and setting sun overhead on a giant blue sky ceiling with painted clouds. Roman soldiers periodically stroll the hallways, and storefronts look like Rome recreations with white pillars, live plants, and Roman statues. The theme at Caesar's Palace, and any exceptional themed location is unified, concise, and compelling.

This theme, then, might be what Dewey referred to as "underlying quality."[20] They are the pieces of the puzzle that include not only mechanical alteration of our world but also an intent to shape emotions and practical distinction in phases that are fluidly connected in a linear fashion. The theme is not distinguishable from the experience but is a fluid throughline of the experience.

The second factor for creating excellent consumer experiences is to **harmonize impressions with positive cues**.[21] These cues are the thoughts or feelings that people take away from the well-defined pieces associated with the theme. Each time a touch point occurs for the consumer, a positive cue should move them through the experience. An usher who simply shows an audience member their seat accomplishes very little, but the one who says, "enjoy your evening, Mr. and Mrs. Smith. If you need anything while being whisked away to Mozart's middle years, let me know" gives a cue that creates an impression that is hopefully themed around Mozart's middle years.

Impressions of negative cues can also exist. In order to have a positive and effective experience, a manager must work to **eliminate negative cues to ease** access. Oftentimes audiences see instructions printed on white paper and taped to walls, explaining which seats are down what aisle. The cue being sent is that we would like you to find your own seat. In fact, anything that does not contribute to the theme is probably distracting from it and therefore should be eliminated.

Dewey found that the pieces of an experience all contribute to the overall aesthetic of the experience, but only in total.[22] For an experience to occur, these fluid pieces, positive or negative, that all connect to one another seamlessly provide the overall experience. There is a visceral or emotional reaction to each piece as it is occurring in the experience, but it is the summation of those pieces and their final consummation with the person having the experience, that actually causes it to be an experience.

A fourth factor in developing an exceptional experience is to **mix in memorabilia**.[23] People purchase the drink in the expensive glass they can take home as a souvenir because they want an object with which to remember the experience. Postcards exist for the sole purpose of sharing or remembering an experience. Tee-shirts and ball caps that recognize an experience are sold at most major events worldwide, and the price point is higher than for a simple piece of clothing because the garment is significant for the memory of the experience in which it was made available.

We consider these objects part of the construction of experience. Dewey eschewed the materialism suggested, and instead focused on how the pieces affect the psyche.[24] Each has its own function individually, yes, but these connections to the real world contribute and become a part of *an* experience, potentially due to their memorability. A semantic issue may be at play between the mechanical notion of mixing in memorabilia and the aesthetic notion of experience. The English language has no single word for the concept of "artistic aesthetic," but rather the words *artistic*, having to do with the act of producing art, and *aesthetic*, having to do with enjoyment and perception. It is easy enough to see these two things as separate and distinct, with one implying or imposing itself upon the other, but this would suggest that because art is a process of creation, enjoyment and perception have nothing to do with it. However, the creator of art actually experiences the art through the perspective they hope the audience has as they create the art. As a result, *an* experience an audience has with art is more controlled than general experiences of life. The perceiver of the process of creation, whether artist or audience, has an experience in the consumption of that creation, and the consumptive experience is purposeful: "The act of producing that is directed by intent to produce something that is enjoyed in the immediate experience of perceiving has qualities that a spontaneous or uncontrolled activity does not have. The artist embodies in himself the attitude of the perceiver while he works."[25]

Finally, exceptional experiences **engage all five senses**.[26] This is a utilitarian function, but every sense has some input into the collective memory that is the experience. As each is engaged, it further cements those neural connections that turn a sequence of events from normal life to *an* experience. As Dewey notes, since art includes the process of perception, the greater we are able to perceive it through multiple senses, the more likely the occurrences are *an* experience.[27]

Final Thoughts on Defining Product and Experience

This chapter identified traditional definitions behind the terms *product* and *experience*. It discussed the basic idea of a product as anything that "can be sold to a consumer for attention, ownership, usage, or consumption." This simple definition is complicated when we introduce the tangibility spectrum: from pure tangible good to intangible service, which exists through a lens of benefits to the consumer. To understand how customers assign value to products, we began with the core customer level, which purely deals with the original wants and needs that drive a buyer to purchase a product, and built upon this with a number of tangible and intangible product levels that included actual, enhanced, convenience, shopping, specialty, unsought, industrial as well as the more elusive idea of ideas, people, organizations, and places. Value is enhanced or diminished by the attributes, quality, features, and style and design of the product in question. In the arts, however, it may be more beneficial to investigate experiences and their ephemerality. Identifying the customer touch points that create a positive experience is integral as we move into the experience economy and away from a product-focused landscape. Though these products are still involved in our search for customer fulfillment, it is the larger array of memories, emotions, physical stimuli, and aesthetic value that differentiates the arts from other products. As Pine and Gilmore note, experiences are "memorable." Through theming, positive cues, memorabilia, and sensory engagement we have the power to make experiences not just memorable, but unforgettable.

7
Product and the Arts

This chapter explores the concept of product relative to arts organizations. Generally, the traditional notion of product is an inappropriate construct for marketing any art, commercial or nonprofit. This statement will be supported by reevaluating the term *tangibility* and what it means for nonprofit arts experience-makers. It will explore the arts' purpose as a tool for enlightenment as opposed to simply a scheme for financial enrichment, or a mechanism for consumer satisfaction. This chapter asserts that the purpose of the nonprofit arts organization is not the same as that of the art that it makes. It will also illuminate the importance of identifying why an organization's art is produced, and how this can be leveraged in the experience economy.

Before exploring the notion of product and the complications that construct presents for the nonprofit arts, we present the case of the Dalicin Opera Company and how they struggled with this very challenge.

The Case of the Dalicin Opera Company

The Dalicin Opera Company, located outside of Austin, Texas, had been in operation since the mid-1980s. Although located near Austin, the company served a small population. On average, the Dalicin saw an annual attendance of about 4,500 patrons. Through the years the company had developed a series of educational workshops to supplement their mainstage season of two operas and a series of four to six solo performers. Though a small company, the organization had a significant donor base relative to their annual operating costs. This donated income allowed the organization to create programming purely for artistic merit, unlike many other nonprofit arts organizations in the United States, that must balance programming decisions with the potential for ticket sales.

By the late 2000s, Dalicin Opera's financial situation allowed their artistic director, Genevieve Plock, to host a wide variety of artists from around the world while taking risks other organizations might be hesitant to take. One such programming decision was to create a new opera composition program through their educational offerings. Through the program, several composers would create new operas with oversight from an experienced composer in residency with the company. A new opera was included in every season as an additional offering bringing their annual season to three operas plus the four to six solo presentations.

In 2012, Anna Ferncroft joined as the marketing director of the Dalicin Opera. Ferncroft loved the arts, and had attended events at the Dalicin since she was in high school. Although her background was in music theater performance, she had always loved opera. "If I had a better voice I might have pursued a career in opera. I didn't think I could cut it, and that's when I discovered music theatre." She went through a BFA music theater program at a nationally recognized university, but after graduating changed her path. Throughout her undergraduate program she had volunteered with her department to create the graphics and programs for their productions. In those experiences she developed a love for graphic design. After completing her BFA, she took a position at a large venue in town. "I had been working at an arts center downtown that welcomes tours," she shared. The center held a large theater which could seat an audience of nearly 2,500. They primarily hosted national tours of Broadway musicals which would run for several weeks, and special guest artists (comedians, musicians, dance events, etc.), who would perform one or two events over a weekend between the national tours.

When the position became available, she applied right away. At the arts center, Ferncroft served as an associate director of marketing, but was transitioning to her first director of marketing position at the Dalicin. She was thrilled to be taking on the new job. "Moving from a presenting organization to a producing organization was so exciting. I had lots of experience with these sort of, 'big name events,' but getting to work on something new, and so niche was exactly where I wanted to be." The transition was also a move from a for-profit corporation to a nonprofit organization. "I'm embarrassed to say it, because it sounds so silly to me now, but at the time I really didn't know the difference. I knew that the Dalicin had a smaller audience base, and that they created their own operas, but I didn't understand the full picture of how the income moved around. I'd always thought nonprofits didn't have many financial resources, but that was certainly not the way it was at the Dalicin."

In her previous position she had a focus on promotion. Her primary work was in coordinating web advertisements, billboards, radio spots, direct mail, and program advertising swaps with other performing arts organizations. She had even arranged ad swaps in the past between the Dalicin and the arts center. This new job as the director of marketing gave Ferncroft a new level of control. She shared that in her first weeks she "wasn't nervous at all. Everyone from the [performing arts center] I was leaving called me nuts. To some of them it seemed like a step back going from these big name performers, to opera singers none of them had ever heard of."

When she started her position, she was focused on the upcoming season rather than the events that were ongoing at the time. David Rocke, the director of marketing whom she was replacing, remained with the organization to complete the season for which he had created and executed the marketing plan. There was a three-month overlap in which they both worked for the organization. Plock told Ferncroft they had set the contracts that way to allow for a smooth transition.

Although they worked separately, Ferncroft was encouraged to share her plans with Rocke for advice. Ferncroft, however, wasn't particularly motivated to share her plans, "You know, I just thought I knew better. It was silly and dumb, but I figured I had done marketing for these big shows so I knew the business." Over those three months they only met twice to discuss the marketing plan Ferncroft was putting together. Rocke was not a fan of Ferncroft's approach, "David was nice, but he just kept telling me that my plan was too simple. 'It lacks depth' I remember him saying. As nice as the guy was, in those two meetings he really ticked me off."

Ferncroft had recognized that the touring shows at the arts center were sold based on name recognition. To sell the events in her last job, she worked to spread the news and the title as far and wide as possible, through as many channels as she could find. These events essentially sold themselves. She knew it would be different at Dalicin, and she incorporated this difference into her plan. "I wanted to be certain that people knew what they were coming to. It's a very important part of marketing, it's really the first thing—people need to know what they're buying, and with famous titles or people they already have that in their minds."

Every year over 4,500 people attended events at the Dalicin. Ferncroft knew that these people would be their primary audience. They already had the knowledge to understand the value of opera and the impact it could have on them. These 4,500 people would recognize the titles and names and needed very little description to consider if they wanted to attend. As a director of marketing, though, part of her job was to increase in the number of sales. In her last position sales numbers were recorded annually and carefully tracked to ensure profitability. To increase the number of sales, Ferncroft saw that she would need to reach beyond the 4,500 who would recognize the organization, the titles, and the performers.

She noted that, "at the time, my mantra was 'do they know what they're buying, do they know what they're buying?' It sounds silly, but I would say this to myself over and over. Everything about our communications was designed to communicate that. Rather than promoting titles, composers, and performers, I focused on describing the plots, the costumes... really everything that would happen on stage." She figured, if they did not know what they were buying from the title, she could tell them what they were buying by describing the product. Rocke disagreed with this approach; Ferncroft saw his approach as antiquated. "I don't know—he would just put the title with a picture, the dates, and how to get tickets. At the time I just thought, 'how boring!' I wanted to tell people what they were getting for their money."

After Rocke left, Ferncroft began to push promotions for the first two events out to the community. The opening of the season was Puccini's *Tosca*, and the second was a concert of songs by Wagner, Rossini, Verdi, and other composers from the Romantic period. The Dalicin's music director determined the selections and invited a select few performers to sing. To promote *Tosca*, the materials downplayed the title and instead described the three acts, told the audience about the costumes, the set designs, and even what instruments were included in the orchestra. Ferncroft's promotion essentially broke apart the event into different components to describe what the audience would get, so that people who were not familiar with *Tosca* or Puccini might purchase tickets. She did the same with the concert, they listed the pieces that would be performed, who would perform them, and what instruments would accompany the concert.

As the opening of *Tosca* neared, Ferncroft looked at the sales trends relative to past years' similar events. "It wasn't good, well, it was bad actually. We were down like 30% compared to the worst opening from the previous 5 years at two weeks out. I met with Plock to break the news about how it was going. Honestly, I thought I'd be fired, but Plock just [said], 'oh okay, our audience'll be what it'll be' and she just moved on to talking about how great things were going in rehearsals. I'd never been so confused." As the opening got closer, Ferncroft continued to push for more sales by sending out additional emails with more information about the show. After its two-week run, *Tosca* closed with about 25% less income than budgeted. The week after closing, Plock called Ferncroft to her office. "I thought I was being fired for sure, I'd never seen an event take such an unexpected loss. I sat down opposite her, waiting for the shoe to drop, and she asked me. . . if I would pick up one of the singers for the concert from the airport because no one from company management was available to do it and she knew I lived by the airport. It was as if no one cared that the event had sold so poorly."

There was a three week space between the end of *Tosca* and the weekend concert of compositions from the Romantic period. Ferncroft reviewed the sales data for the concert, and though she could not remember how low the sales were in comparison with similar events, she recalled that sales numbers were a lower percentage than for *Tosca*. As before, she notified Plock of the slim sales, and Plock seemed disinterested in the conversation. The concert was undersold, and like *Tosca*, it did not recoup the costs of production. Although both productions were produced at a loss, both were hailed as successes internally. Plock and others at the organization pushed forward with business as usual, but Ferncroft was determined to increase their sales and attendance.

For the next event, a new opera developed by a student in Dalicin's education program, Plock took a different approach. Ferncroft felt that, of all the events, promoting the audience experience rather than a title was most appropriate. She also knew that simply breaking down the performance components would not be enough. "This was something no one had ever seen before. It was called *Honor and Faith*. Which is clearly a title no one was familiar with, but it was a unique offering because it was created by students of the education program. That became the angle." Ferncroft created promotional materials based around the experience of creating this opera. Promotional materials included information about the composer, what went into a new production, and how special it was to experience a brand-new piece of art.

Even before reviewing the sales data for the event, Ferncroft knew there was a difference. "People were just so much more responsive to the materials. Our social media was more active with comments and questions, it was really a shift." As the event drew closer, Ferncroft doubled down on the messaging about how unique the offering was and how special the experience is to hear music for the first time. Their open performance was nearly sold out, and they turned a profit for the first time that season. "There was real energy in the audience," Ferncroft recalled, "you could feel their excitement."

The following week Ferncroft dropped into Plock's office to check in about the event. Despite the overwhelming difference in the income and audience size, it was as if no change had occurred in attendance. "She just said, 'wasn't that a wonderful new opera? I wonder which student's work will be selected next year'? I was really shocked, I thought we were going to celebrate." It took Ferncroft some time to realize that the culture of the organization really was not focused on sales or income. It also wasn't focused on audience impact or community either; they were solely focused on the production of art.

Ferncroft learned some valuable lessons from marketing those first three events. "I shifted my messaging to focus more on the audience rather than exactly what the product is. I wanted the message to focus on how the audience experiences the product and how they are actively involved, even if they are just there in the seats. It makes them a part of it." Of course, under the engagement edge, the product of the art is the total experience of the audience members rather than only what occurs on stage, so our lines of thinking are slightly different from Ferncroft's.

She realized another key about communication that is tied to education. "I always knew that not everyone knows about operas, but instead of segmenting the messaging to people based on what they know, I lowered the bar to try to include everyone, and probably alienated some opera buffs in the process—oops." Ferncroft had sent the same materials out to everyone, so those who would have recognized the title and immediately opted in instead had to work through the promotional material to find it. With the new opera created by the educational program, the messaging could be more simplistic. "Everyone was in the same boat here. No one knew anything about it so everyone was pretty much able to get the same stuff."

She shared her final thoughts about her early days at Dalicin, "What I wish I had done is, rather than communicating about what was going to happen on the stage, I should have driven home what it feels like to see it. That, as an audience member you are a part of something really special. It's

> what I always loved in high school. I felt like I was a part of what was happening when I was there, it wasn't just a presentation for me."

Is Art a Product?

Before unpacking the idea of a product, we must address the main argument about the concept. Many nonprofit artists will boldly and logically argue that art is not a product. We have referred to John Dewey's tome from the 1930s, *Art as Experience*, which details quite clearly, even if in a dated philosophical fashion, that art is not a commodity with utilitarian value like many other products or services.[1] Even entertainment such as Netflix provides a utilitarian purpose. Though one may argue that part of what the nonprofit arts does is entertain, many artists will agree that the primary function of art is not to entertain, but to enlighten. **Enlightenment is part of the experience that makes art unique when held against a traditional product or service within the marketing mix structure.** Enlightenment occurs within the consumer, and it is because this ineffable enlightenment is the primary function of art that it is perceived uniquely by every consumer. Making statements and assessments about the average consumer to derive appropriate marketing mix placement for a product may be conceptually consistent with sound logic; however, doing so for art is not.

There is, however, another side to this argument, and it is the one made by marketing experts: Of course art is a product. Anything that we create of value that we can put for sale is a product. Another argument marketing experts make is that the conceptual framework of product also includes services *and* experiences. Therefore, art is as much a part of the definition of a product as a hotel, car rental, or Disney theme park ticket. Although the utilitarian value of the former two is clear, the utilitarian value of theme park is less clear. A theme park is considered an entirely complete construct under entertainment, which has its roots in products. Entertainment has utilitarian value, as does the hotel room and the car rental, but art has no utilitarian value beyond the secondary or perhaps a tertiary and byproduct function for entertainment. Commercial art is designed for entertainment (or at least commercialism) as its primary function and can generate greater revenue for the production value, just as a theme park does. Yes, it is an experience that borders very closely with the work of nonprofit arts organizations, but because the primary function is utilitarian, we leave theme parks in the realm of service.

The origin of the term *product* helps us understand its limitations for the arts. It comes from late Middle English, originally gleaned from the Latin word *productum*, meaning something produced for use. The term is also used as a verb, *producere*, which means "to bring forth." Essentially, the word *product* comes from the concept of producing or manufacturing something from raw materials and bringing it forth for use. At first glance, this original definition of the term implies that anything produced and brought forth would be a product. The implication, however, in the original definition is that something is brought forth for a person's use—to be grasped, and tangible, exactly how a product is conceived by most. In the strictest sense, then, art is a product when it is not actively included in the engagement process, meaning concrete products that include art objects could be included in this foundational definition, to a point. But what about paintings, sculptures, and other objects of art meant to be viewed but not touched? What about performance art? How do these mediums fit into the definition of a product?

We should also understand the divergent definition of the word *tangible* when applied to the arts. The engagement edge's function is to shift our thinking from the traditional sales and marketing model to a collaborative one. With the notion of engagement, we are not producing something to "bring forth" for the consumer in the tactile sense. It is here that the word *tangible* takes a turn. The intricate nature of the word *tangible* includes that which is observable, measurable, and perceivable. The concept of *real* as related to a tangible object becomes the authentic quality of a product of artistic endeavor. The palpable undercurrents—the tone, feelings, and emotions of experience and the engagement it embodies—exist in the viewers.[2] Even if we are discussing physical art pieces that are only observed, art does not exist until the consumer is experiencing it, so we cannot bring it forth or produce it without the consumer's participation. Unlike a tube of toothpaste, or even a hotel room, the result of the creative artistic process does not reach its full potential to be complete until it is formed as a memory in the mind of the consumer.

Disney

The middle ground between art and product is evident at Disney theme parks, where an understanding of the experience economy has led to success.

Although we may argue all art is designed as an experience that occurs within a consumer, we also find that memories created by the experience are as vital to art as all the pieces that go into its construct. The Disney experience, like most, if not all, commercial art, can be replicated precisely for the purpose of entertainment. Though the nonprofit arts do entertain, their contribution to the milieu of arts, in general, is primarily one of engaged experiences. This argument is derived directly from Sinek, who encourages businesses to look at "why" they create what they create.[3]

One question that arises as we consider product is that of equilibrium: If the core item of value to the consumer proves to be unsatisfactory, does this negate the desire to return for another experience, even if the overall experience is satisfactory? In other words, if an evening at the symphony turns out to be a lovely affair, but the audience member is dissatisfied with the art, does this in and of itself negate the desire to return? The art's function is to enlighten, not to entertain. If it fails to have a positive impact and it still enlightens in some way (perhaps negatively), it is therefore still a valuable part of the overall experience.

So, what does enlightenment mean in this context and why can we not purely rely on consumer satisfaction? The overall satisfaction provided by art includes memories of the experience that surrounded and included the art. When McCarthy said that a product or service is "the capacity to provide satisfaction, use, or perhaps the profit desired by the consumer," he blanketed everything he possibly could in this statement.[4] This statement, however, was written before 501(c)(3) organizations as we now know them existed. When McCarthy said that the product or service provides satisfaction to some degree, he was referring to the satisfaction of needs and wants. The enlightenment of the artistic experience is unique and different from the entertainment value. Following Sinek's logic, the "why" we create nonprofit arts is to generate enlightenment in terms of awareness and an understanding of art, to bridge the gap between the artists and audiences, and bring local communities together through the world of art. Even a poorly received piece of art in an otherwise exceptional experience will achieve some form of enlightenment in its audience. By doing so, we satisfy Sinek's "why" and find ourselves outside the realm of McCarthy's product as defined by McCarthy and his successors.

How is art created and what purpose does it serve? Products and services are designed to satisfy a specific need or want in a consumer. They have the specific function of satisfaction, as we have seen from McCarthy, and they are created with this purpose in mind, typically based upon substantial consumer research. On the other hand, art is not simply created for the audience or specifically to satisfy the consumer. Instead, art is created with the intention to develop a reflection of the world. The goal of its creation is to develop this relational experience where the viewer and artist come together. When a commercial product line is scalable, such as at a Disney theme park or a Broadway tour, it moves beyond the ethereal notion of creation. It moves into the realm of entertainment, where it becomes a commodity that can be sold as a service or product.

It is in this window where we see the importance of understanding your "why" in the experience economy. Recall that the subtitle of the book *The Experience Economy*[5] is *The World Is Theatre and Every Business a Stage*, suggesting that those purveyors of traditional products and services should consider moving closer to the arts in the fourth economy. Although providers of products and services could provide experiences, such as a Disney theme park, they cannot profitably achieve the same goals as the nonprofit arts community. **Disney's "why" ultimately is to sell tickets, and that is done by creating an experience. In the nonprofit arts, the "why" is to generate enlightenment by having experiences with art and members of the community.** Yes, tickets may be sold, but that consideration is secondary to the function of nonprofit arts and is necessary only for sustenance, not profit.

Why Art Is Not a Service

Art is not designed with the intention that it will act on behalf of others. If we assume that the definition of service is "the action of working for the good of others," then it is clearly shown that, although the nonprofit arts organization's primary function is service, the function of the art is not. Nonprofit organizations exist to serve the public. These organizations exist to serve the public good and create art at times, such as producing local performances and educational outreach activities, but **that makes the organization a service, not the art itself.** The organization utilizes its skills and abilities to support, develop, and further artists and their endeavors.[6] It then opens the arts offering to the public, where its service continues as it educates, creates, encourages, and engages its community, building a pathway between art and society. Ben Cameron asked, "What if we no longer think of ourselves as self-contained organizations and institutions, but as platforms designed to aggregate creative energy?"[7] In agreement with Cameron's logic, the arts organization is a steward of the art, where artists and audiences can be brought together by the organization through the collection of creative energy.

Experience and the Collaborative Process of Art

In many ways, art is a process and is not about an end-product at all. Consider that the performing arts always present something that has never been presented before *because it is live*. Even if it attempts to replicate the performance from the day before, the event will always be different. Endless rehearsals would still never allow the art to unfold exactly the same way twice, meaning that the performance occurs as the audience experiences it.

Strictly visual arts can also be described by their process, although the end result may be seen as a finished piece of work. The physical work of art does not deviate from its finished state, but in process art it is the very process and means of creation that is the art. Process art is a movement within the art world that formally began in the 1960s and popularized through the 1970s. The origin of process art, however, is said to go back as far as the 1940s and the abstract expressionism movement embraced by such artists as Jackson Pollock.

The paintings of Jackson Pollock, with splattered, sprayed, and dripped paint adorning the canvases, demonstrate the process used by Pollock. The final artifact of the painting reflects the moment in time when Pollock reflected on society through his painting; all expressed through his process. We posit that because art is process-oriented, it is neither product nor service, but experience. The Pollock painting has little relative value as paint on a canvas. The sum of those parts has no greater utilitarian worth than a few dollars. **It is Pollock's interpretation of the world and his use of materials that send out a message and create value.** In Pollock's case, as with all process art, the message is demonstrated by the process behind the work.

Today, a form of process art has evolved in contemporary artistic endeavors by using multiple media and materials. There is a robust following for expanded forms of process art that is about not only the means but also the materials used, such as in sustainable art, rubbish or trash art, recycled art, eco-art, and much more. Through these media forms, artists use specific materials and incorporate the use of these materials in their process to send their messages. Twenty-first-century art also includes other process-laden means such as digital art, street art, collaborations with engineering concepts to develop animatronic art, and much more.

It is assumed that art is a completed object or performance, ready for audience consumption, but consummation cannot be achieved without **audience participation**. It is important to consider that the artist conceives art as an interpretation or reflection of something, even if those viewing it may have a very different experience. The visual arts bring about different thoughts, feelings, and emotions based on the viewer, their circumstances, and their personal history. All art forms are in a constant state of flux, allowing for continuous interpretation and appreciation, and can be conceived as a collaborative experience. The audience participates in that once a connection has been made, there becomes an inward observation, and the encounter becomes a personal experience.

The art does not exist as an artistic expression if that communication is not received. The distinction here is this: the tube of toothpaste does not require a toothbrusher in order to exist. It is a product that has no home until it is promoted and purchased by a consumer. The same can be said for the hotel room lease. It exists as a service, whether it is being used by a consumer or not. **Art, however, does not exist until it occurs in an audience, so it is neither product nor service.** It is a participatory process which requires the consumer of the process, and without whom the art becomes simply a rehearsal or paint on a canvas. As we will demonstrate in chapter 8, though the art is actually an experience engineered by artists to some degree, it requires the input and participation of an audience in order for its purpose to come to fruition.

There is a fluidity to all art: process art figuratively morphs with varying perceptions and meanings attributed to it by the viewers. Literary art is unique in that it illustrates how a finished work can evolve through another art form, often performance. Shakespeare's plays are a good example of literary art that continues to bend, shift, and reshape based on current artists' interpretations. This fluidity, however, is restricted in commercial art. It is *designed* as a product in the strictest sense. McCarthy never considered "process" as part of "product," though we do see "process" as part of the artistic experience. In commercial art, there is a right way to approach the art, with clear instructions on how to go about creating it most effectively. The ultimate goal is to have a final product that is as close to perfect as possible and sell a maximum number of pieces, which means that the focus cannot be on imagery or inspiration because it must inherently focus on maximizing the potentiality of sales or attendance.

The *Problem* with Traditional Arts Marketing

Consider the product from an entrepreneur's perspective. This is the ground zero of marketing. The basic functions of marketing are to solve a problem with a product or service, find the consumers who need that problem solved, and then remind the consumer of their problem and provide an explanation of how the product or service will solve it, and then get the product or service to the consumer. The process is problem-driven.

One issue with this approach is that it assumes the only function of marketing is to solve problems. Sometimes, marketers will diagnose a problem that consumers do not even know exists to push their product or service onto the consumer. Additionally, not everything in life is a problem, nor do we need a solution for every issue that occurs in life. From the artist's perspective, marketing and problem solving are challenging because art is not intended to solve problems. In some cases, art may not even serve to solve a desire. Although many products and services exist to solve problems, this is not a fundamental feature of the arts. The pervasive attitude that marketing functions to solve problems tends to overshadow much of the purpose of the arts.

Art is created to have meaning, not to solve problems. Those meanings can be visceral, emotional, and intrinsic. They have individual value to the person consuming the art with no absolute value outside of that context. We choose to appreciate art for the feelings it stimulates, and the desire to share in the imagery, creativity, and ingenuity brought to the surface drives us to consume art. In some sense, this desire seems almost instinctual for those who have been introduced to it. Other than an interest in the investment potential of owning a piece of art, and rather than solve a problem, it is the ability to experience certain emotions and feelings produced on a repeated and recurring basis that impels a person to purchase art. Art is not about solving problems; it is about having meaningful experiences.

Traditional marketing, in turn, puts pressure on artists to consider their making of art as a process designed to solve problems, a consideration that can impact the free-flowing nature of artistic creation. The goals of providing a reflection of society, stirring emotions, meaning, and the like are the artist's goals, and though art may lead to awareness and understanding of societal problems, this is not the core function. Arts marketers, rather than focusing on engagement, must convince consumers of the problem that exists ("you need art in your life") to sell them on purchasing the art. The focus of marketing a product is fundamentally flawed when considering the nonprofit arts.

Product Has Never Worked

Artists have long known that the conceptual framework of product, whether they understand on an academic level or not, does not work for the arts. We can also see why none of the traditional elements of the marketing mix fit the nonprofit arts. The notion of "product or service" has an additional structural issue that sets it apart from the nonprofit arts: It implies commerce. The idea of price, which supports the construct of product or service, falls apart when considering the nonprofit arts. It is this relationship between the elements of the marketing mix that presents another failure for the concept of product in the nonprofit arts. Although the nonprofit arts have taken advantage of some theoretical constructs of the P that represents promotion, the remaining two Ps, price and place, have minimal or no construct under which the nonprofit arts can use them effectively. Because the marketing mix requires an appropriate balance of the four Ps, the nonprofit arts are left with promotion that works to help create brand recognition and product, which is an incomplete construct and cannot be appropriately mixed with price or place.

Final Thoughts on Product and the Arts

This chapter discussed the definition of product and its role in arts marketing today. It also explored why this term is ineffective in arts marketing, chiefly because art only occurs in the presence of participation. This participation results in an *experience* as opposed to a physical product. The next chapter explores how traditional marketing can be reframed to include the term *experience*. It then explains the components of building an effective artistic experience and explores how the other Es of the engagement edge can support this process.

8
Experience and the Arts

In 1934, philosopher John Dewey published the book *Art as Experience*, and Dewey's thoughts robustly shape our ideas. Dewey stated,

> Experience in this vital sense is defined by those situations and episodes that we spontaneously refer to as being "real experiences"; those things of which we say in recalling them, "that was an experience." It may have been something of tremendous importance—a quarrel with one who was once an intimate, a catastrophe finally averted by a hair's breadth. Or it may have been something that in comparison was slight—and which perhaps because of its very slightness illustrates all the better what is to be an experience.

Dewey goes on to add, "There is that meal in a Paris restaurant of which one says 'that was an experience.' It stands out as an enduring memorial of what food may be. Then there is that storm one went through in crossing the Atlantic—the storm that seemed in its fury, as it was experienced, to sum up in itself all that a storm can be, complete in itself, standing out because marked out from what went before and what came after."[1]

Chapter 6 explored common perspectives of both product and experience and chapter 7 unraveled some of what has been traditionally accepted as true about the term "product" and the entire concept embodied in that term. A product (good or service) is quickly becoming more and more outdated as our society continues to shift from a service economy to an experience economy, as the product can only assume a partial role in the relationship developed between a consumer and a producer. This relationship is at the heart of the engagement edge. Although we cannot speculate on where this shift may present itself in the marketing mix, or in for-profit businesses, we know that for the arts, the notion of "experience" is much more representative of what we create and sell than the term *product*.

In his book *The Entrepreneurial Muse: Inspiring Your Career in Classical Music*, Jeffrey Nytch discussed how best to proceed as an entrepreneur in a classical music setting.[2] Part of his argument encompasses the notion that art does not exist in aesthetic bubbles surrounded by other items of value but that the art is the center of a larger experience we seek to partner in with an audience.

Social Experience

One of the unique features of the arts is that its appreciation does not occur in isolation. Even for an audience of one, the artist exists, either physically or metaphorically, in the exchange of thoughts, ideas, and emotions that occur between art and audience.[3] In most cases, the audience is not a gathering of one but of many. It is in this realm where the consummation of the experience occurs. **The arts require community in the sense that it is designed to be experienced as a social function, where shared norms, ethics, customs, values, and traditions among the audience are a part of the overall experience.** A play designed to be witnessed by a full audience cannot fulfill its primary function of centering the entire experience if no one is present to experience it. This scenario is in stark contrast to a product or service that continues to exist regardless of whether or not it is used. Art, perhaps because it is in some way a reflection of society, requires a swath of society to participate in its existence in order to fulfill its function. The consumer is actually part of the art in this sense.

So why is the product (or the arts offering) not simply at the core, with other additions that add value becoming part of the *enhanced product*? Because all those values add up to nothing until they are being consumed. They have no value without the presence of an audience to experience the art. Art is social by nature, and it is in this vein the engagement edge takes precedence over the traditional marketing mix for the nonprofit arts.

The case of Sally Taylor and *Consenses* illustrates this notion beautifully. To Taylor, the art simply cannot exist, and she intentionally creates it to be this way, until the audience has put it together in their minds, thoughts, and emotions.

The Case of Sally Taylor and *Consenses*

In 1998, Sally Taylor had a vision for an arts project centered on an exploration of perception. Taylor had no idea at the time that it would one day bring together hundreds of artists from different mediums to create unique arts experiences for thousands of audience members. The project was called *Consenses*, and in 2014 on Martha's Vineyard, an audience experienced it for the first time. Jay met with Taylor to discuss her inspiration, process, and vision for *Consenses*. Her genuine passion, energy, and curiosity seemed to infuse everything that she had to share.

She shared that since she was a child, she has been obsessed with the notion of perception and that she sees perception as central to the way we experience art and the world. She believes that "art doesn't happen until somebody experiences it, and a visitor or audience member is just as much of an artist of what is happening as the artist who created it." When Taylor lived in Colorado, she had an interaction that helped shape her ideas about perception and what it meant to be an artist. "There was a man who was sort of a hippie, and he only owned what he could fit on his bike." One day Taylor stopped and gave the man a cup of coffee. He accepted the coffee and was looking off into the distance at the mountains. She recalled that his eyes got very big, "I asked him what was going on, and he responded, 'you know, I can't believe that I've created all of this.'" Taylor asked what he created, and he responded, "well, all of these mountains and the smell of this coffee, and this cement." Taylor backed up slowly, she thought, "clearly, this dude is out of his mind, but I realized from this that we are each artists. We are each creating a worldview everywhere we go." She sees art as a primary tool to share a worldview. "There is so much more that could be understood if we had the capacity to understand each other's worldview, and one way we can do that is through the senses. I think that's what art is, it's the offering of an internal worldview to somebody who only has access to their own otherwise."

Her initial idea for *Consenses* began while she was living in Colorado. "It started with a dream of owning a house and that I would invite six artists of one medium to come and live with me for a month." Taylor wanted to select different stimuli, and each artist would respond to one piece of stimulus with their art. Essentially, they would stay with Taylor in residence and create art inspired by what she provided. "After that month, they would leave the art in the room that they were staying in, then another artist of a different medium would come in." These artists would respond to the first artist's work without knowing what the catalyst was that Taylor had provided. "Let's say musicians were following photographers. The musicians would not know what the photographer was responding to, but they would create music based on the photograph in their room, and at the end of the month leave [a recording of their] music." *Consenses* is like an artistic game of telephone in which each artist responds to another artist's work without seeing the full chain of what has come before. "A month later, dancers might come in, and they would dance to what's in their room. After all of the senses had been represented, the last of the artists would move out and the house would be opened for an audience to experience the art for themselves in each of these rooms." This was Taylor's initial conception of *Consenses*.

The name *Consenses* came partially from her love for the Spanish language. *Con*, meaning with, and the English word *senses*, so that the title meant, "with the senses." It also seemed appropriate because, ultimately, her goal was to create what she called "an expansive sort of consensus, where everybody's complete interpretation exists, is allowed, and is welcomed." She was inspired by the idea that the art pieces created would come to consensus when the audience member experiences the pieces together and tracks the process from beginning to end through the art. Taylor designed *Consenses* to culminate as a constructivist experience as the audience members construct their own unique experiences from each chain of art. "The idea was that art isn't art on its own—each person who views it is creating a new piece of art as they experience it."

After much consideration, naming the project, and even some initial planning, Taylor put her idea on hold. She thought, "Oh my god, if I do this, I would have to live with all these crazy artists. No brainer, that's not going to happen, no way." For years, the dream of creating *Consenses* would pop into her head, but the logistical challenges of coordinating such an effort always seemed too great. In 2012, Taylor was spending time in Thailand. "While there, I was vehemently shaken by the inspiration that was living in my heart and my head, and I knew that it was time. I grabbed a pencil and piece of paper and drew out what I had long known that I needed to create." She recognized that technology had changed and that because of the internet, she could be in touch with basically any artist with whom she wanted to work. It seemed that the possibilities were endless since the creation of *Consenses* could now be a worldwide effort connecting artists from many cultures rather than being based within one city. "Suddenly, I could do this better than before, and it didn't have to be in my living room."

Taylor launched the first *Consenses* using images of nature. She selected images from her home, Martha's Vineyard, Massachusetts. Rather than the artists being in residency with Taylor in her house, they would create their art from wherever they were located. The artists began creating pieces based on the images that she sent them, and the artist would send the art back to her. "I would then ask myself, who does this art want to have dinner with? You know, I would get like a glimmer. So, a photograph I would get inspired by and say, 'Oh my god, I need to hear violins. Violins need to respond to this.' So, I would go online and ask a violinist if they would like to participate."

For the first *Consenses*, Taylor started with twenty-two of these images of nature from Martha's Vineyard as the catalysts. Most of the artists she was reaching out to, she did not know. "It was a learning process, I didn't know how different artists and different mediums work and how much time they would each need." She started by sending all the images to musicians. Once the musicians returned a piece of music, she sent the music to dancers or filmmakers. All different forms of art were included. "Sometimes I would get something back and say, 'oh, clearly this needs to be interpreted by a jeweler or perfume artist.'" For the first *Consenses* there was an enormous number of moving parts. The twenty-two chains included more than 140 artists from around the world and took over two years to complete. "It was daunting and scary, but I felt so invigorated and motivated by it. I just couldn't stop. It drove me instead of me driving it."

Since the first catalyst for consensus was images of nature on Martha's Vineyard, Taylor wanted to present *Consenses* back as a gift to the island. "It was about water, farmers, and seafarers. It included frost, flowers, and sand. I wanted them to experience it and to see the essence of Martha's Vineyard captured from artists around the world through these various mediums." This first iteration was essentially a three-day arts festival. Taylor shared that she could only rent the space for those three days and had to coordinate setting up all the exhibits. "It was so much work, but it was so inspiring."

At the center of the experience was the audience. Unlike traditional artist collaborations, where artists work closely together to curate an experience for the audience, the audience was the first to experience the full picture. Though all the art pieces were provided for the audience, each referred to the previous one so that the audience member was the link that brought it all together. Bringing all the pieces together occurred inside each audience member rather than the artists collaborating to create the full picture.

Taylor shared that the most common audience reaction to this first iteration was a desire to respond creatively. They think, "Oh my god, wait a minute, I can create and react artistically instead of phonetically or literally to something." Another common response was being overwhelmed. They had to make an unexpected trip to the store to buy boxes and boxes of tissues because "So many people were saturating all of their senses, and then bursting into tears. We have evolved to expect artistic experiences to be two-dimensional. We have been subsisting off visual and sound as our sensory information rather than smell, taste or touch." It can be overwhelming to consciously open up to an artistic experience that uses all of the senses.

Taylor compared the process of *Consenses* to the generations of a family. Many people know very little about their ancestors, yet through *Consenses* you can see the ancestor of a piece of art and how individual perception has shifted through time. The audience is, of course, then experiencing their own perception of the shifting perceptions of the artists. "Life is taking in information through stimulus, then followed by interpretation, then followed by action. And, that's what *Consenses* is. Ultimately, it's about the audience member who brings it all together."

Since 2014, Taylor has taken several different approaches to produce versions of *Consenses*. She has produced it as all live performances where artists perform onstage with rehearsed art developed over months. "It's just so versatile. When we do it live, we have dancers and poets, paintings are projected, and perfumes and different teas are passed around to the audience to create a multi-sensory experience." The stimuli Taylor selects are incredibly varied, she shared that one of her favorites was drawings from fifth graders based on their interpretations of love and fear.

To Taylor, *Consenses* is really saying one thing: we are all artists. Even without physically creating something, as the audience experiences *Consenses*, they are creating in their minds. "In the process of this, I've come to realize that art is really one thing. Through these different languages and senses, inspiration comes in, gets explored in our heads, jumbled up in our hearts, and then it's often expressed out. This expression doesn't have to stick to [one medium], I can open up a different door. I started as a musician, but I've been painting recently and knitting in a very creative, furious way using fiber arts."

Taylor estimates that she has worked with well over five hundred artists from around the world since she began producing *Consenses* in 2012. Several thousand audience members have experienced one of the many different iterations. Recently, Taylor has been producing educational experiences which further blends the roles of audience and artist in creating the chains.

Like all art, the art with *Consenses* does not exist until the audience experiences it. For many arts projects the creation is solely process-focused, and an audience later experiences what was created. *Consenses* provides an excellent example of how an arts project can provide an audience-centered experience without being what many of us consider commercialized art.

Customer Experience

It might be wise to address how "customer experience" is perhaps a misnomer for the term *experience*, as used in reference to the nonprofit arts. Customer experience looks at the touchpoints along the consumer's route in relation to the product or service and considers the cumulative impact of those touchpoints on cognition, memory, and emotion up through and including the use of the product or service. However, there is no actual interaction with the creator of the product or service as there is in the arts. As stated in previous chapters, **the art process becomes an experience only when it is fully consummated, a process that generally requires artists, and audience members.** Although the art can be presented for an audience of one, it is typically intended for an audience of many, and the cognition, memories, and emotions of many, particularly if viewing the arts simultaneously, affect the way the art will be perceived. This is where the typical audience experience becomes *an experience*, and it is a moment that does not exist for traditional goods, products, or services. The tube of toothpaste may provide a customer experience at its touchpoints along the purchasing path, but it lacks both the interaction with the creator of the toothpaste and other consumers of the toothpaste to allow the experience of purchasing it to become *an* experience. Of course, buying a tube of toothpaste can be an experience, but it is still a tube of toothpaste. On the other hand, viewing art is often a complex, immersive, significant, and thought-provoking experience. It is ephemeral and experiential and is, therefore, by definition *an experience*.

Use

Let's look at the key distinction that we have been suggesting: **For art to exist as an experience, use must occur. The same cannot be said for a traditional product or service.** For art to exist as art, it must be consumed. It cannot become art until an audience consumes it: the *point of consummation* as Dewey called it.[4] A hotel room is still a service, as is a rental car, or even a seat in an auditorium, leased to an audience member for a ninety-minute show. An arts offering becomes art when the intended audience consumes it. We say "intended" audience because artists are purposeful, we hope, that their art is for someone to experience.

Moreover, the offering remains art and an experience until there is no audience left to appreciate, absorb, examine, consider, and feel the art. Pine and Gilmore noted that, as we shift into the experience economy, businesses will start charging for the experience of engaging with the product or service.[5] **Because art cannot exist without consumption and consummation, it cannot be a product or service in the sense that McCarthy intended and is instead an experience, as Dewey made clear in 1934!**[6]

Components

The concept of McCarthy's marketing mix considers all four parts (product, price, place, and promotion) as intermingling parts that must be mixed and balanced appropriately to successfully engage the function of marketing. We see that the construct of product, though distinct in one sense, is influenced by the other functions of the marketing mix. A product is made of its component parts, including the place function (as distribution channels), the price function, and even the promotion function. Experiences are made of their raw materials, the labor and capital required to put them together, *and* the constructs of education, environment, and ease of access. The parallels between the marketing mix and the engagement edge do not make them simply semantically unique, but similar in that they have to do with connecting with consumers. The process, however, is substantially different in the two approaches. **The engagement edge works with a point of view that could not be considered when the marketing mix was developed since 501(c)(3) nonprofits, as we now know them, did not exist at the time.**

Changing the Experience

Uniqueness is the ingredient that turns an experiential event into an *experience*. With this in mind, places like Disney theme parks are regularly updating and changing the overall experience so that it is consistently new and fresh. In the arts, we tend to update the experience by changing the core piece of art at the center of the experience. **In the case of performing arts, however, the art is transformed in a sense at every performance because the audience is integral to the art experience, a part of the art in many ways, and always unique to each viewing.** Although we cannot control the unique nature of each audience, and though we try to manipulate audience etiquette, their reactions will change the way others around them perceive the art. So, art, unlike most tangible products, is changed by the audience as they experience it in the present.

Lived Experiences Inform Value

If audience reactions affect perceptions of the art, it also holds that the lived experiences that shaped these reactions will affect the overall *artistic* experience. Those who have lived experiences that resonate with trauma might react differently to art with a traumatic focus. That reaction, or the very real sense of audience "energy," as artists like to refer to it, will have an effect on other audience members enjoying the experience. **The entire experience is altered based on how the audience, as individuals and a whole, chooses to appreciate (or not appreciate) the art.**[7] Because nonprofit arts presentations tend to be of limited duration or run, there is scant time for a presenter to determine the general response of the audience and how that will affect the value of the presentation. Interestingly, then, the organization will not have the time to respond to observed value in order to adjust pricing factors.

The Pillars

Pine and Gilmore developed five pillars to transform products or services into experiences,[8] and Dewey's earlier notes about experiences make it clear that the two are in alignment.[9] How could those five pillars work in practice?

The following sections examine all five of them and provide examples of how arts organizations can apply each in creating experiences.

Theme the Experience

Dewey talked about the connection of moment to moment, all interconnected as part of the "underlying quality." He suggested that this can be manipulated, but the intent of shaping emotion and physical distinction in phases, seen or unseen, was how an experience might be thought of intellectually. Pine and Gilmore said the theme need not be known to the consumer but must exist and used the example of the Forum Shops at Caesar's Palace. What about a Dali exhibit at a local museum? One can imagine surrealist-looking educational materials, walls decorated with Dali-esque colors and patterns, melting clocks sold at the gift counter, the scent of Spanish tapas wafting from the café, curators explaining painting methodology, and more. The idea is that the theme is immersive but not requiring action on the part of the consumer (though some active participation can be possible as well). This creates the artist aesthetic Dewey discussed.

Harmonize Impressions

The idea of harmonizing impressions means ensuring that each touchpoint, interaction, or piece of the immersive experience should have very structured connective tissue from one to the next. We think of this as the map that leads every consumer through the experience. For the consumer to have a truly aesthetic and immersive experience, the manager should develop a plan that looks at every aspect of the process of viewing the art, considers how the experience connects with and has a bearing on that art, and then plans how the consumer will be led through the touchpoints. This can be as simple as an usher tearing a ticket and sending the patron to "Suzie standing at door two who can tell you about the ballet you will see." Does this mean that every usher must be trained to answer questions and discuss the content of the core art? No. That is not a required touchpoint to harmonize impressions, but it certainly could be.

Eliminate Negative Cues

For the engagement manager, walking through an entire experience can help spot and ultimately eliminate negative cues. It seems remarkable that a theater company might spend weeks or months rehearsing every aspect of a production, only to have the *entire experience* never rehearsed or even checked. A savvy engagement manager will behave like a patron, wait to request tickets until prompted by education or educational materials, schedule a visit, dine out beforehand, try parking like a patron, take advantage of all the parts of the experience available, and search for negative cues that could distract from or damage the ultimate experience.

Memorabilia

Many people intentionally save theater programs and ticket stubs as memorabilia from an arts experience. There is great value in sending someone home with memorabilia, particularly if it is labeled in such a way as to stimulate discussion with others about the artistic experience.[10] In this way, our patrons, with their memorabilia, become educators to potential future audience members. Memorabilia also serve another purpose: it is a tactile visual representation, and an educational tool that can become a multi-sensory experience. We encourage our audiences to engage with a physical object associated with the art, and this piece of the experience adds to the final consummation.

Engage Five Senses

Although memorabilia may engage the sense of touch, it is not as easy to engage both the sense of smell and the sense of taste. Still, every sense should have some engagement in the process of an artistic experience. Disney now pumps scents into rides at key points, orange blossoms as one soars over California orange orchards, and freshly mown hay over the fields of the Midwest.[11] Some rides have misters spray out when riders pass by an ocean. Note that the misters are so subtle as not to become negative cues. What about taste?

As a child, Jay grew up just north of Boston and frequently went with his parents to North Shore Music Theatre (NSMT). NSMT was a nonprofit regional theater in Beverly, Massachusetts. As a family, they would attend performances at the theater several times each year. In the lobby of the theater was a concession stand. One of the few options available was mint Mentos. For Jay as a child, going to the theater and having mint Mentos at intermission became a part of the experience. Clearly, NSMT as an organization had not worked to create this connection, but even now, the flavor of mint Mentos reminds Jay of NSMT. For Jay, that sensory experience does not remind him of specific moments but rather of his connection with the organization as a whole, since Mentos became a consistent part of his trips there.

For Anthony, a similar experience occurred having to do with the sense of smell. When he was twelve, his father took him on a special outing with no other family members to see the Cy Coleman musical *Barnum*, starring Jim Dale. The experience was memorable not only because it was a chance to see a big Broadway musical but also because it was a special outing with his father. As they were handed their programs and took their seats, Anthony remembers the distinct smell emanating from the program, caused by the specific ink used in the printing process. To this day, the smell of that particular ink brings up positive memories of the theater and that specific trip with his father. It reminds him of his love for theater and instills a desire to attend again.

Improved Experience

As noted, entertainment venues such as theme parks are charging for the experience and then charging for additional products and services associated with the experience. In the case of Six Flags Magic Mountain in Valencia, California, they have upcharge products that allow park-goers to tailor (and improve) their experience. One such product is the FLASH Pass, which allows riders to bypass ride lines for a steep fee. It comes with three different ways to tailor and improve the experience. These range from cutting line waits by 50% at the lowest price to cutting line waits by 95% at the highest price. That park also offers a single price for dining all day if a guest is inclined to take advantage of that offer. These two products are clearly designed to allow consumers to tailor their own experience at the park—for a fee. Although the idea of charging for add-ons to enhance an experience has yet to take a stronghold in either the commercial sector or the nonprofit arts, with the Six Flags Magic Mountain example, or even the nonprofit arts concession stand offering drinks for an extra price during intermission, we see experiences being enhanced with value added offerings that sometimes come with their own price.

Spontaneity

One aspect of experiences that makes them distinct from products and services is that an experience can also occur spontaneously. Although it can be carefully planned and structured with touchpoints delicately marked and connected, and negative cues eliminated, it can also be impromptu. In chapter 11 the case study discusses pianos as site-specific art, and will provide a good example of how experiences can occur spontaneously. Even in that case, one will see deliberateness to the unplanned nature of the art. Once the spontaneous experience begins, however, it is less controlled to allow the audience to appreciate and shape it the way they wish. Products and services do not occur spontaneously, nor do they present themselves spontaneously in a way that the consumer can appreciate and shape them. It is in this vein that we can engage through *an* experience. The experience that we curate is transferred to a consumer who can tailor, adjust, appreciate, and shape it as they wish. In the engagement edge, control of the experience is shared once the audience engages in the experience. With both the organization and patron having an active level of participation, the engagement in the experience allows it to be consummated, as Dewey has suggested.

In this sense, attendees are almost all co-creators of the nonprofit arts experience, even if they are not co-creators of the offering. This distinction between product and experience makes the shift in the engagement edge more than one of semantics or approach. In the nonprofit arts, the consumer is part of the experience, is a co-creator of that experience, and, therefore, must be engaged to participate fully to the greatest extent possible.

The Other Es

Part of the experience of a nonprofit arts presentation is influenced by the environment in which the experience and its various touchpoints take place.

Part of the experience also includes how nonprofit arts organizations educate consumers about art experiences. The engagement edge suggests that the nonprofit arts educate rather than promote, and must do so in an interactive and engaging way to be effective, as described in chapter 5. Ease of access is also a part of the experience, as this is where the arts organization eliminates negative cues from the experience. Much like in McCarthy's marketing mix where the four Ps mix to work together,[12] the four Es all work together. None are independent of the others, and in order for the engagement edge to at its best, all must be planned, coordinated, and allowed to occur in the engagement process.

Conclusion

In this chapter we clarified the term *customer experience* as a series of touchpoints that result in the activation of memories, emotions, and thoughts for audience members. This is a definition that cannot be satisfied by McCarthy's "product," which has little concern for audience participation. Nonprofit arts professionals that understand the significance of this shift know that art is changed through audiences' reactions—reactions that are shaped by lived experiences. They also know that an effective experience can be promoted through careful theming, a keen attention to touchpoint transitions, a dramatic reduction in negative cues that hinder the experience, and a deliberate education through memorabilia dissemination. Finally, they understand the effect that sensory cues have on individual experiences as well as the benefits of tailored experiences and the fickleness of spontaneity. Part IV will illuminate the *environment* that these experiences occur in and why McCarthy's "place" is not suitable for nonprofit arts organizations.

PART IV
ENVIRONMENT

Part IV examines the constructs of place as it is defined in the marketing mix framework, and environment as it is defined in the engagement edge. It follows through each of the two concepts, exploring how they do or do not work appropriately for the nonprofit arts.

Chapter 9 focuses on definitions for the terms *place*, as intended within McCarthy's marketing mix, and *environment*, as the term is generally used today. It explores the different facets of each term and finds distinction and commonalities for both. Although both these terms have a generic definition having to do with location, the chapter provides greater depth to our understanding of the terms. Though human interaction with environments may not seem the perfect match for the nonprofit art, the definitions make it far more logical to apply environment as part of the engagement edge than McCarthy's place.

Chapter 10 reviews the notion of place as it refers to the supply chains and distribution channels of a business. It presents some of the major and various facets of the notion of place, and demonstrates why their structure may be suited for commercial and for-profit operations. It then investigates how those same reasons often lead to failure when attempting to implement them in the nonprofit arts.

Chapter 11 explores what the notion of environment might look like in the nonprofit arts. Following terms from environmental science and environmental management, we see that the functions of an environmental manager, at least on a macro scale, are equivalent to those skills that will best serve the arts organization and its patrons in the process of engagement.

The Case of Felix Barrett and *Sleep No More*

Few artists have used environment as well as Felix Barrett in the delivery of art experiences. Barrett is the founder and artistic director of Punchdrunk, a British theater company that develops theater experiences that challenge the notion of traditional performance spaces, and engage audiences in new ways. With Punchdrunk, Barrett has created revolutionary theater experiences that defy audience expectations while remaining audience centered. The company's most famous work, *Sleep No More*, was created in London in the early 2000s. It was further developed in 2009 at the American Repertory Theater, a nonprofit theater in Cambridge, Massachusetts, and has been running at the McKittrick Hotel in New York City since 2011.

Jay met with Barrett to discuss the development of his approach. Barrett is deeply passionate about creating theater experiences and discovering how environment is the shaping force that drives audience engagement. He pinpoints his focus on changing the way theater is delivered to a time when he was a student. He shared that he "went in feeling underwhelmed by conventional proscenium arch theatre, in that all the status was given to the performers, and the director and the back of house crew, while the audience was often neglected." Barrett saw that many theater performances were stale and felt that audience experience was an afterthought in the art creation process. "I wanted to do theatre which would give power back to people. It would make [the audience] the epicenter of it." Barrett was driven to return theater experiences to a time when audience and performer were collectively in an experience together, and that the audience would remain active throughout, "like in Elizabethan times, you could throw cabbages, you could leave halfway through. With too much theatre now you have to endure it, even if you're not liking it."

In 2000, Barrett founded Punchdrunk to do just that. He began producing work that undid established audience expectations and protocol for audience behavior through changing the typical performance environments. Barrett's approach to theater performances provides audiences with unprecedented control to move and interact with performers. *Sleep No More* and his other productions generally have the audience on their feet throughout, in an environment designed to always keep the audience guessing. He said,

> Whenever we're in a process, if in doubt, [we think] what would the audience expect us to do next, where would they expect it to go? And then

we'll do the opposite. If the audience can ever preempt what we're going to do they start to settle back and then we're losing them because they're becoming passive. We don't want passive spectators, we want active participants.

To increase active participation, Barrett sets productions in nontraditional performance spaces. As noted, *Sleep No More* is performed in the McKittrick Hotel, a once abandoned building that has been transformed into a performance space. The performance takes place over five floors of the building as audience members follow actors and explore the environment while the performance takes place around them. As a result, it is impossible to see every part of the performance in a single visit.

Barrett shared that in selecting environments for his productions, the first consideration is audience safety, and explained, "it needs to be secure and safe for the audience to promenade, as they're moving under low levels of light, up and down stairs. It must also be easily accessible so that people with disabilities can approach it." Barrett was quick to point out that a close second consideration for him is finding a space that, through controlling the environment, the illusion of danger is developed for the audience. "You want that feeling of danger and a level of apprehension that triggers fight or flight and adrenaline because we want the audience to be in a heightened state. We want heightened senses so that they are ready to go. It's a fine line, we spend most of our budget on health and safety, then we layer on a facade of danger, it's just artifice."

Barrett provided an example from a production of *Faust* that Punchdrunk produced more than fifteen years ago. Various signs were used to warn the audience of hazards that (of course) did not exist. "We put up massive signs outside saying, 'Danger Asbestos!' It was just so our audience thought as they arrived 'this can't be the place.' And in doing that we got a volatile audience that was already triggered. So, whether they like the show or not, because of the active environment we create, it's going to go much more deeply under their skin than it would do if they were just passively consuming." The point Barrett was making is that by creating a theme to the environment, he creates an active experience that goes beyond what happens on a traditional stage.

For Barrett, stepping beyond proscenium arch theater means applying the environment in unexpected ways. In the example above, the experience of *Faust* began even before the audience entered the venue. The environment Barrett created included an experience on the street outside. In designing environments, he shared that the goal is "always a series of rug pulls. With what we do, we have to keep the audience guessing." His vision of the environment extends well beyond the beginning and end of what some might consider the typical theater-going experience. "We're creating that slow plunge into the depths. I think the design of space echoes that as well." He is adamant that the experience often begins in an environment before even entering the address on the ticket. "Maybe it begins when the audience enters the building, but maybe it starts before. Maybe it started when they got off the subway, or when they were on it. Maybe it started with the phone call they received the night before . . . and maybe it's different for each person."

The environment Punchdrunk creates invites a cross section of the community rather than being focused on a few demographics.

> Something like *Sleep No More* is properly accessible. It's *Macbeth* and pretty much every line of the Shakespeare is there, if not spoken verbally, it's in the physical language or the set design. So it's appealing to Shakespeare scholars, but if you're a kid who has never been to a theatre show and you like playing your PlayStation, hopefully, you'll see it as an open world adventure and gain just as much. So we find we get a real cross section from people in their teens through your normal theatre audience.

Since the audience member chooses their own path through the environment, they have agency in their own experience.

Barrett shared that *The Cherry Orchard* was one of the first productions Punchdrunk created. It was presented in a townhouse in a small town in the southwest of England. The environment was clearly established by staging the production in a real house, and the audience could move through the house as they experienced the play. He recalled, "there was a group of American tourists who walked into the house and froze. For about 15 minutes they just stood there, and then gradually backed out." For these audience members, the environment of the house and being so close to the performers may have made the experience feel too real or uncomfortable. A crucial aspect of creating environments is maintaining the audience's level of control so that they can remain within their comfort levels. Barrett calls this an "opt in level of theater." He adds, "it's the opposite of going to a circus and the clown saying, 'hey you, volunteer to come on stage and be humiliated,' this is supposed to be about empowerment, rather than humiliation."

Barrett noted that the environments he creates "really depend on the manner of the show." He recalled one of his favorite productions, *The Crash of The Elysium*. It was a production for children ages six through twelve, and guardians were instructed to tell the children that they were going to a museum rather than the theater. "You know how you get an exhibition of some sunken vessel. So, there would be dredged up tea cups and stuff. The kids will come in with their parents, and we made the initial area as deliberately dry, banal, and boring as possible. It was bone crushingly tedious. There was an actor saying, 'here is a section of hull from 1869.' And just as the kids glaze over and say 'mum, this is terrible.' Alarms go off." Actors came in and whisked the children away for a Doctor Who–themed adventure through a totally different war-torn themed environment that included a one hundred thousand square foot quarantine zone. In this event, audience members moved through differently designed environments which built the experience.

Regarding productions of *Sleep No More* in New York City, Barrett noted that many people consider the performances to be nightlife. Because the environment Barrett created is beyond the bounds of traditional performance venues, and the performances attract audiences that may not attend what some consider traditional theater, he believes *Sleep No More* challenges long-held elitist ideas of what theater can be. Barrett shared that for him "it's a real source of pride." In 2016, Punchdrunk launched a production of *Sleep No More* in Shanghai. Barrett shared that "as the experience economy has grown, people's perceptions of [*Sleep No More*] in Shanghai is more that it's 'a cool thing to *do*' rather than, 'I'm going to *see* that show.'" The experiences create engagement and excitement within the community, and as a result, Punchdrunk "spends basically zero on marketing." These perceptions and level of word of mouth are tied to the experience that develops directly from the environment Barrett creates.

Of course, not all nonprofit arts organizations should use Barrett's specific tactics, but this approach illustrates how influential environment can be to an arts experience and the level of control an organization can have over environments. When a nonprofit arts organization offers art to an audience, so often the focus fails to extend beyond the curtain going up and coming down. Part IV of this book explores how environmental considerations can enhance the arts experience before, during, and after what so many nonprofit arts organizations would consider their core offering.

9
Contrasting Frameworks
Place and Environment

The idea of *place* has to do with the location where our product is distributed to our consumers. For big businesses, this typically means that place is a *collection* of places, beginning with those who distribute all the supplies and parts to create the product. These are the *upstream distribution channels*. The *downstream distribution channels* are all the distributors who carry, store, promote, and get the product into the consumer's hands. Both streams are invaluable to a large corporation, and even when they operate in a business-to-consumer relationship, they are still vital to the companies with strong relationships with their partners in the distribution streams. The idea of place and distribution is crucial in the marketing mix.

Conceptually, the notion of place and distribution has been well studied and researched. As chapter 10 describes, there appears to be very little correlation between the typical P of place and arts marketing unless you consider the actual space where viewing art occurs to be essentially the entire manifestation of *place*.

The word *environment* evokes the natural world and its elements. There has been ample study of the environment, in myriad ways and through multiple lenses and disciplines. In the context of the engagement edge, however, the term *environment* is meant to convey those places or surroundings in which arts consumers interact with any aspect of the offered experience. Note that this definition extends beyond the idea that the environment is only the physical space where the art is presented. Instead, it encompasses the entire environment beginning when the consumer is made aware of our existence, and through their final interaction with the arts organization. Suddenly, the notion of environment may seem even larger in scope than it appeared in the *Sleep No More* case.

What Is Place?

The supply chain feeds into the distribution process, but most marketers focus on the delivery network or *distribution channels*, as it is there that direct contact is made with consumers.[1] Previous chapters mentioned the product of toothpaste. In business, suppliers provide the raw chemicals for the paste, the plastic for the tube, the ink for the printing, financing for the machines that assemble them all, and more. These are the upstream channels. Once the toothpaste is created, it is given to a distributor, or multiple levels of distributors, who store, inventory, control, distribute, and promote the toothpaste both to the supermarkets and drugstores where it will be sold as well to the public at large. These are the downstream channels. In the arts, we see little comparison other than perhaps to a ticketing service such as TicketMaster or the traditional Broadway tour. Even both of those are the work of for-profit corporations.

Movement of Goods

When toothpaste is made, hundreds of thousands of tubes are created simultaneously. It would be inefficient for the producer of the toothpaste to then distribute each tube, one at a time, to consumers. Instead, the organization hires an intermediary to distribute those tubes to all the various consumers. Because the distributor has the appropriate connections, network, shipping, and storage facilities, they are used to minimize the expense of distribution to the organization creating the product, even if they must add on a cost for their services.

For a large organization, the distribution network may have many levels. Each level consists of one intermediary between the producer of the good or service and the consumer, with the number of different intermediaries making up the *channel length*.

Direct and Indirect Marketing

For most marketing practices, direct marketing may be too costly or difficult, or require too much expertise to work effectively. A toothpaste company selling directly to the consumer would struggle mightily. In the arts, however, most relationships with consumers are a result of *direct marketing*, where there are no intermediaries between the company making the product (the arts offering) and the consumer. In the nonprofit arts, essentially every touchpoint with community members is direct. The only example that comes to mind for the nonprofit arts that is indirect are ticket offices that work under consignment or as a contracted service. In contrast, in for-profit corporations, most distribution approaches have an intermediary. For example, TicketMaster would be considered an *indirect marketer*.[2]

Occasionally, the missions of organizations partnering in a distribution channel may conflict. Channel conflicts occur when two organizations within the channel have competing objectives or differences of opinion.[3] Arts organizations do avoid such conflicts by engaging in only direct marketing. The disadvantages for nonprofit arts organizations in a for-profit centered marketplace are clear.

Horizontal and Vertical Marketing

In a horizontal marketing system, entities partner together at equivalent marketing channels to accomplish a single sales goal.[4] The Starbucks Coffee retailer located inside some Target stores where consumers are shared is an example of *horizontal marketing*. Global alliances such as airline alliances where flights are codeshared is another example of horizontal marketing.[5]

In a traditional marketing channel, the producer of the goods or service works with a wholesaler and a distributor to get the product to the final retailer or consumer. In theory, because experts are working at each level, it is expected that the process would be seamless. In vertical marketing, the producer typically (though not always) takes on the leadership role to ensure that the channel processes are effective and fluid.

Contractual System

Another type of distribution system is the contractual system. This approach has three potential means of contract.[6] The first is a *franchise contract*. Under the franchise system, to maintain consistency and quality throughout the brand, franchisees are responsible for following rules, regulations, and policies set by the corporation. A second contractual system is the *retail sponsored system*, where retailers initiate a partnership with an organization or several organizations to supply a product, but the retailer maintains independence. A *retail cooperative* is the third type of contract. It is similar to a *sponsored chain system* or *wholesaler system* in which someone agrees to use the name of an organization, such as a hotel chain, for example, while the individual business is independently owned and operated.

Disintermediation

One interesting change occurring as our world becomes more globalized and connected through technology is that organizations are cutting out intermediaries in the supply chain and reaching more directly to the consumer. *Disintermediation* is an interesting development because it can reach consumers more directly, and is currently a social trend toward more direct interaction and buyer options. It also happens to be a shift toward the traditional arts organization distribution model.

Analyzing Needs

As mentioned, the function of each level of a channel is to move a product or service from the manufacturer to the consumer and do so in a way that adds value for the consumer. To appropriately design a place/distribution channel, one must know what the consumer wants and needs. For example, do the consumers want close proximity and easy access to the product? Do they want lower prices? Multiple colors? Various other options? Do they want easy customer service? Delivery? Returns? Repairs? More? Each of these options may require a different intermediary to deliver and meet the needs of the consumer.

The Internet as a Distribution Channel

The creation of the internet has granted companies the ability to sell directly to customers who are at home. This direct link to the customer has allowed many companies to connect with previously unreachable consumers. By selling products directly to the customer, companies control more of the downstream distribution channels. Through the elimination of the retailer, the producer of the product can suddenly build direct relationships with customers while, at the same time, reducing expenses. This online model of direct distribution and relationship is similar to distribution models in the arts. With the growth of online sales came new channels for distribution—online retailers.[7]

In 2019, Amazon surpassed Walmart to become the world's largest retailer. Online retailers use machine learning to recommend products to consumers based on their perceived interests and prior purchases. They allow the producers of products to take advantage of sophisticated technology to accurately reach their target market—for a fee. Though online retailers drive prices down and take a percentage of each sale, companies that produce products see increased sales by using the online retailer for distribution.

Setting Distribution Objectives

To ensure that the corporation reaches multiple targets, they must establish what levels of service they intend to offer consumers and differentiate those levels. For example, toothpaste users who want easily available bargain toothpaste, and those who want high-priced, specialty, whitening toothpaste may shop in different locations and must be targeted differently in the distribution channel. The organization may also consider the size and scope of the distribution when making decisions about channel objectives to maximize efficiency and profit. Large distributions may require more intermediaries, competitors may affect distribution or promotion, and even the economy can affect objective decision-making.

Intensive, Exclusive, and Selective Intermediaries

Once an organization has determined its channel objectives, it can then decide who the intermediaries will be. Some intermediaries can take a product directly to the consumer, while others take the product to a retailer, who then provides the product and service to the consumer. Large manufacturers prefer to use multiple channel designs and multiple intermediaries to reach buyers of different sorts. These organizations, however, must also determine how many intermediaries will operate at each distribution level. There are three types of distribution to consider: *intensive distribution*, *exclusive distribution*, and *selective distribution*. In intensive distribution, the organization places its products or services in as many retail outlets as it can find. Consumer goods such as our regular toothpaste are often found this way, in multiple retail outlets. Exclusive distribution is a process where the manufacturer limits the number of intermediaries that are handling a product. Typically, this is seen with high-end purchases or expensive products considered luxury items. Exclusive distribution allows a product, good, or service to have elite status. Consider that, generally, there is only one distribution system available for the arts. One can see one reason why the arts are often considered to be elitist. The final type is *selective distribution*, where the organization chooses some of the intermediaries to carry the company's products but not all available intermediaries as in intensive distribution. Selective distribution can allow for higher profit margins while still allowing the product or service to be available to most consumers.

Channel Management

Although it was once simple to hire an intermediary and forget about them, that is no longer the case. Instead, corporations focus heavily on partnership management and ensure that their partners are satisfied and have all the tools necessary to accomplish a strong distribution system. This practice is known as motivating and managing channel members. Corporations often use customer relationship software designed to ensure that the relationship between the consumer and the distributor is working efficiently and effectively. Likewise, partnership management software accomplishes a similar task for the relationships between the distribution partners and the organization.

Distribution Logistics

Because the globalized world has become so interconnected, sometimes distribution can become incredibly complex for the organization to ensure that consumers have the right products in the right assortments with the right variables at the right time in the right location. The process of getting the product or service from manufacturer to consumer is called *logistics*. Logistics involves the planning, organizing, implementing, leading, and controlling of the product or service process from its point of origin up to and through consumption by the buyer in a way that maximizes efficiency and profit. Though organizations used to develop a product and then examine different means for getting the product to the market and the consumer, **savvy companies now utilize consumer data and preferences to determine how best to create a personalized experience for the customer in a process termed consumer-centric logistics.**[8] The distribution process includes the following: *outbound logistics*, getting product or service downstream to the consumer; *inbound logistics*, the incoming stream of supplies and services to create the product; and *reverse logistics*, where returns are handled. The entire process of coordinating the logistics is *supply chain management.*[9]

As shown, the P of place is a complex system of distribution management that focuses on the movement of parts, supplies, money, and talent. It is a detail-laden, multi-faceted puzzle designed to take advantage of those with the greatest skills and talents at each level of the supply chain.

What Is Environment?

To many, the term *environment* refers to nature, and the rolling expanses of the planet—uninterrupted, unspoiled, and without human interaction. In a more general sense, environment takes into account the form, design, and circumstances in which something exists. Environment means surroundings or *environs*. The *environment* is the surroundings of any entity, individual, thing, or group of people, organizations, or systems. Although we may think of an environment as the place where we operate as individuals, environments are a place where relationships exist, occur, intermingle, and develop. In turn, those relationships and the individuals and things involved in them are influenced by the environment. The concept of an interrelationship between those parts in the environment is vitally important as we discuss the engagement edge.

When an environment is created or adjusted by humans, there is often a level of intention that goes into the creation and maintenance of the environment. Some environments are strictly designed to serve a function, while others are created to enhance or create aesthetic experiences. These are the environments that are the most essential for consideration as part of the engagement edge. Although these environments may be intentionally designed, human interaction typically occurs within them and affects how the environment is experienced. In this way, even environments that are carefully designed by people operate as a complex ecosystem.

Environments and Nature

As noted, many people immediately think of nature when they hear the word *environment*. Though nature as environment is distinct from how we will consider environment in the engagement edge, elements of the concept relating nature and environment are useful to consider, especially through the notion of complex ecosystems.

An *ecosystem* is the intermingling of living and nonliving components within the environment. These interactions are the relationships to which we refer when we speak of environmental science and environmental management. These areas of study deal with changes in various environments and how one relates to the other. Disruptions or changes in one environment can lead to changes or disruption in other systems. Consider how changes in our human-made environment have affected global climate change, as a prime example. Scholars often view ecosystems in nature through a *systems analysis* approach.

The systems analysis approach sees ecosystems as complex, with many parts that affect other parts in the system. Ecosystems are incredibly fragile and are easily destroyed. In order for a person to maintain and control an ecosystem, they must be purposeful and intentional in their approach as they cannot control every aspect of the system that impacts the whole ecosystem. The process of attempting to maintain and control ecosystems is called *environmental management*.

Because environments are complex systems with multiple organisms functioning within them, it is inappropriate to say that environmental management is about completely controlling the environment, as it would be impossible to control all organisms and their actions and impact on the environment. Instead, we can think of environmental management as the management of human activity and its effect on the environment.

To apply this idea from nature to arts, consider Barrett's theater company, Punchdrunk, from the introduction to part IV of this book. Although carefully designed, the environment was shaped not only by the artistic director, the actors that he chose, and the location and sets that he used, but also by other audience members, the audience member's trip to and from the venue, and even the expectations and perceptions of audience members. Barrett's artistic ecosystem was vast and interconnected, and he recognized elements that he could and could not control within the environment that he created. Yet, his experimentation with recognizing the causative effects that each factor produced was integral to his success.

Human-Designed Environments

Although ecosystems and systems analysis provide a useful framework to consider the complexities of environments, as noted, for the engagement manager a consideration of intentional and designed environments is most useful to the engagement edge. Both natural ecosystems and environments that people intentionally design have components that are beyond any manager's control. Yet, many people have created environments that function remarkably well. Though some elements of a designed environment serve key functions, other elements of designed environments create space for aesthetic experiences or to, at the very least, impact the emotions and perceptions of those within the human-designed environments. Three examples illustrate this concept of human-designed environments and their application well.

Doctors' Offices

One type of human made environment with a strong emphasis on aesthetics are doctors' offices. Though these environments obviously have many practical elements and safety considerations, it is important to create a space in which patients feel comfortable and safe. Patricia Milne, a director of the Canadian Medical Association Centre for Practice Productivity, notes that "patients want to feel they are people, not numbers," when they are at the doctor's office.[10] The environment "affects patients the moment they enter the office" and can have a significant impact on the patients' (and the doctors') experiences. Design factors in the doctor's office environment include layout, aesthetics, and decorations.

A larger, open concept waiting room can increase mental comfortability for patients. Comfortable seating, relaxing music, and pleasant reading material promote physical and mental comforts for patients. In return, Milne notes, the patients are more likely to be in a positive mindset for their appointment and are more likely to have friendly, productive discussions with the office staff. Visual aesthetics such as artwork, wall color, and decorations also play a large part in patient experience in the medical environment. Landscape paintings are a common genre of artwork found in hospital settings, and they contribute to the "therapeutic" nature of visual aesthetics.[11] These landscape paintings, which portray serene illustrations of meadows, lakes, or trees, in conjunction with calming paint color on the walls, can create a soothing environment for patients and staff in which to conduct their core purpose: providing healthcare. Although patients are the "attendees" of doctors' offices, it is the doctors, nurses, and other staff who spend the majority of their days in the office. J. Swartz recognizes this concept relative to environment and adds, "what better reason to make sure that the office is attractive and efficient?"[12]

Coffee Shops
Coffee shops are less controllable environments than doctors' offices, but they are also human-designed to use aesthetics to create an intentional environmental experience.[13] The environment of coffee shops promotes coffee shop culture through various aesthetic elements. Although coffee shops are for-profit businesses selling a product, much of their existence depends on aesthetic elements that bring people together to uplift community, culture, and the overall consumer experience through the environment. The experience a consumer has at different coffee shops varies, and depends on whether the coffee shop is a part of a chain corporation (like Starbucks or Dunkin' Donuts) or is a privately owned or family operated coffee shop. For example, a consumer could have a virtually identical experience at a Starbucks in Florida or a Starbucks in Michigan in terms of the interior design, ambient music, and the uniforms the staff wear. These similarities in the environment create a sense of comfort for the consumer, and consumers may be more likely to visit whatever Starbucks is in their vicinity, even if they are traveling in a new city just for the aesthetic environment.[14]

In contrast, locally owned coffee shops create a unique environment for the consumer as different coffee shops will feature different decor, floor layouts, and some offer outdoor/patio seating. The environment at a local coffee shop may feel more authentic than a chain coffee shop to the consumer, and will invite a different demographic of consumers.[15]

Jaishikha Nautiyal emphasized the significance of "ordinary" aesthetics in coffee shops, and how these aesthetic elements create an environment that is as special as it is simple. She references Catherine Tucker's account of the coffee shop environment, which noted "conversations create a quiet background murmur... a comfortable ambience with stained wood décor, stylish wall art with a coffee theme, sofas and easy chairs around low coffee tables, and small circular tables with simple wooden chairs."[16] This depiction of the environment illustrates what is true in many coffee shops, yet it still invokes the personal memory and feeling of experiencing the coffee shop environment. Of note, only portions of the environment Tucker shared are actually within the control of a manager.

The Marie Antionette Factor
Not all human-designed environments are built to function for businesses. In 1786 Marie Antoinette had a themed environment built so that she could imagine herself in a different role—placing herself at the center of a constructed environment. The Chateau de Versailles in France was the site of the Hameau de la Reine, or "The Queen's Hamlet."[17] This idealized environment was part hamlet, part garden, and part farm and was designed for Marie Antoinette's pleasure. Marie Antoinette, who was the ruling queen of France at the time, desired a space where she could "play peasant" and escape palace life by pretending to be a poor commoner. Hameau de la Reine is an environment built with an emphasis on aesthetics and enjoyment. The "peasants" who "lived" in the hamlet were royal servants who acted as members of the pseudo community. One servant was tasked with continuously baking bread so that the hamlet would always smell like fresh bread. To create the illusion of farm life without the mess, servants would pre-clean newly laid chicken eggs for Marie Antoinette before she came to collect eggs. The Hameau de la Reine was also a fully operational farm and was the site of the first Anglo-Chinese garden.[18] Every element of this environment was carefully considered to give the main attendee (Marie Antoinette) the most idealized and enjoyable experience. As a result, this ornamented farm created an illusion of charm and pleasure that best suited its attendee.

Although the French Revolution may have rendered the Hameau de la Reine an environment useless without participants, the hamlet has been preserved in the years since the French monarchy's demise. Hameau de la Reine is now a retreat for visitors of Versaille. Tourists can experience a small taste of the environment once reserved for the queen of France. Though the environment of Hamleau de la Reine now serves only a pleasure-based purpose today, it has become an environment of historical significance.

Final Thoughts Defining Environment

Environment is a key factor in the engagement edge, because all arts experiences are nested within an environment of some type. Environments in nature provide a useful perspective through the concept of ecosystems. As complex systems components within the ecosystem impact each other and, thus, the ecosystem as a whole. Ecosystems and environments are not fully controllable, even with careful planning. Human-designed environments are the most suitable environmental consideration for nonprofit arts organizations in applying the engagement edge. Human-designed environments often serve to affect people's emotions and perceptions. In doctors' offices and coffee shops they lead to greater comfort and help to serve the core purpose of each entity. The unique example of Marie Antoinette provides a focus on environment that developed an experience one might even call engaging.

Conclusion

In this chapter, we explored the term *place* and identified its significance in the marketing process. After looking at the complex system of distribution channels, intermediaries, and distribution logistics it is clear why the arts require a more fitted term. The experience that one has in front of a Dali or at an immersive theater production cannot be inventoried by a distributor or presented as a franchise. The term *environment*, which focuses on the relationship between attendee, location, and touchpoints is more appropriate, as we will see in chapter 11. Before chapter 11 more deeply explores environment at the arts, chapter 10 will further explain the limitations of the term *place*, and why a shift from place for the nonprofit arts is essential.

10
Place and the Arts

Chapter 9 discussed the broad concept of place and what it means in business. This chapter discusses "place" from interaction to objective, breaking down exactly why this concept cannot distribute the experiences that we explored in chapter 8. We note that this failure may be largely due to the arts maintaining control of every aspect of their business and not hiring out expertise in other areas. The ephemeral core of a personally crafted artistic experience is incompatible with detached, impersonal distribution streams.

As a caveat, arts organizations do frequently have a suitably sized *upstream* distribution channel where suppliers and distributors provide the goods or services necessary to create the organization's offerings. However, downstream distribution channels are limited in nonprofit arts. Aside from ticketing services that contract admission sales, the art offering generally remains fixed in the location determined by the arts organization. There are also instances where the location of the art experience has been fixed by the *artist(s)*. An environmental art event, for example, might be transient or moveable, where the audience might be asked to change locations for complete appreciation of the experience. Mobile art, such as app-based or online-based theater, is currently an exception to the rule and pushes the boundaries of the artistic experience.

Arts organizations may also choose to outsource promotional efforts, and in this case, we do begin to see the emergence of a downstream distribution channel, but these are far more elusive than in big business, which can have multiple downstream partners that actually distribute the product. **The reason place is not suitable for the nonprofit arts is that place is about moving products through distribution channels. You cannot move an arts experience through a distribution channel.**

In the case of the Manscott Puppet Club, we can see how the notion of place simply does not stand up to the needs of a nonprofit arts organization, and why the construct so often cannot be included when looking at marketing for a nonprofit arts organization.

The Case of the Manscott Puppet Club

Otis Monk speaks with infectious energy. He has held many different jobs in his life. At various times Monk was a taxi driver, a fisherman, a hotel manager, a golf course landscaper, and a marketer for an arts organization. When he was ten years old, he started taking classes at the Manscott Puppet Club in Washington, DC. As the name suggests, the Manscott Puppet Club focuses mostly on performances featuring puppets. Though many people expect that puppets are geared only for children, many of their performances are dramas and created for mature audiences. The Manscott Puppet Club frequently presents art that challenges the status quo and deals with social justice issues. As Monk explained it, about one-third of their programming is produced content for adults, one-third is content for children and families, and one-third is education.

The education program includes courses in many styles of puppeteering, puppet construction, voicing puppets, and acting classes geared toward stage performance. It was in one of these acting classes that Monk was first introduced to theater performance. "Oh man, I was hooked. After that first day, I told my dad I needed to take more classes. He told me I had to wait to finish that one before I could sign up for any puppeteering ones. But every week, I asked and asked, and finally, at the end of the eight-week session I was in, he let me sign up for two classes. Then eventually three, and finally by the time I was fourteen, I was taking four classes at a time." Monk suspects that from the time he was ten to when he aged out of the youth program at seventeen he may have taken more courses than anyone in the history of the Manscott Puppet Club.

Monk remained active with the organization as a performer in their adult and family performances. "I took some courses at a local college, but I really didn't like the academics. I had to be more active, I just had to." Monk explored a number of career paths but remained consistently involved with the Manscott Puppet Club. After several years of exploration, Monk moved with a friend to Nova Scotia, where he found work as a fisherman. He was born in Canada and maintained dual citizenship. Growing up, he often traveled to Nova Scotia to visit his grandparents. He spent six years in Nova Scotia, and shared, "being a fisherman for that long was enough being active for me. I really missed Manscott and the big city."

After his time in Canada, he returned to Washington, DC, and became involved again at the Manscott Puppet Club. At this time, he found work as a taxi driver, but taught courses in Manscott's education program and performed in their performances. Six months after Monk's return, the current marketing manager had a child and was taking eight weeks off, so Monk offered to step in to assist. "It was a sort of part-time job I did along with driving. I was, basically, supposed to do the marketing plan just as it was written. And of course—I did that. But they knew me. I'm sure they thought 'Otis will probably do his own thing,' and if they thought that—they were right."

Monk was now in charge of executing the marketing plan for the theater. The problem, however, was that Monk felt he did not know anything about marketing. He spent his afternoons researching marketing methods and learning about McCarthy's four Ps. "Those four Ps are fascinating stuff," he shared, "we were doing some of [the Ps] but not all of them—and they are supposed to work together." He realized that the plan he had inherited was a promotional plan rather than something that encompassed the four Ps. He expressed that he already knew what the product was, and that people liked it, and felt the price seemed reasonable, and he had a promotional plan. "But we only sold our tickets in one place. [Distribution channels] were what we were missing." For years, the Manscott Puppet Club sold tickets through a box office and online. All their sales were purchased and tracked through a ticketing software system.

"This was the place I could make my mark. Distribution! I thought we should triple or quadruple the number of places we sold tickets so then we'd triple or quadruple our sales." Monk presumed that by selling tickets in multiple locations, the Manscott Puppet Club would exponentially increase the number of sales based on the number of distribution points. "I thought it was pretty clever. We could always add more shows as we sold more tickets. I wanted five more places to sell so that we could multiply our current sales by six and earn enough to maybe build myself a job there when the real marketing person came back."

Monk was hard at work. In addition to coordinating all the plan's promotions, he laid the groundwork to sell tickets through more distribution channels. In his second week on the job, he met with the box office manager. "She really didn't get what I was doing because she knew nothing about marketing. But two weeks before, I knew nothing about marketing, so I don't judge." Monk explained his plan. He wanted to select five businesses in the area and offer that they sell tickets. They would take the contact information for the purchase, collect the money, and distribute the tickets. Each day the business would inform the box office of all their sales and batch payments to the Manscott Puppet Club. The box office would then input the sales into their ticket system. In exchange, the business would collect the fee the box office typically took per sale, and they would receive 10% of the overall ticket purchase.

The box office manager did not see the benefit to Monk's plan. "She still didn't get it, and she didn't know why another business would want to sell our tickets. But money talks." Eventually, the box office manager agreed to give it a shot. She printed two hundred tickets for Monk to their next event. The event had ten performances, so each of the five businesses would receive four tickets to each performance to start. Monk felt that only four tickets to each performance per ticket outlet was insufficient. "I wanted more, but she wouldn't give them to me. She said once they sold, she would do another bunch." They could seat 110 in the performance space, so Monk wanted to divide the house by six and give each distributor (including their own box office) eighteen tickets per performance.

Monk then started to identify possible businesses to sell tickets. "It was great because as I drove the cab if I saw a good business, I could just drop in." Though his drop ins were informal, they were also strategic. His goal was two toy stores, two cafes, and a local library. In his initial visits, he struggled to find decision-makers who could approve selling the tickets. Each asked that he come back later or call to make an appointment. Over the next week, Monk managed to make an appointment with five managers (one from each type of possible distributor). By the end of the week, only one toy store and the library agreed to his plan. Because of the library's status as a public institution, they agreed to sell the tickets for the Manscott Puppet Club at no cost. Monk distributed a ticket ledger and 40 tickets to each.

Monk recognized that he needed to meet with at least twice as many businesses the next week to meet his goal. "The corporate type places really weren't interested. I needed to go to the small family-owned type of place. But I was shocked that they weren't all jumping at the chance to sell our tickets. It didn't cost them anything, and there was no risk." That next week, Monk met with at least ten possible vendors for the tickets. Ultimately, he found two cafes but no second toy store willing to sell tickets.

He set up a display with information about the performance at each location and a sign that said, "buy your tickets here!" Since he only found four vendors to sell through, he distributed fifty tickets to each with five tickets to each performance. In the first few days, he only heard from the library that they had made any sales. When he called around to the other locations, he could not reach anyone who knew about the ticket sales. "When I had downtime in the cab I started stopping by the cafes and toy store to see the plan in action. It was a little depressing. People would come up to the counter and not even ask about the puppet show—and the sign was right there." By the end of the first week of sales, the library reported that they had sold four tickets, but none of the other businesses had sold any.

Monk was five weeks into the temporary position and was starting to panic. "I was getting really frustrated. I wanted to make a difference, and I only had three weeks left to figure out how to make the plan work." In the promotional emails Monk was distributing, he added the names of all the locations where tickets were available around the city. He hoped that by promoting the simplicity of being able to purchase at any of the geographically different places that more people would use the vendors. In his visits to the sites, he also noted that no one had asked about the event. "I know what we needed, and I still stand by it. Bigger signs. So, I made them." Monk produced larger promotional materials for the distribution sites to attract more attention, but only the library was willing to put it up. "If we had bigger signs in all the sites, people would have been more aware and would have got more excited, I think. But when I brought them, people didn't get it. One of the cafe owners was very rude. He said, 'I have a business to run, I can't do this anymore for you,' and he took down the sign and gave me the tickets back. I don't know, exactly, what he did for me. It's not like they ever actually sold any tickets."

Over the course of Monk's final weeks, the toy store sold four, the remaining cafe sold a pair, and the library sold eight tickets. "I just felt like I'd failed. It still doesn't make sense to me why it didn't work." When the marketing manager returned, she was grateful for Monk's work on the plan she had left him, but she didn't understand why he had tried to create a distribution plan. Monk shared that he feels it wasn't all in vain, "they actually did keep the ticket sales going with the library, so I guess that was my mark on the place."

He continued to work with the Manscott Puppet Club as a teacher and performer but no longer in marketing. "Honestly, I was just so done with it all. The thing that I never got, though, was that it seemed like that 'P' shouldn't be there because it doesn't really do anything. If you already provide people one place to buy something, and they're used to it, they'll just go there to do it. Why split it up when people will find you either way?" He refers to the fact that most of the people who purchased through the library, the cafe, and the toy store were already regular attendees. Although Monk may not see it this way, place does have a use and purpose in the for-profit marketing world. Large corporations especially need McCarthy's place to move products through distribution channels to reach a wide consumer base. At least in this circumstance, place was of limited value to this small nonprofit arts organization.

Interaction

The conceptual framework of place is guided by the principle that business interaction is necessary to provide a product or service efficiently and effectively to the consumer. In upstream distribution channels, businesses have little or no interaction with the consumer. In downstream channels, generally other businesses sit between the corporation providing the good or service and the consumer, often interacting directly with the market as a representative agent of the business providing the good or service. This model does not fit the arts. As soon as a representative agent assumes a position between the art and the consumer, the artistic experience would become diluted. The social connection between art, artist, and audience is ephemeral and real.[1] The very notion of "jobbing out" portions of the artistic process to maximize efficiency and increase effectiveness would do the reverse.

Arts organizations are fully capable of building and using an appropriate upstream distribution channel yet rarely find a modicum of downstream distribution channels. Sometimes one of those downstream channels is customer service, provided by a service expert working as an agent of the businesses providing the goods or service. In the arts, this would suggest that part of the experience, in this case, customer service, would be contracted out. Although this may be true for a centralized box office that provides tickets to the artistic experience, there is little customer service beyond the ticketing transaction. Customer service largely occurs through the arts organization's own ticket office, house management, administrative staff, ushers, and the like.[2] By providing the service directly, arts organizations maintain control of the overall experience had by the consumer. Because the arts sell an experience rather than a product, we maintain that any business participating in that process provides something that aids in creating the experience is, technically, an upstream channel.

Distribution Models

There are limited models of distribution for arts experiences, and what does exist, as already mentioned, is the distribution of contracts (tickets) of access to the experience, not distribution of the experience itself. Danny Newman listed a series of methods of getting these contracts of access to consumers and detailed a collection of distribution methods.[3] Newman argued that the largest number of sales would come from return consumers, either as renewing subscriptions or buying subscriptions after having been a single ticket buyer or lapsed subscriber.[4] Newman then added other unique distributors to his list. For example, Newman noted that arts organizations should ask current supporters to send letters to their Christmas card lists inviting them to attend.[5] This practice is one example of place where the intermediary, the holder of the Christmas card list, promotes and distributes access contracts. How many for-profit businesses use the Christmas card lists of their consumers? Similarly, Newman also presses commission sales and bloc sales to businesses as means for increasing attendance. In both, the intermediary is promoting and distributing access, but not the actual arts offering. No intermediary distributes the actual experience in nonprofit arts organizations, though the previously mentioned commercial tour does look more like a traditional distribution model.

Nevertheless, it is insufficient to only say that the methods of distribution are vastly different for the arts. Because arts organizations' primary function is to engage in providing experiences, even the modest distribution channels noted by Newman and others could be part of the overall experience. Most arts experiences are social experiences, and having a friend urge participation will likely enhance that experience. This is word-of-mouth, but the word-of-mouth, no matter how far removed it may seem, is part of the artistic experience.

Economies of Scale

For corporations, there are distinct advantages of using intermediaries in the distribution process of place. It typically allows for larger quantities of products or services to be distributed at a less per unit cost than if fewer products or services were produced and distributed. The volume allows for discounts and savings by making supply purchases in bulk. This process is called *economies of scale*, and it allows a company to reduce prices to the consumer based on the higher volume of sales.[6]

Consider a ballet company, then. If the company schedules a performance for eight nights in their five-hundred-seat venue, they have a total of four thousand seats for audience members available. To maximize economies of scale, the ballet company simply must add performances, with each adding availability of an additional five hundred seats. Of course, this works because the initial cost of producing the outing, the cost of the scenery, lighting, costumes, directors, designers, and the expense of rehearsal time must be incorporated into the cost of every ticket sold. Those costs must be amortized over the total number of tickets sold. The more tickets sold, the lower the cost of each of these start-up items is as a percentage of each ticket. *Running cost* is the amount of money it takes to maintain the production of each performance, with the largest expense typically being payroll.

This limited scope represents the total of the ballet company's economies of scale. The company cannot and does not take advantage of having intermediaries warehouse the performance, store the performance, distribute the performance, service the patrons, and so forth. Those aspects of "place" simply have no bearing on the ballet company or most, if not all, nonprofit arts organizations.

Channel Length

Channel length is the number of steps between the producing corporation and the consumer. In nonprofit arts organizations, the channels are very short, if they exist at all. Aside from the aforementioned centralized box office, where one organization provides the contracts of access directly to the consumers of several arts organizations, our channel lengths tend to be nonexistent. Even in instances where a centralized box office is utilized, much of the customer service is generally not provided by the box office but by the organization providing the artistic experience. The longest our channel length gets in the arts is typically between zero and one step. If we consider the interaction between the ticket agent and audience member as part of the arts experience, then ticket agents are not actually intermediaries at all.

Not having complex distribution channels has certain advantages for arts organizations. Besides the potential for losing sales from one organization to another at a centralized box office, a rare occurrence given that the presenting organization typically handles the promotion of an artistic experience, there is little to no chance of channel conflict occurring.

Horizontal Marketing

Horizontal marketing is a process whereby two or more companies work together to achieve greater economies of scale. One instance of horizontal marketing that might occur in the arts, though we are hard-pressed to find any examples other than advertising in playbills, would be if one art organization sold tickets at the arts experiences of another arts organization. We may see an example of horizontal marketing in arts passes, where multiple organizations band together to each present one or two artistic experiences as part of a bundle of multiple experiences at multiple venues. Likewise, we may see horizontal marketing when tickets are sold for multiple venues or artistic experiences simultaneously; however, it would be a stretch to say that this is what was meant by horizontal marketing. The Starbucks in the Target store is certainly a much clearer example.[7] In the arts, we must stretch to make a decent comparison. In every case, the arts organization is not distributing an actual product or service through intermediaries, but rather they distribute tickets. The tickets sold by an intermediary, as noted above, are part of the experience, and their environments have an impact on that experience. Although one may simply identify this as customer service, we maintain that considering the environment in light of the artistic experience is a much better approach for the arts.

Leadership in Channels

Chapter 9 mentioned that one specific problem with distribution channels is that, occasionally, the leadership of those channels can be lost, confused, or nonexistent. In traditional, vertical marketing design, frequently, the business that sells the product or service takes the leadership position over the channel partners. We might make a stretch here to illustrate a point. For a symphony orchestra, the leadership over artistic experience comes from, at present, the conductor. This person also happens to be the leader of what would equivalently be the director of research and development and the leader of manufacturing. This person, however, is not responsible for the overall environment in which the consumer will have the various pieces of their experience, nor are they responsible for the overall experience. Instead, their focus is on the performance, the core piece that is, "a part, but only a part, of what we are called to do" ("we," being the arts organizations), as Ben Cameron has stated.[8]

Contractual Systems

In chapter 9, contractual systems as forms of place for businesses were addressed. These included both franchises and retail cooperatives. For franchises, a license from the franchise company grants the right to use the name, logo, types of equipment, customer service plans, and all other aspects of the business that have been designed, patented, and trademarked by the company.[9] Though any business can be franchised, it is most common in the fast-food industry, which has many independently owned and operated stores. A franchise system does not exist in the nonprofit arts, nor could it. A franchise requires precise replication of a specific business model.[10] If an arts organization were to franchise its systems, the result would be the replication of art. Moreover, whether we choose to accept that the nature of art can also include replications of art, the suggestion that one community to the next can and will appreciate exact replicas of art as a substitute for the original makes the franchising concept in the nonprofit arts untenable.

In the case of a retail cooperative, such as some hotels or gas stations, for example, the business agrees to purchase a collection of trademarked supplies to use the name of the global parent company. In these cases, systems designed for each independent hotel are typically not provided by the parent company and are handled at the local level. This local oversight allows for certain freedoms and makes it far easier to change brand names at the end of the contract.

On the downstream side of distribution, one situation that is like a retail cooperative are companies that have sought out collaborative partners to resell goods or services: For example, Spas.com partners with independent day spas to sell gift cards that are good at any participating spa for services. Bedandbreakfast.com offers a similar product to its consumers, who use the card at their participating bed and breakfast of choice. In these cases, there is some retail cooperation, so we can define this aspect of these businesses as place. The I Amsterdam case at the beginning of part V of this book is another example of downstream cooperation. However, to the best of our knowledge, there is not a service such as arts.com that provides a retail cooperative for the arts. One might consider the consolidated ticket office that sells tickets for several organizations as another form of retail cooperative, but it is really more like commission sales, as the consolidated ticket office's primary function is not to promote the sales of tickets, but merely to handle the financial transaction. Both spas.com and bedandbreakfast.com assume responsibility for promoting the sales and use of their gift cards. The recently deceased MoviePass, which allowed unfettered access to partner movie theaters, was similar.

Disintermediation

The rise of spas.com and bedandbreakfast.com speaks to industries where little or no intermediation existed, much like the arts. The void filled by these companies has allowed for some semblance of place to appear, though as noted previously, the same process for the arts could only work if each arts offering is created as something unique. In business, disintermediation occurs when businesses reduce (or eliminate) layers of intermediaries and bring themselves closer to the consumer through fewer layers.[11] This movement seems to signal a shift in the experience economy.[12] Disintermediation allows for greater control of the environment in which the consumer purchases products since there are fewer intermediaries standing between the business and the consumer. Since arts organizations typically have fewer intermediaries than for-profit corporations do, they have better control over the environments in which audience members have experiences.

Channel Design

The function of channel design is intended to maximize profit by ensuring that the greatest volume of income can flow from the design's structure, which is why organizations establish either intensive, exclusive, or selective distribution systems. By mere definition it is clear that this process is not appropriate for a nonprofit arts organization, as the goal is not to maximize profits but to best execute the organization's mission. Channel design works to maximize profits in distributing products. Unfortunately, for nonprofit arts organizations, part of the construct of place connects businesses and consumers as tangible products are pushed onto the market. Because arts organizations are not able to use place effectively, their ability to find and to interact with the maximum number of community members is reduced.

Because the arts lack the P of place in their business models, there lies a distinct disadvantage when attempting to capture the largest number of consumers. As stated earlier, the arts are not in a position to extend part of their work to intermediaries.

Internet Distribution

The internet is certainly an excellent distribution channel and allows businesses to connect direct-to-consumer if they choose, and it allows for a more do-it-yourself, tailored buying experience without the interference of salespeople, driving to a store, and standing in line.[13] In the nonprofit arts, the internet as a distribution channel has not been incredibly effective, except in cases of art as commerce, where a hard artifact is sold to a consumer. Ticketing for the performing arts, even the commercial arts, remains dominated by two major players: LiveNation Entertainment, owner of TicketMaster, and CTS Eventim in Europe.

In 2015, Amazon.com, now the world's largest retailer and distributor, launched Amazon Tickets as a way to capture both the commercial market for the arts as well as the untapped nonprofit market. Though the effort was not launched with huge fanfare, Jeff Bezos, CEO of Amazon, said this of the effort through a job posting: "Our vision goes beyond selling tickets as we aim to disrupt the entire live entertainment experience, including what happens before, during, and after the show."[14] Note that by talking about the live entertainment experience and what happens before, during, and after the show, Bezos refers to the environment in which the experience and its associated pieces occur.

Two years later, the project was shelved, purportedly because "promoting is only lucrative when ticketing and promoting took place together," within the same environment as part of a complete experience.

The convenience of securing a contract of access via the internet certainly allows the consumer some ease of access to the art. However, to ensure that said internet sale is part of the environment of the arts experience, the website selling the tickets should develop unique parameters designed only for that individual arts experience.

Objectives

Chapter 9 suggested that businesses need to determine objectives for each product or service and set objectives for distribution based on the nature of the product. For example, an essential commodity such as toothpaste, sold as a consumer good with intensive distribution, requires one set of parameters, while that pearl whitening, diamond-filled, luxury toothpaste requires a very different distribution system. This example appears as two unique experiences framed around the particular product of consumer or luxury toothpaste. Since arts organizations do not use intermediaries, they instead manipulate the environment and experience for each unique type of target user.

Using intermediaries, unless arts organizations can specifically control their environments, simply dilutes or causes damage to the overall arts experience. Given this dilution or damage to the artistic experience if nonprofit arts organizations use intermediaries, they find themselves set apart from the businesses that use multiple channel designs and multiple intermediaries to reach buyers of different sorts.

Consequently, the P of place does not and cannot work for the nonprofit arts, and as a result, the arts likely will continue to struggle to gain an increased foothold in the marketplace. Certainly, if the option were available and workable, nonprofit arts organizations would have long ago approached an intermediary about assuming intensive distribution for us. **Instead, the arts tend to be seen as elite, reflecting a distribution system that is extremely exclusive and almost unbending.**[15] As much as the arts try to shake their elitist mantle, they are currently pigeonholed into a marketing model that places them there.

Conclusion

The word *place* is marginally deceptive in business and is even more so in the arts. The term is a noun that implies a fixed location in space. That location, or in the case of multiple distribution channel partners, locations, has to do with a physical presence. Although the term *environment* is also a noun, it has to do with the surroundings of one or several fixed locations. One may choose to quibble semantics, but the distinction is very real. For an experience, the environment in which the experience and all its various components take place is more logically associated with the art than the conceptual notion of distribution known as place.

11
Environment and the Arts

It may seem strange to connect the term *environment* with any business, and perhaps even more odd to connect the term to audience engagement efforts in the nonprofit arts. As noted in chapter 9, however, the term *environment* is far more than the images of nature that the term initially brings to mind for many people. Environment means surroundings. For the nonprofit arts, the surroundings of a work of art are vital to developing the experience in which the art exists and will be consumed.[1]

Effect of Place

Chapter 10 explored the concept of place and all the facets that go into its construct. It noted that place has to do with distribution channels, supply chains, and the means of transporting goods or services from raw materials to the final destination. The P of place is designed to capture everything outside the realms of product, promotion, and price. For the small business, however, though some supply chains may exist, it is very rare to see distribution channels in play. The small business owner (and the nonprofit arts) is going to be hard-pressed to find a way to turn the notion of place into both supply chain and distribution, with the exception of a distribution channel of direct-to-consumer. Although the construct of place, and how it mixes with the other Ps, makes sense for a larger organization that is trying to focus, specialize, and streamline, for the nonprofit arts, it is a stretch, if not an impossibility, to calculate the cost and effects of distribution into a marketing mix. Without one of four ingredients, the recipe turns into a disaster.

Environment as Backdrop

The term *environment* represents the world in which we live and function and, in some ways, all those aspects of life that surround us in any given, defined, or undefined space. Environments can be large or small, subsets, or the entire planet, solar system, galaxy, or universe. We refer to the environment as any of these things, meaning the surroundings in which all aspects within an environment interact. The concept of environment is not only the physical place in which we occupy space but also the emotional and mental aspects of that place. For artists, part of what they do is enmeshed in the notion of environment because they do two things: (1) intentionally manipulate the environment to provide their art, and (2) use their art to reflect society through the environment in which it exists. Environment is not only the backdrop for art, but the reason art exists, as art is designed to record and reflect the world the artist sees or envisions within an environment.

Environment and the Collaborative Process of Art

One transformational form of community advocacy related to environment is the idea of creative placemaking.[2] "Creative placemaking takes place when artists, arts organizations, and community development practitioners deliberately integrate arts and culture into community revitalization work—placing arts at the table with land-use, transportation, economic development, education, housing, infrastructure, and public safety strategies."[3] The creative placemaking approach puts the arts front and center in the local community environment and asks artists to work to shape that environment around or with created art. "Creative placemaking animates public and private spaces, rejuvenates structures and streetscapes, improves local business viability and public safety, and brings diverse people together to celebrate, inspire, and be inspired."[4] A reflection of our society and the local community placed into a cohesive environment for the purpose of rejuvenation, animation, and improvement is creative placemaking. It is a concept inextricably linking the arts and environment, and it is a notion that is growing in popularity due to consistently successful results.

Qualities of Environment

When the engagement edge uses the term *environment*, it refers to the actual surroundings and the qualities of each aspect the community member encounters. A simple example is the state of the restrooms attached to the lobby of a theater. Their condition or quality contributes to what makes up the environment for the arts experience. The qualities of environment(s) can include virtually everything in the defined environment. In the arts, **think of the environment as the qualities of those locations where audience members go during the entire process of the experience.** This description refers to the qualities of places where interaction occurs from the moment the consumer becomes aware of the offering up to, and even after the point when, the entire artistic experience is consummated. This context of environment includes visits to a ticket office, phone calls, restaurants before and after the experience, and the physical environments in which the patron will travel through to arrive at the location where the art is presented. We cannot control the qualities of all these environments, but **a solid plan considers the most frequent touchpoint environments and seeks to control or quasi-control as many qualities as possible.**

Environmental Aesthetics

For the engagement edge to work, the environment plan should place the focus less on locations (places) and more on aesthetics in an environment. As noted, aesthetics refers to the branch of philosophy that looks at beauty and matters of artistic taste. Because the nonprofit arts present an artistic experience, the environment plan should follow the same characteristics as the design of the art itself. It is for the attendees and concerns the details of environmental aesthetics when possible.[5] Typically, this would be in the physical location where the art is presented and should represent a change in environmental characteristics from offering to offering. It is here that the theme of an experience, as Pine and Gilmore have explained it, can be created. As the engagement office travels further from the physical location where the art is presented, it is proportionately more difficult to control the environment. The gallery is already under environmental control, as are the lobby, concession stand, and other parts of the facility's accessible areas. The walkways between the parking lot and the building may be slightly less controllable, and the parking lot even less controllable. The local restaurants are uncontrollable without a plan to steer attendees to specific restaurants, where specific environment plans can be put in place.

Control

In the marketing mix, the notion of place is completely controlled, even when handing over responsibility to multiple intermediaries. The authority to assign any fulfillment obligations still allows the marketer to maintain control of the entire place function. The concept of environment in the engagement edge has aspects that are controlled but includes ancillary, related, and adjacent elements outside of the organization's purview. For areas that arts organizations do control, the theme of the experience can be carried throughout.

Environment Plan

To develop an environmental plan, the engagement manager must do a broad sketch of all those locations that a consumer is likely to encounter as touchpoints in their arts experience. Although there may be crossover from one experience to another, such as attendees passing through a lobby every time they attend an experience. It is vital to decipher which touchpoints may differ with each new experience, as the environment that we can control can be changed to make each experience unique. The list of touchpoint environments contains three levels: those that can be manipulated, typically, with people, décor, and additional offerings of value; those that can be partially controlled, such as partner restaurants that can work with the organization to ensure a quality experience; and those that attendees will pass through that cannot be manipulated. From these lists, an engagement manager works with defined options and makes conscious choices about lesser controlled environments.

In those middle areas, we find partners who can assist in controlling the environment, such as local restaurants that partner for experiential offerings centered around a specific piece of art. The partners become what some might refer to as arts organizations' distribution channels because they appear similar to those found in the marketing mix P of place. Because we have defined the offering of the nonprofit art as an experience, arts organizations then do have distribution channels in some sense that assist or participate or cannot avoid being part of the overall experience. **Because the experience is not fully consummated until the audience member has had an opportunity to complete their viewing of the artistic endeavor, the definition of distributors falls flat.** Everyone outside our control with whom we can work to assist in developing environments that support the experiential theme can be potential *environmental partners*.

As Experience

Environment is inextricably linked to experience. One's experience occurs through a collection of touchpoints that are seamlessly connected, and each of those touchpoints can be defined by the environment in which they exist. The case of Sing for Hope Pianos provides a nice example of environment both as creative placemaking and as a series of touchpoints for community members. The relationships that occur within each of the environments contribute to the overall experience as appreciated by the arts attendee.[6] Experience and environment cannot exist or even function effectively without the alignment of one another. **The engagement edge seeks to plan and execute appropriate engagement strategies by aligning and controlling experience and environment simultaneously.** Although one might argue that a product also exists within an environment, the function of that environment is often less pertinent to the nature of the product itself. Additionally, because the arts have a function that intermingles with and reflects upon environments, the concept of the arts experience and arts environment appear even more indelibly linked.

> **The Case of Sing for Hope Pianos**
>
> Monica Yunus and Camille Zamora, both opera singers, became best friends while studying at the Julliard School. Their initial bond was built on more than a love of music; both are fiercely passionate about serving their communities through the arts and providing artists opportunities to serve their communities. Together they would eventually lead one of the world's most renowned public arts projects through the nonprofit arts organization they cofounded. The number and variety of locations of the art project made the consideration of environment a crucial component of their approach. Earlier in this chapter, we described environment relative to creative placemaking. Sing for Hope Pianos is a key example of large-scale creative placemaking as it puts the arts at the center of the

community environment and includes the community in creating and shaping the environment through art.

Jay met with Yunus and Zamora to discuss Sing for Hope Pianos and how their love for serving the community through the arts began. Zamora shared that the attack on the World Trade Center on September 11, 2001, was a defining moment for them in the way they saw and experienced art. They were students in New York City on September 11. The Julliard School shares a city block with a firehouse that was one of the first responders to the attacks. "We went in and sang for the fire guys that day. It was a way to find and bring a piece of the arts out in a time of crisis." She noted that the performance was not just for the firefighters, "it was [also] a way to make ourselves feel better."

Five years later, Yunus and Zamora officially incorporated Sing for Hope as a nonprofit arts organization.[7] This experience of responding to a critical situation with art became one of the foundational principles of their organization. Sing for Hope provides New York City–based artists resources to give back to their community using the arts. Over several years, the nonprofit developed programming in schools, hospitals, and community centers. "By 2010," Zamora shared, "we basically had this robust arts peace corps in New York City that centered on artists responding to crisis and dismantling barriers to access."

Around this time, Yunus and Zamora decided to develop a symbolic project celebrating the successes of Sing for Hope. After weeks of considering possibilities, they read about an arts project that had developed organically in the United Kingdom. Zamora went on, "Basically, there was a guy who was moving, and he owned a piano. Well, when he arrived at his new place, he couldn't get his piano up the stairs. So, he left it on the street with a sign that said, 'play me.' It became a viral sensation in his little town." The excitement in the town was palpable, and it created a dialogue about public music-making. "An entrepreneurial artist from Bristol then scaled the idea to a couple of different cities, including London, and their program took off."

At the time, there were no large public music projects like this in the United States. Yunus and Zamora were so inspired by what they saw in Europe that they decided they had to bring it to New York City. "It's such a symbol and celebration of the idea that art is for everyone. Monica and I talked and said 'okay, let's just do this,' we decided to go big and do the world's largest version. We decided to put out 60 pianos across all five boroughs."[8]

After the decision to move forward, Yunus recalled, "all we needed was funding, a city partnership, pianos, and spaces to put them . . . So, we realized that we basically needed everything." Over several weeks, they developed a consortium of philanthropic supporters and managed to meet with key decision-makers at City Hall. City Hall helped to connect Sing for Hope to a contact in the Parks Department to determine sites and permissions for the placement of pianos, but they did not provide the actual instruments. Zamora shared, "I think a lot of people just assumed that these pianos fall like manna and that they're funded by City Hall. That's not the case at all. We [fundraised] every dollar to make the project possible."

In determining piano placement, Yunus and Zamora aimed to ensure that pianos were readily accessible in every geographic part of New York City. This element was one factor in convincing City Hall and the Parks Department to participate. Since the pianos were to be installed outdoors in public spaces, controlling the environment was more limited than most performance spaces. Rather than intentionally manipulating the environment where the art experience was provided, they carefully and purposefully selected existing environments that matched their needs. The pianos were purposefully placed in areas where environmental noise would be as limited as possible, where groups of people could easily gather without hindering the flow of busy New York City streets and sidewalks, and where many people could use and experience the pianos. Although they carefully selected the locations to ensure a conducive environment, the message of Sing for Hope Pianos was that art can exist anywhere. The diversity of locations the pianos were placed in was the purpose for the overall project, so the geographic location of each piano was a factor, but the actual placement within the geographic location was carefully determined. For Sing for Hope Pianos, the environments (though carefully selected) did not have to be manipulated to provide space for the art, but the presence of the art impacted and changed the environment. In for-profit marketing ventures, improving its distribution channel is never the purpose of a product; in the nonprofit arts, changing an environment can be the function of an artistic experience and art project. Likewise, the environment also impacts the way the art experience occurs to each audience member.

Sing for Hope Pianos launched in the summer of 2010 in all of New York City's boroughs, and Yunus and Zamora reached their goal of sixty piano locations. "We were very fortunate in that the final list of the 60 locations was quite widespread. The locations really represented the socioeconomic backgrounds of all New Yorkers." Adding to the aesthetic experience, artists designed a paint job for each piano. Many of the artists were inspired by a theme, and most used bright colors. The designs intentionally made the piano stand out in its environment and create a welcoming feeling that invites passersby to stop and play. Yunus noted the great variety of people who participated that first summer. "One of the wonderful things is that you saw every kind of person engaging, we've had many videos of homeless people sitting down and playing with the passerby lawyer looking on. The environments we select create an opportunity for unique interactions and breaking down barriers. It takes a lot to get us New Yorkers to look at one another. These pianos get people to stop and interact around this language of music."

When asked about the reactions from audience members, Zamora shared that early on, responses were largely positive, but even one of their board members registered some concern. "One board member basically said, 'I can't be a part of this and see instruments like these left outside.' We totally understood and respected their opinion, but we said, 'this is what we think the arts are meant for, and though this eighteenth-century instrument may not be able to withstand winter, it can certainly withstand a summer with all of the precautions in place.'" The environmental considerations included how and when people would interact with the instruments and keeping the pianos safe from the elements. To protect the pianos and to develop greater community engagement, Sing for Hope was intentional in building out systems to ensure that each piano had a "piano buddy" who would care for the piano while it was in its location. The buddy was usually a volunteer who would keep the piano dry with a tarp in case of rain and remove the tarp and reset the piano for public use once the weather was again conducive for people to gather.

Others early on were concerned about vandalism. Yunus shared that this is a question they received frequently, but, since launching Sing for Hope Pianos, they have never had a single case of vandalism. On the contrary, the communities where Sing for Hope installs the pianos take great pride in what the pianos can do for their environment. "It's amazing the grassroots community engagement and the development of a sense of ownership that people take." As noted earlier in this chapter, the notion of environment is not relegated only to a physical location; it also includes the emotional and mental perceptions of the place. The way the environment occurs emotionally impacts the way each piano is experienced in its environment.

Regarding audience reactions, Zamora addressed that Sing for Hope has very little hard data about audience response. "The overarching question we've had since we started is: how do you measure joy? How do you go beyond the anecdotal because our anecdotal evidence is astonishing, and will bring tears to your eyes every time, but how do you capture data around that? We have many stories of transformation, but people have such a preference for [quantitative] data." Sing for Hope Pianos is an especially challenging project for the organization to collect quantitative data around because the environment of a piano in public means that no tickets are sold, and organization representatives are rarely present when the experiences occur. Both Yunus and Zamora believe that Sing for Hope Pianos can provide arts experiences that change communities. "It's changed peoples' perception of New York and made them want to travel [to New York]. It's made neighborhoods feel happier. It's an economic driver. A local deli guy shared that he sells so many more sandwiches when the piano is there. We also have a strong suspicion that the presence of the pianos reduces the rate of crime."

Yunus and Zamora believe Sing for Hope Pianos landed at just the right time, given what was happening in the world. The economy had not yet recovered from the great recession, and New York City saw a record number of tourists filling the streets. Yunus expressed that it was a particularly long and hard summer in New York. "It was also the summer of the BP oil spill, and it was so hot—we had just all had it. It was a moment where the world wanted some good news. We happened to have launched these pianos, and it became the lead story in every news show." Sing for Hope Pianos got more impressions than any other public art project in the country that year. At the end of the year, they opened New York Magazine and, "The lead story was a collection of reasons to love New York City, and [Sing for Hope Pianos] was one of the central features."

At the end of the summer in 2010, they considered the press coverage and audience reactions, and Yunus and Zamora decided to make Sing for Hope Pianos an annual event rather than a one-off arts project. "We took a deep breath after that [summer] and said, 'You know what, let's, let's try to ensure that we can continue to do this for years to come.'" At the end of summer 2010, Sing for Hope began partnering with New York City schools to place the pianos from the project into schools to promote their continued use.

In working to create sustainability for the Sing for Hope Pianos program Yunus and Zamora developed an implementation manual that described all the steps to operate the program successfully. Although the project primarily operates in the summer, Yunus noted the consistent rigor involved year-round in continuing the program. She shared that Damian Woetzel, who serves as the chair of their programming committee on the board of directors (and happens to be the president of the Juilliard School), introduced them to the phrase "Artistic habits of mind." This is a phrase they use often and for them means "teamwork, rigor, excellence, but also empathy and a passion for the art and service." These qualitative components, the technical information about determining piano placement, and even best practices for loading pianos in and out of their trucks are all included in this document that promotes creative placemaking for their organization.

Sing for Hope Pianos has installed more than five hundred unique pianos in New York City in the past ten years. Even though they have placed more than five hundred pianos, the environment is a key determining factor for the precise location of every individual piano. Though they acknowledged that their quantitative data is limited, they estimate that Sing for Hope Pianos impacts around two million people annually.

As Education

One of the educational topics engagement managers need to address with potential audience members is what the environment will be like when they attend an arts offering. In this same vein, arts organizations continuously educate their audiences about the brand as well as educate them about the process of attending arts experiences.[9] A part of the branding process, then, is in the education the organization provides about the environment and what it will be like for attendees.

We also mentioned earlier that "it is . . . important to identify the right location for providing education. Is it at a community center, classroom, church basement, club meeting, museum, theater, or other entertainment venue, or perhaps even a mall or store front? Determining what *environment* will best assist our learners is critically important." Note that the term *environment* is intentionally used as the experience actually starts as the organization begins engaging through education with the potential audience member. The location in which they provide and engage in that education is as essential as the environment in which the offering occurs. **The educational environment is simply one touchpoint in the process of the experience, but the environment should be conducive to learning, the theme of the organization as a whole, and its brand.** The educational component may also be part of the environmental plan for an organization's specific offering, but as discussed at length in chapter 5, to develop a solid brand, the education and the environment in which it takes place must be carefully considered.

As Ease of Access

The four Es of the engagement edge are closely connected. They not only have a great deal of interplay, which is why they all work in tandem, but they are interlocked. Not one of them can exist and function without the other three in the engagement edge. For example, one way we ease access to our experiences is by educating our community about who we are, why we exist, and what we provide for them. The process may require interactions, exercises, games, lessons, discussions, or other pedagogical tools. The education eases access to the experience, and it **takes place in an environment that, according to Dewey, is one of many environments that flow from one to another to make an entire experience.**[10] The four dimensions of the engagement edge do and must work together in order for them to be successful. This is, in part, why Monk's distribution plan failed in the case of the Manscott Puppet Theatre. Though Monk expanded the distribution chain, he did not expand the environment, or engage through education.

How Environment Finds Balance

Although there are multiple environmental touchpoints a consumer will travel through in order to consummate the artistic experience fully, and they are seamlessly connected in the experience, the environments themselves can function more like a womb than a setting. Within each environment is an opportunity to nurture and grow the emotional relationship between the patron and the art offering. It is within these locations where countless interactions and relationships occur and intermingle. Though we cannot control the occurrences within each environment, we can *influence* those occurrences and relationships. Part of the environmental plan then becomes looking at how people will interact within each environment they pass through. It includes understanding how the environment contributes to the overall artistic experience in an aesthetically pleasing way and determining how to ensure that interactions are free from negative cues, as Pine and Gilmore have suggested.[11] This strategy suggests that environments that are not part of the core art are a part of the overall artistic experience and must be treated as if they are as equally as important as the core art itself, at least to the consumer.

Disruption

One key issue for the engagement manager to consider is how the environment and interactions within it can impact or be impacted by outside influences. Anthony recalled a time when he owned a boutique hotel. Most of the time, couples arrived for a lovely, romantic getaway, smiling and happy and ready to enjoy their stay. Occasionally, however, a couple would arrive at the front desk tired, upset, angry, or frustrated from something that occurred in an environment outside the hotel. Their unhappiness would be visible from the moment of their arrival. Whatever affected couples such as this tended to carry itself through their entire stay. They would call the front desk repeatedly to complain, be upset about how the restaurant treated them their first night in town, bicker over the breakfast buffet in the morning, and would eventually check out with glum faces, completely dissatisfied. Whatever had occurred in those earlier environments had disrupted the hotel service. Anthony could not have done anything to ameliorate whatever relationships and occurrences happened before the guests' arrival.

There may have been an opportunity to manage those environments at least to some degree. For example, on occasion, an argument in the car on the way to the retreat hotel was a contributing factor. He developed a series of facts and local topics designed to be explored during the car ride to the hotel. This handout was supplied to everyone who booked a room. We cannot control every interaction outside of the artistic experience. We can, however, look for ways to address potential issues and take a modicum of control over outside conditions to support an overall satisfactory experience.

For the Artist

It may be discouraging to think that environments outside of the actual artistic core offering have any part in the artistic experience. Art is seen as the purview of the person who creates the painting, sculpture, play, ballet, symphony, opera, or other presentation. How can we treat the lobby of a theater, halls of a museum, parking lots, and local restaurants as part of the artistic experience? Artists recognize that those environments are organized and controlled by people who are not trained or skilled in creating arts offerings. Art, however, is a collaborative function. From selecting a frame for a piece of art to the placement of the painting in a gallery, or the layout of the halls leading to each space, every decision made impacts how the audience experiences the painting.[12] Everyone involved in the process of creating art to deliver it to an audience member is part of the environment in which the experience takes place and is, therefore, a part of the collaborative experience. The artistry of creating appropriate and controlled environments has certain artistic challenges more daunting than those of the creator of the core art. The environment must be manipulated to please the greatest number of people while following the theme of the artistic offering. **The artist and engagement manager are partners in creating the environment, each working to ensure that the environments they control are focused on the goal of fully immersing the audience into the artistic offering as a culmination of an artistic experience that occurs within a collection of environments.**

PART V
EASE OF ACCESS

Part V of the text explores the various elements of the P of price from the marketing mix and the E of ease of access from the engagement edge. The chapters walk through various aspects of each of these notions, comparing and contrasting them in terms of the nonprofit arts as well as other for-profit organizations, demonstrating which concepts work better for which type of organization, and why.

Chapter 12 attempts to define the term price, as meant in the marketing mix. The concept of price is a collection of pricing strategies. Pricing is loosely understood in the arts and few of the pricing strategies that arts organizations do use function for nonprofit arts organizations. The chapter then begins to explore the concept of ease of access by describing common perceptions around the words ease and access.

Chapter 13 takes a deep dive into the notion of price. It details the various main strategies used by organizations to price their products, and discusses the relationship between price and product. It then explores how the arts have unusual issues associated with their nonprofit status, mission, and function. These elements often force the notion of price, the only one of the four Ps dealing with revenue, to fall flat.

Chapter 14 follows with a discussion about the concept of ease of access. It creates the paradigm for what ease of access really is, goes deeper into defining what it means in practice, and considers it in relation to the arts.

Before beginning chapter 12, consider the two brief cases below. One describes a nonprofit's role in creating ease of access in the city of Amsterdam since the 1990s. The other presents a vision for how access to the arts may be eased in the future with the continued development of technology.

The Case of the I Amsterdam City Card

The I Amsterdam City Card is an offering by Amsterdam & Partners that serves to encourage cultural experiences and create ease of access for people interested in arts experiences in the city. Amsterdam & Partners has nonprofit status in the Netherlands and receives government funding to support its mission. The I Amsterdam City Card is a service that helps to reduce barriers of access to arts experiences. Jay met with Sandra Ahmadi of Amsterdam & Partners to discuss their approach to providing access.

Ahmadi shared that the I Amsterdam City Card was initially developed to encourage tourism and ease decision-making for what types of cultural events potential audience members might enjoy. She explained that "the City Card started in the 1990s to help people discover all that Amsterdam had to offer, and to help change the way people interacted with the arts in the city. People can choose how long they would like access anywhere from 24 hours to five days." Although tourists are the primary target, many community members from in and around the city use the card. The card provides access to hundreds of cultural experiences throughout the city, "We partner with museums, theatre, comedy, dance, visual arts, opera, gardens, a zoo, if it's a cultural offering in the city of Amsterdam you can access it through the card." The city is home to more than seventy museums and nearly all of them participate with the access card.

The card goes beyond creating access to the cultural experiences. It also provides access to public transportation around the city and reduces dining costs at many restaurants. Although more expensive than a single museum ticket, Ahmadi shared, "the purpose is really to create access for people who want to experience culture across the city. Part of that access is making transportation, dining, and other experiences around the core art experience easier. Another component is reducing the cost to keep it accessible. We are always seeking ways to reduce the price, because we do not believe that money should be a barrier to culture." The organization also provides clear descriptions and partners with other community organizations to provide education about the arts experiences.

When the City Card was first developing, the founders were primarily focused on museums. Within the first few years, however, the board sought to open the offerings to more experiences throughout the city. Initially, there were many questions as to what could or could not be considered a cultural experience. "Many of the big museums at the time wanted to control what would be part of the card. They wanted it to be the big museums only. Through time we have really expanded what is considered a culture here in the city. It's created a more inclusive environment." Ahmadi estimated the card launched with between twenty and thirty partners, "now, there are hundreds of partnered arts organizations and related businesses."

The card has led to more equitable opportunities for new and small cultural organizations in the city. Smaller organizations receive enhanced exposure and financial benefits through participation. "We hear it all the time. People go through some of the large museums, then visit some of the smaller ones that they otherwise would not have attended. When this happens, the smaller museums see an increase financially they would not have otherwise, and they serve more people. As partners, all of the cultural experiences receive the same rate for every visit." Amsterdam & Partners sees the I Amsterdam City Card program as creating sustainability for small cultural organizations and assisting in developing and ensuring more diverse experiences for audiences. The audience, of course, receives the benefit of easier access to cultural experiences they otherwise may not have.

As the level of ease increased, Amsterdam & Partners recognized a change in the demographics of who was using the City Card. Initially, the target audience for the City Card were people more than sixty years old. "It was really just something for older couples. Honestly, at the time, going to the museum was mostly associated as something older people did." Ahmadi recalled that through the years, a wider cross section of people began to purchase the card as costs were reduced and transportation options were added. "In recent years we have seen many young people using the card because it makes everything simple, and it's really relatively inexpensive."

Amsterdam & Partners sees the I Amsterdam City Card as an offering that has altered the perception of the city. "It's really changed the image of Amsterdam abroad and resulted in increased tourism. People hear about how wonderful the cultural experiences are here, and when they hear how easy we make it, they come." Ahmadi believes the program has benefited macro and micro levels of culture in the city. As a whole, Amsterdam is increasingly seen as a cultural center, and small cultural organizations benefit through simplified access for audiences.

Although Amsterdam & Partners is not a typical nonprofit arts organization, their approach to easing access provides an excellent starting point for considering ease of access against McCarthy's pricing strategies. Both ease of access and McCarthy's pricing strategies will be explored at length in the following chapters.

The Case of Commonwealth Shakespeare Company and Hamlet 360

Steve Maler is on the cutting edge of applying new technology to create ease of access. This application of the technology is so new that when we first heard about it, our first thought was, "how inaccessible." As inaccessible as the approach may be now, Maler and his company, Commonwealth Shakespeare Company in Massachusetts, have set their sights to the future. Commonwealth Shakespeare Company partnered with Google to create the longest theatrical production ever produced and distributed through virtual reality: *Hamlet 360*. Although the equipment necessary to experience the production may be financially out of reach for many people now, Maler believes as the cost for the equipment is reduced over time, virtual reality will ease obstacles many people face in experiencing the arts.

To learn more about the company and how virtual reality could someday ease access to arts experience Jay met with Maler and visited Commonwealth Shakespeare Company to experience *Hamlet 360* firsthand. Since Maler founded the theater company in 1996, it has been dedicated to enhancing access to Shakespeare performances. Maler shared that the founding of the company was initiated in response to his question, "Why aren't more diverse audiences in the theater? I looked at the audience and said, 'I'm not in this audience,' as a young guy in my 20s. I looked around and didn't see my friends in the audience. So the company really launched with this idea of how do we break down the barriers?"

Like the Public Theater in New York City, which is described in chapter 14, Commonwealth Shakespeare Company offers free, outdoor, public Shakespeare performances every summer to their community. Maler acknowledged that price is often a barrier to attendance, "we wanted to first and foremost remove that pricing barrier, but it's not the only barrier. We recognized that many people didn't feel then, and still don't feel now, like they belong inside of these buildings and physical edifices that have been created to house art, music, dance, theater, visual art, they don't feel like they belong." Chapter 14 includes a discussion of reducing elitism and the barrier of low self-efficacy. To respond to this issue, they "blew the walls off to the theater, and put the work out in the park with no gates or even fixed seats to create a completely porous experience for the audience."

For years, Maler and Commonwealth Shakespeare Company created access through the Shakespeare on the Common performances and by bringing Shakespeare into schools and other environments to enhance access. The step toward virtual reality is an investment in providing a new path to access in the future. "We see [virtual reality performances] as a direct extension of our mission of making these plays available to anyone and everyone everywhere. So the way I pitched this to Google is that this is a way of the company scaling its mission to the world."

Google signed on and invested hundreds of thousands of dollars to help develop the project as a prototype for how virtual reality could change performing arts experiences. The investment in the recording and implementation of the technology was significant, and Maler acknowledged the obstacle of financial accessibility to virtual reality experiences. "The barrier to entry is challenging because of the gear. Not everyone has a VR headset right now." To start distributing the experience, Maler noted that a donor purchased twenty-five VR headsets for the company so that Commonwealth Shakespeare Company could partner with local schools to tour the experience right into their classrooms. Some schools already do have the technology for their students to experience *Hamlet 360*. The production has been shared around the world, including a school in Brazil which Maler video called with to discuss the performance.

Jay was surprised by the experience of actually seeing the performance in virtual reality. In a film, the focus of the audience is determined by the director. That is a part of that medium's art. In a virtual reality performance, the audience member has total control of what they look at, and can adjust the focus of their eyes to clearly see objects or actors close or far away. Maler noted that "the medium is not a proxy for live theater. It's a new medium, it's a different medium, it has attributes of theater, it has attributes of film, but it's really something somewhere in between those two spaces."

Virtual reality provides new agency to the audience that they lack in traditional venues with fixed seats. "If you're in the back of the house because you can't afford the front row seat in a big Broadway theater, you're having a very different experience of that show. With VR, we have placed the viewer in the optimal space to experience the content, and we've shaped the experience for that viewer."

Beyond serving people across the world, arts experiences delivered through virtual reality may become valuable for people within the community who are not able to travel. Although they have not begun developing programming yet, Commonwealth Shakespeare Company is considering how to deliver arts experiences to aging populations. Maler believes "the aging population is incredibly culturally sophisticated. They spent their lives going to and attending live events and engaging with literature. Just because sometimes their mobility decreases doesn't mean that their interest in participating culturally has decreased."

Although technology has not yet caught up to make virtual reality arts experiences widely accessible, Maler and Commonwealth Shakespeare Company are dedicated to preparing for when it does. He sees the development of accessible art as a responsibility of arts organizations. "We must develop new streams to reach new audiences in ways that make it truly accessible to everyone." For Maler, virtual reality is not the only way to do this, but it is one way that has great potential for the future. "So whatever we can do, whether it's setting up a stage on the Boston Common, or partnering with a school to bring some really great education into the classroom, or using technology to reach audiences that are homebound or can't get to the city center to experience the cultural riches of that community, it's an extraordinary opportunity and obligation, I think, of us as a society to make this work easily accessible."

12
Contrasting Frameworks
Price and Ease of Access

This chapter presents the basics of both *price* from McCarthy's marketing mix and *ease of access*. It defines key elements of these components so that the terms are understood in the context of the following chapters. In the strictest sense, price has to do with the amount of money consumers exchange for a good or service. Price, however, amounts to the total of all those values that the consumer is willing to exchange for the good or service.[1] Traditionally, price has been the main factor that affects the buyer's choice between products. It is also the only part of the marketing mix that produces revenue. Price is incredibly flexible as it can typically be changed easily. It is challenging to determine appropriate pricing, and many marketing managers (especially in the arts) prefer to focus on the other parts of the marketing mix.

Ease of access is the process of reducing obstacles to help provide access to an offering. It considers more than the exchange between individual and organization. Sometimes, like when organizations provide free offerings, there is no exchange. Even in a free offering from an arts organization, obstacles exist that can hinder potential participation from community members. People experience varying levels of ease of access depending on how many obstacles exist, how those obstacles impact them individually, and how those obstacles occur to them.[2] This mix of obstacles means that some people have an easier time accessing arts organizations' offerings than others. Ease of access focuses on reducing obstacles for *all* current and potential audience members. Before building on this idea, a description of the traditional approach to price is in order.

What Is Price?

Because price can be one of the most difficult pieces of the marketing mix to establish appropriately, it is important to review the various factors that go into pricing methodology. Experts have explored these factors in many ways, but the list has been narrowed to those most prescient.

Cost is a primary factor in determining a price for a product or service.[3] Businesses cannot ignore the cost of producing the product or service they create. Businesses must sell the product at a price that is high enough to offset the cost to produce the product or service. The price, however, must also be low enough that it generates sufficient demand.

Demand greatly affects the price of a product or service, and it must be considered before setting a price. If there is high demand, the price can be set higher, and if there is low demand, the price must be set lower. Likewise, if there is a high supply of the product or service, the business may choose to set the price lower to exhaust supply, or if there is a shortage of supply, the business may choose to increase the price.

Competition is an important factor in setting prices. A competitor who has an enormous market share, market strength, or influence on the market can be the leader in price setting, and a corporation with a lesser share will have to follow prices set by the leader. It is vital to look at competing prices or competing goods or services to determine appropriate pricing tactics.

The **purchasing power of the consumer** must also be taken into consideration when determining prices. The corporation must know who the buyers of the product are and their bargaining power over the price set. Of course, individuals have little bargaining power unless they are purchasing in substantial quantities, at which point, a corporation may need to negotiate or set prices lower to meet the consumers' needs. If the consumers have little bargaining power, the organization may set a higher price if it seeks to generate a substantial profit. They have an **objective** of setting the price higher. If they are more interested in expanding their market, the price may be set lower. Obviously, what the objectives are for the organization will have some bearing on price setting.

Many products and services are susceptible to fluctuations in the **economy** when there is a large number of unemployed workers or when wages are stagnant. Often, prices need to be set lower. Luxury prices, in particular, may drop when the economy is in a downturn. Government regulations can also be a significant factor in pricing products or services, depending on what those regulations control over the product or service.[4]

Marketing Mix Issues

Price can also be influenced by what marketing method is used and how the other elements of the marketing mix are combined.[5] If, for example, distribution lines require several intermediaries, the price of the good or service may go up. If consumers are provided service after their purchase, that service may add on costs that will increase the price. In fact, different prices may be charged for the same product or service if the product or service has additional value added through the distribution channel. A product or service that may be in the decline stage of the product life cycle could lower the price from the original price set.[6]

Pricing Strategies

A business has a delicate balancing act when setting a price. The lowest price a business will offer (typically) is the cost to produce and distribute the good or service.[7] Anything added to this amount is profit. At the other end of the spectrum, the highest price a business will offer is one that does not eliminate demand. Any higher, and demand will not be great enough to sell the products or services. Within the "sweet spot" are places where profit is less or more—finding the exact location where profit and demand meet can be challenging, particularly given that the strategy to do so requires an understanding and analysis of many internal and external factors.

Cost-Based Pricing

Cost-based pricing, also known as cost-plus pricing or markup pricing, is a strategy whereby the business calculates the total cost to create the product or service and then adds a percentage onto that total cost to set the price.[8] The difference between cost and price is the profit level. If a company selling toothpaste spends $2.50 to produce the toothpaste and wants to make a 50% profit, the price of the toothpaste would be $3.75, with $2.50 going toward cost and $1.25 going toward profit. Generally, providers of physical products are more likely to use cost-based pricing than are providers of services, which are typically less costly to produce but provide greater value to the consumer.

Value-Based Pricing
For a business that is extremely aware of its consumers and their willingness to purchase and pay for a product or service, value-based pricing can work to build relationships and strengthen the brand. In value-based pricing, the business allows the consumer to pay less than the amount they feel the value is worth by setting a price lower than the consumer is actually willing to pay.[9] Value-based pricing allows the business to increase customer loyalty and provides an opportunity to focus on the consumer in areas such as service and market research instead of generating the largest, immediate profit. The aim of value-based pricing is to increase market share and profits over time.

Penetration Pricing
Penetration pricing may not generate a profit as its function is to enter a market or disrupt it. In penetration pricing, the business sets a substantially low price compared to value to make a sudden impact in the market and quickly generate a presence.[10] Because penetration pricing generates presence and not profit, it is not sustainable in the long-term, as the company will come into the market with an extremely low price. Once the brand and product are established, the corporation will transition to a different pricing strategy.

Competition Pricing

In competition pricing, or competition-based pricing, businesses look at competitors who offer similar value and weigh the price based on the competitor's pricing.[11] If consumers feel that a business offers greater value than the competitor's, the business can then price the product or service higher. If consumers feel the value offered by the competitor is higher, the business may set a lower price than the competitor. In competition pricing, businesses must be aware of what sorts of offerings provide similar value to a consumer. This comparison can be tricky, especially when most or all of the value derived from a product or service is exclusive to the consumer.

In competition pricing, a business must also know the strength of the competitor's offering. If the competitor offers a poor product in exchange for a lower price, the business may add value to its product or service in order to charge a premium. If the competition is priced high compared to value, however, the business may lower prices to maximize sales and outsell the competitor. The purpose of competition pricing is not to beat or even match a competitor's prices but to set sales prices in such a way that value and price compare favorably to the competitor's, to maximize value to the consumer.

Price Skimming
Price skimming is at the opposite end of the spectrum from competition pricing. A business utilizes price skimming by entering the market with an extremely high price compared to its value in order to generate the largest profit.[12] Over time, the price is lowered as demand for the product at the higher price recedes. The advantage to price skimming is that it allows the company to make up for advanced costs for research and development of the product or service. As the product or service becomes less relevant, the price can be lowered. The initial high price of a cell phone, which lowers as later models are released, is an example of price skimming.

Psychological Pricing
As the name implies, a psychological pricing strategy has to do with the psychological perception of the consumer. People may wonder why a product sold for $0.99 is not simply priced at the exact dollar value, one cent higher. The marketer is choosing to play on the consumers' psychology. Ninety-nine cents appears to be a better bargain than one dollar. The same is true with $1.99, $2.99, or any value ending in $0.99. This strategy is sometimes referred to as the *left-digit-effect*.[13] As Lin and Wang describe the effect, in three-digit integers such as $4.99 and $5.00, with different leftmost digits (the 4 and 5), consumers perceive the price discount to be larger when the left digit is smaller (the 4).[14] The ninety-nine cents stall the progression to the next full dollar (the leftmost digit) and, therefore, seems deceptively less expensive. Another form of psychological pricing is placing a less expensive item next to a more expensive item to entice the consumer to think of the less expensive item as a deal. Psychological pricing is often used with the discount methodology of *Bogo* or *buy one get one*. Finally, changing the color, font size, or shape of pricing information can also affect the consumer's psychological perception.

Bundle Pricing

The process where two or more products are bundled together is called bundle pricing.[15] Products or services may be sold separately or as a bundle. In some cases, products or services may only be sold as a bundle. In either case, the idea is to create higher customer satisfaction with a product offering of improved value.[16] Most consumers prefer to purchase a bundle if it is a discount over the individual prices of the included products or services. Bundle pricing can also allow the consumer to be introduced to a second product, which they get as part of the bundle. For businesses, bundle pricing usually drives sales and results in higher profits. It is also advantageous to businesses because it can lower marketing costs by promoting multiple products using the marketing and sales resources of a single product.

Premium Pricing

In premium pricing, also known as luxury pricing or prestige pricing, a company sets the price high to communicate that they have an exclusive, expensive product or service.[17] The focus of premium pricing is on the product's total value as perceived by the consumer and less about the actual cost of producing the product or service. Premium pricing is directly related to brand awareness and brand perception. Brands that use premium pricing are known for their high value relative to their competitors. Often, premium pricing appears in fashion or technology, where products can be priced high and considered luxurious or exclusive.

Optional Pricing

Optional pricing is the process where the company has a base price for a product or service that offers multiple options, each with an additional charge. The options themselves add value to the initial product. Cars are an excellent example of optional pricing, as the base model car comes with a particular sticker price and all sorts of options are available, such as sunroofs, sound packages, and more. Computers are also an excellent example of optional pricing, as the base model of a computer will have several add-ons available at additional cost.

Product-Line Pricing

In a product-line pricing strategy, the business needs to consider all the products in a distinct product line in relation to one another. Prices must be stepped into levels by value, quality, and price that reflect the cost of each individual product. The price must also reflect the relationship of each product to the others in the product line. For example, some customers may want a high-end product, and others might prefer to spend less and buy a low-end or mid-range product. This strategy often includes "horizontal differentiation," where features, add-ons, and aesthetic differences are what separates the product levels.[18]

The Pricing Mix and Balancing Price

Determining the best pricing strategy can often be difficult because the ultimate goal relies upon how consumers will respond to the price. The price, however, must be set in such a way as to, ultimately, generate a profit for the company. Determining how to price the product or service requires a balance of many different factors. For example, as discussed, overall product development costs are an important factor in considering a price, but manufacturing costs are also important. As noted, price can be affected by its relationship to competition. Additionally, corporations must determine the level or margin of profit required and determine what discounts or seasonal effects might occur that could change buying habits. They must consider the product or service's lifecycle when determining the price and decide on what price-setting methods they intend to use.

What Is Ease of Access?

For each of the three previous Es, education, experience, and environment, we have shown the structures and frameworks that encapsulate each of those terms as concepts. Also noted were the works done in specific fields with the notion of experience being relatively new to the management world, though perhaps not to the arts. Each of those constructs brings to mind the type of work being done within them and shows how that work parallels nicely with the engagement edge and where it purports to lead us. The concept of ease of access, however, is not a construct as readily understood or deconstructed, as it relies on two words, *ease* and *access*. Although common terms, they have a more complex meaning when used together. To unravel the notion of ease of access, we start by defining what the words mean in other usages to explain how the concept of ease of access functions in the engagement edge.

Ease

Ease is defined as "comfort, relaxation and freedom from pain, stress, or anxiety." Certainly, arts organizations work to ensure the comfort of their audiences, so this part of the definition fits us very well. One might make the same argument about relaxation. However, arts leaders cannot always guarantee that an artistic experience will be relaxing. Of course, they want audiences to be free of pain, but this is really outside the purview of the engagement edge. Freedom from stress and anxiety, however, is a vitally important component for arts organizations to consider, as many potential consumers do not attend because they may feel that the process of attending the arts creates stress and anxiety. In this window, engagement becomes vital through education, and where we see the construct of ease of access having its greatest impact.

One can also "ease" the agitation and worry of others. In this sense, we see the full-throated strength of the term *ease*, because in the nonprofit arts, we see education as the path to easing agitation or worry about what is to happen. It is from this place that educational objectives for our potential audience emerge.

Another usage of the term *ease* that fits the model of the engagement edge is the practice of easing into things, moving slowly, carefully, and deliberately toward an end state. In the process of engagement, we look for an opportunity to do exactly that. To be fully engaged, one must be eased into the engagement, so ease is a part of that process.

We might also think of the word *ease* as a means to loosen the tension or pressure felt in a situation. The function of ease is to make the process of connecting two things manageable. The engagement edge considers two elements: the nonprofit arts experience and the consumer. The nonprofit arts organization must ease new audience members into the experience carefully while simultaneously reducing, lowering, and eliminating barriers.

One might also think that a life can be at ease if it is free from financial burdens and stress. Ease can mean the state of being free from stress generally and totally, not just free of financial stress.

We can loosen tension and burdens when we ease the pressure on them. In this sense, ease focuses on physical restraints themselves, causing those restraints to be minimized, reduced, or eliminated. In the nonprofit arts, restraints abound and vary from individual to individual, but the arts organizations can ease some of those restraints. They can make things less difficult and reduce the challenges obstacles can present by easing issues to manageable levels. The engagement edge recognizes the manageable levels that become key to increasing participation in the nonprofit arts experience. Although price is certainly one of those obstacles, it is by far not the only one. It serves as a nice example, however, of how barriers like price can be lowered, minimized, or even removed.

Arts organizations offer a respite; The nonprofit arts experience that may be a break from the daily burdens of life in the form of intellectual and emotional escape. This sort of respite is a means for providing ease. **Although there may be myriad ways arts organizations can provide a hiatus from daily life through experiences, we do not see this as a primary driving factor of the conceptual framework of ease of access but see it as a secondary benefit. In other words, providing respite may not be a goal of our engagement efforts, but it is certainly an anticipated byproduct.**

Access

When originally developing the engagement edge, we considered the construct of *exchange* as a replacement for *price* but found the usage too utilitarian, and primarily focused on money. Since money is the explicit challenge, mission-driven nonprofit arts organizations struggle within the context of price, and so it seemed imprecise. We toyed with *ease of exchange*, drawing on Pine and Gilmore's strategy to reduce obstacles and impediments for the consumer, but still struggled with leaning toward the dominant term being *exchange*. Although an exchange does occur in this construct, there are many obstacles a potential audience member must overcome that are not based on an exchange in which two parties exchange value. Many of these obstacles are intangible, unmeasurable, and not elastic enough to allow us to determine where a perfect balance exists, particularly because the total obstacles may be fluid and change from person to person. Instead, we chose to consider that the exchange required constant assessment to make it easy for a potential audience member to gain access. Hence, the construct becomes ease of access, something that works with and for the other Es of education, experience, and environment.

Arts organizations can think of *access* as the permission or means to use, approach, or enter a physical location or experience. Primarily, what we mean when we discuss ease of access is an attempt to make the experience in its physical location as barrier-free as possible. The term can also mean the permission to use, approach, or take advantage of the emotional discharge of the art itself. This emotional connection is certainly a second way we grant permission to access, but the idea is much more deeply ingrained in the individual than the notion of physical access.

Access can also mean not only that we can use or enter a physical location, but it can mean that we have the right to do so without impediment or interruption. Access means, or at least implies, that barriers have been removed to the point that usage is unencumbered.

Access can also demonstrate an outburst of emotion. One might say a person had an access of rage. Though this older usage may not seem perfectly fitting to the engagement edge, it is not lost on us that the intrinsic value of emotional exchange from art to consumer (and occasionally from consumer to consumer) is related to the notion of emotional outburst.

Finally, access can be used as a verb to mean that we have accessed or can access something. This is the usage of access that is vital to the Americans with Disabilities Act (ADA) in the United States. The ADA prohibits discrimination to access based on disability. Issues related to the ADA are essential considerations for nonprofit arts organizations. Chapter 14 further explores ADA issues in venues.

Final Thoughts Defining Ease of Access

Our definition of the construct of ease of access sees the concept as the processes through which an individual or group works for the benefit of others to make use or attendance less complicated through any means necessary. This idea implies that the overall function of ease of access is to seek access points, and to reduce, lower, or eliminate barriers and obstacles that could deter use or participation. **Ease of access is about finding every connective point and making certain it is as open, inviting, welcoming, and as barrier-free as possible.** In this sense, we see the parallels to the social construct of accessibility, and believe the two views are compatible. Chapter 14 further defines the construct and application of ease of access.

13
Price and the Arts

It is impossible to consider the concept of price without first reiterating what a product or service is, as the price is affixed directly to that product or service. In the strictest sense, price has to do with the amount of money we exchange for a product or service. This definition, however, is limited to actual monetary exchange and neglects to consider the other costs that the consumer must expend. If the price requires a consumer to travel to a ticket office to secure their ticket, there is the additional expense of fuel, insurance, and wear and tear on a vehicle as well as their time. The total of all the values that consumers must put forth to access the product or service is what makes up the notion of price.

Before the chapter digs into the failings of the price construct for the arts, it begins by examining how the marketing mix defines product or service to align the construct of price appropriately. First, we have noted that products are items for sale and anything that can be sold to a consumer for attention, ownership, usage, or consumption, all of which must satisfy a need or want. As McCarthy wrote, a product or service, "has the capacity to provide satisfaction, use, or perhaps the profit desired by the consumer."[1]

The seller possesses a product or service that the consumer wants or needs. The buyer has something that the seller wants or needs—money—and they are willing to invest their time and effort into getting their money to the seller in exchange for access to the good or service they have available to satisfy the buyer's need or want. The *total product* is a combination of the *physical product* plus the *extensive product*, which is made up of things like the company's brand, packaging, service, promises, and more. This complex notion of product is then affixed with a price that some consumers are willing to expend to access the product. According to McCarthy, the product does not have to "include a physical product at all," and can be exchanged with "either taking away or giving you anything tangible," as long as it "satisfies needs, and therefore provides a product in the sense," that we use product.[2]

The case of Judith Drexel and Concert Pricing presents examples of pricing issues that regularly challenge and hamper nonprofit arts organizations.

The Case of Judith Drexel and Concert Pricing

Judith Drexel has worked for classical music presenters and producers since she was in college. Her love of music began as a child. "My parents used to play all types of classical music for us when we were children. By the time we were ten or eleven, my sister and I were begging my parents for violin lessons." Drexel and her family lived in a rural part of Kansas, where access to a violin teacher was challenging. Instead, they were both enrolled in piano lessons. "Neither of us got very far in our studies. By high school, we had other priorities, and classical music just fell off my radar."

For Drexel, that all changed in her sophomore year of college when she volunteered to usher at a local symphony to earn required community service hours. "I couldn't believe that they would count it as community service. I got to help people find their seats, talk with them about the concert, and experience the concert for myself." By the end of the semester, she had earned the forty hours of community service required for the year. "I liked it so much that I told a white lie and said I needed to earn another 40 for the next semester. For some reason, I felt that I needed to provide a reason I wanted to come back rather than just saying that I enjoyed volunteering." She signed up for every possible time that she was available and continued to work with the orchestra that summer rather than going home.

Over the summer, she assisted in the box office and worked as an assistant to the house manager for their summer concert series. By the end of summer, she knew everyone who worked in management and many of the patrons as well. During the next school year, she stayed active with the organization by taking on a part-time job in the box office. "That fall I seriously considered changing my major to music, which, in retrospect, was a terrible idea since I didn't play any instruments other than those couple years of piano from middle school. I just knew that whatever I did when I graduated had to be something in the music world."

In her sophomore year, one of her courses had her create a hypothetical public relations plan for an organization of her choice. She selected the local symphony and wrote several press releases for upcoming events as part of the hypothetical assignment. "My first attempts weren't very good, but throughout the semester, we adjusted our writing with the teacher's feedback. By the end of the class, I had a couple of press releases I was really proud of." She shared the project with some of the staff members at the symphony. "Lisa [Shelley], who had been writing all of their press releases, invited me to do a few drafts and work with her on announcing the next season. It felt like I finally found something that I could contribute from my studies."

Drexel's involvement with the orchestra went on for the remainder of her time in college, and finally, when she graduated, they offered her a job. "I didn't fully realize how lucky I was at the time. But, they really changed my life." Her job was in public relations and marketing. At the symphony, public relations and marketing were both managed by Shelley, and Drexel was hired into a new position to be her assistant.

One of her first tasks on the job was to recommend pricing for the following season. "I'd always figured that determining the price was a box office job or the executive director's job rather than marketing. I had no idea where to begin other than looking at the prices from the previous year." Shelley had shared that they wanted her to determine how to make the income from ticket sales as high as possible without losing their audience base. Their audience was primarily made up of senior citizens who purchased tickets with a senior discount. "The discount really felt like a gimmick, they would save maybe two or three dollars on their fifty-dollar tickets, so it wasn't much of a savings."

Shelley advised Drexel that they could only bring the price up slightly for each type of ticket, or the audience would notice. "To me that just seemed like a strange way to price something. Basically, we were trying to hide how we valued the symphony. It didn't feel right, so I started doing some research." Drexel started by comparing their pricing to other symphony orchestras around the country of a similar size. She found that pricing was remarkably varied. Orchestras of a similar size and caliber in similar cities charged between $26.00 and $72.00 for their tickets. Their orchestra was somewhere in the middle, with most events topping out at $55.00 for the most expensive ticket. "Initially, I figured we could just price ourselves at the same prices as the most expensive similar orchestra. Lisa didn't like that idea because she felt that the people wouldn't want to pay much more than they had been."

Drexel decided to reach out to a teacher from her college. She had taken an introduction to marketing course and recalled that the teacher had talked about pricing. "I went to his office, and we talked about the symphony and my pricing project. He gave me so much material about how I could determine pricing." Although she was initially overwhelmed, she returned home and went through the pricing options he recommended step by step. None of the strategies he recommended seemed to match the incremental annual increase the orchestra had been doing.

The first possible method, and where her former teacher recommended she begin, was with cost pricing. Cost pricing is when the customer's price is determined based on the cost to produce the product. She didn't like the idea of cost pricing because each concert had a different budget, and she knew that the orchestra would want price consistency across the different concerts. Also, if she took the budget for each concert, and split the operating expenses of the administration among them, the total price per ticket far surpassed even the most expensive of the comparable orchestra ticket prices.

She reviewed penetration pricing, but since the orchestra had been in existence for so long, they certainly didn't need to reduce pricing to gain a market advantage. Competition pricing was also not a match since their closest competitor was more than one hundred miles away. "I remember thinking, well, there is no real competition for symphony orchestras, so I didn't have any organization to try to undercut. And besides that, we wanted to raise prices."

Drexel was drawn to price skimming as a possible strategy. Price skimming had the higher established revenue potential that Shelley valued. The orchestra had the added benefit of having no local competitors, so Drexel thought a higher price would not cause audience members to select another orchestra. Over time, however, price skimming is meant to offset the advanced costs of a product and later be reduced. People who want the best, newest products will pay the higher price; others who are more price-averse will opt to wait until the product is available at a lower price. "The idea of offsetting the high production costs was really appealing; I didn't see how that could possibly work at the symphony, though, since we only held concerts for one or two weekends at a time. We would need to run for months to do any kind of strategy like [price skimming]."

Drexel thinks that she may have reviewed more than twenty variants of pricing strategies. "Honestly, I was just getting frustrated. Most of the pricing strategies are about bringing new products into the market. And that's really what we do since we were constantly producing new concerts. At the same time, though, I had this feeling like somehow it wasn't always a new product, but it was a variation on our service." Drexel had clearly identified a challenge in pricing the arts. She was faced with a decision: treat every concert like it's a new product or consider the full season of concerts like a single offering with different components. "Neither felt right, but I had to choose. We rolled out each concert as its own event, with different poster art and a splashy announcement, so yeah, I decided each concert was a new product. But all these years later, I still go back and forth on this."

Ultimately, Drexel settled on premium pricing as her lens in establishing price. This method seemed the closest match for their audience base because it indicated a high-end product produced by an established brand. The orchestra was the only one within the geographic area, so they were certainly the most established. Premium pricing also centers on the consumer's perceived value rather than on the actual cost of the product. "In that way, it seemed like a perfect fit because when I considered cost pricing, there was no way to get the ticket price anywhere near covering the cost of production. So, by premium pricing, I got to ignore the actual cost and focus instead on the quality of the concerts."

This focus is, of course, the opposite of the function of premium pricing in for-profit corporations. The cost to produce the product should be significantly less than the product's price in premium pricing. The corporation does not factor in the cost to produce the product because they charge more for exclusivity and high prestige. For example, when purchasing a handbag from Walmart, a customer expects to pay a low price. Walmart's pricing structure is a cost-based pricing system in which a percentage of profit is added to the cost of each item. When purchasing a handbag from Louis Vuitton, the consumer expects to pay a much higher price. Although the cost to create the Louis Vuitton handbag is greater than the Walmart bag, their costs are far closer together than the pricing for the items because Louis Vuitton uses premium pricing.

Drexel began putting her proposal together to do premium pricing for the orchestra. With Shelley's permission, she reached out to one hundred patrons with a survey to establish how they valued their experience at the concerts. "Doing research is such an important part of managing a business, and this was the first time the orchestra had ever done any type of survey." Drexel was surprised by the results. Most patrons indicated that they felt the orchestra was worth more than the pricing they were currently paying. They also indicated, however, that they would be unwilling to pay more than the current ticket prices. Several people even raised concerns that the orchestra might eliminate the senior discount. "It was clear from the results that our audience felt that the orchestra was a world-class experience, but that they wanted to receive discounted prices. I decided to combine the premium pricing to create the world-class type of perception and provide deep discounts to maintain the loyalty of our base."

For the proposal, Drexel recommended transitioning the highest price ticket from $55.00 to $90.00 each. The $90.00 was the premium price which would then be discounted to a new high price of $70.00. Under her proposal, the average ticket price for the organization would rise between $10.00 to $15.00. This difference of $10.00–$15.00 per ticket would cause the meaningful change that Shelley had indicated the organization needed. "I'd never, and still haven't seen a mouth drop open quite like Lisa's did when I proposed a $90.00 top ticket price. I explained my reasoning and the survey, but she made it clear that it was not going to happen." Shelley was concerned about the initial sticker shock of a $90.00 price for tickets. Instead, they used Drexel's plan and created a top ticket price of $68.00 with a discount of $10.00 to make the top ticket price $58.00. "In the end, we just raised the ticket prices a couple of dollars and created a lot of confusion for our audience. We basically sold the same number of tickets that we always had and ended up with about a 5% boost in revenue." Shelley was very happy with the increase.

The following year, Drexel shared, they decided to eliminate the discount, which was causing customer confusion, and simply moved the price to a $60.00 top price ticket. "That didn't go so well. We tried to eliminate the confusion of the high price from the previous year, but everyone still expected to get $10.00 off . . . which we, obviously, weren't going to do on a $60.00 ticket. They still got their senior discount of a couple of dollars, but they weren't happy with that anymore." Over time, the orchestra's audience got used to the slight annual ticket increases. The organization did not see any significant changes in the number of audience members each year.

Drexel shared another experience she had several years later when she worked at a new classical music festival. She was working as their PR director and was asked to weigh in on the pricing. "At first, I really didn't want to after the last pricing situation, but the [festival] management was much more flexible in what the pricing could be." She had heard of some arts organizations offering "pay what you want" or "pay what you can" pricing. They decided to set prices for most of the events but offer several "pay what you want" concerts. "It just felt good to me not to have to tell people how much to pay. I liked the idea of it. Many people would come and ask what we suggest they pay, and I would just say, 'you get to choose what it's worth to you,' but many people still didn't know how much to give." Previously, you have read about how the product of the arts is not complete until the audience experiences it—since the experience is the product. Asking people to value the product in advance of the experience causes a real challenge. How can they be expected to value something that doesn't yet exist? Drexel indicated a similar sentiment, "I really should have asked them to pay on their way out. The concert was so good [that] it was difficult not to be swept up in the emotion, which I guess might have added to the experience and caused people to give more."

Drexel still works in both PR and marketing. She often has assistants who work on all aspects of her PR and marketing, including pricing. "When they come to me now, I say, go and learn about pricing like I did. But I always warn them, pricing in the arts isn't a science. At the end of the day, we're just going to pick what feels right, and price will be the amount that's the most we think the audience will pay."

Donations

The arts actually provide two core products, one with the art at its center, which we have referred to as the arts experience. Arts organizations traditionally think of it as the product. However, nonprofit arts organizations typically have a second offering that exists to mediate the issue of pricing the art: donations.

One might think of the donation as a voluntary way to pay more than requested by the organization, but this does not negate the fact that the donation satisfies personal needs or wants within the community member, separate and distinct from the art itself. Although one may want to think of a donation as something inseparably linked to the art, that is not the case. The donation, like the art itself, is linked to the organization. By every standard and unique definition of product readily available and applicable, in the way the marketing mix defines a product, the donation is indeed a product: a product that did not exist in its current, 501(c)(3) tax-exempt form when the marketing mix and the four Ps were proposed.

The donation is important to price because, as stated, it mediates the actual aggregate amount of money consumers spend to access the artistic experience. The oft-heard notion that the organization brings in only 60% through ticket sales, makes it clear that the remaining 40% of revenue required to run the organization and provide the art comes through donations. So, in total, every ticket sale brings in only approximately 60% of the money required to achieve a revenue-neutral position for that sale. An additional 40% must be secured from that patron or elsewhere to cover the total cost to the organization for providing said art.

Price as Access

The concept of price as a monetary figure is part of a larger construct, and semantically, McCarthy used the term *price* because of the P, but the construct is clearly more than the understood concept of money. We might want to think of price as the "price of access" or the monetary cost associated with access to the product or service. In this way, there are other items in addition to price that affect the overall cost of access to the consumer. **The fact that donations have a varying effect on the total financial resources of the organization is paramount. Price in the arts is a moveable target, never standing still long enough to be labeled accurately.** That is true because price is connected to donations. It is impossible from one minute to the next to know where the total price must land to meet overall expenses for creating and presenting the art.

It is not surprising, then, that regardless of the price charged to the arts consumer, and no matter how concerned arts organizations are about pricing their art at the highest possible level, the demographic profile of the consumer does not appear to change.[3] The same demographics are noted even when there is no admission charged, such as at a free museum. This statistic is in direct contrast to the traditional approach of offering multiple prices for different targeted segments. The organization could maximize efficiency and create an artistic experience that is a luxury good for those wanting a premium experience and a deal for bargain hunters.[4]

Prices to arts experiences, however, tend to remain fixed or static with some discounting based on seating location, age, affiliation, or other factors (regardless of donation income). A dance troupe charges $30 per ticket, regardless of the total cost of creating and presenting that event and the total value to the consumer. In the arts, the intrinsic value varies drastically between patrons, but determining a dollar value with a numerical measurement appears to be the only way to set price as traditionally, intangible property such as an arts event is priced strictly by monetary value. For this reason, price is disassociated with value when referring to the nonprofit arts. Certainly, intrinsic value exists for any purchase, but because the arts offer an experience that is almost entirely determined by the value gained individually by each attendee, a generalized monetary price cannot accurately reflect the full value of the event.

Further, the concept of price has to do with the maximum amount a company can charge for a product or service relative to cost as a means for maximizing profit. **Because nonprofit arts organizations do not concern themselves with profitability, but rather sustainability and service, price as a monetary construct does not belong when discussing nonprofit arts organizations as its function is uniquely different.** Through the larger construct of ease of access, monetary price is a piece, but only a piece, much like the monetary price is only a piece of the larger construct of price.

To explore more deeply, we see price assuming the mantle of average perceived value, with the assumption that the two ends of the spectrum of perceived values do not sway too far. For example, all consumers at Walmart likely have a sense of the perceived value of goods purchased. The same can be said of customers at Mercedes-Benz. For the arts, however, some audience members might perceive the value to be in the Walmart range, and others might perceive it to be in the Mercedes-Benz range. The average price between those could easily dissuade both those parties from purchasing. When access is eased for the consumer, however, it becomes possible to consider access at the individual consumer level, providing both value and increased monetary exchange for individually crafted experiences resulting from consumer engagement.

Unlike price, ease of access is a welcoming term, and it is intended to be so. **Price suggests a sacrifice on the part of the consumer. Ease of access, of which price is a part within the engagement edge conception, implies that the burden caused to the consumer in the exchange is being reduced or eased.** Because the arts are an experience, expanding the analysis of product value beyond a one-dimensional exchange is essential in order to capture the value generated in intrinsic rewards to each consumer. We have attempted to capture this value by using average pricing based on monetary value, but we know this falls far short of truly capturing a consumer's determination of worth, especially when donations are factored in.

The Lease

Like most leases, we think of the use of an artistic experience as an opportunity to occupy a space for a limited period of time. The seat in the theater or the room in the museum is the location that will be of value when value is added to them. The lease is of little value during any period when no artistic offering is occurring, but while the art offering occurs, the value proposition is raised. Other value-added benefits simply increase the overall value, but the offering itself has the greatest power in determining value for the consumer. Viewing the core product as space to lease helps "us look at how we go about creating value for the arts consumer because it starts with a blank space, an empty room, or an empty seat. It also helps us to understand the total value we add to that space."[5]

Pay What You Can

"For ages, street musicians have used this [*pay-what-you-can*] pricing mechanism to make a living; museums, such as the Metropolitan Museum of Art in New York, and other not-for-profit organizations routinely let visitors decide how much they pay."[6] This method is a unique way to determine or establish the value of any offering. It allows the determinant of the value, the consumer, to assess the value in terms of monetary price. When attending a street performance, however, the audience member can pay for their viewing before, during, or after. In the case of Judith Drexel, pay what you can pricing did not work because audience members could not know how they valued the concert until after they experienced it. The pricing approach also provides an opportunity for people with less privilege who may otherwise not be able to visit the venue. Beyond the arts, there are very few examples of companies permitting the consumer to set the price. Whether implicitly or explicitly, arts organizations that do this have recognized the incongruency in the P of price and have shifted to allowing each consumer to make their subjective opinion of value. They then trust that the consumer will pay the appropriately determined amount based on its worth relative to what they can afford. It certainly allows for greater ease of access, though no matter who throws darts at the pricing dartboard, the audience or the organization, the end result is no different. Price does not appropriately capture value in the arts, and there may be no way to do so accurately.

It is incumbent upon the arts organization to clearly understand the total overall value to the consumer. This range, however, exists on a very large spectrum, based on intrinsic decision-making by consumers. Sheth suggested this issue as leading to a newer marketing paradigm because this practice requires the organization to have its pulse perfectly on the perception by the consumer, which determines how the organization reacts to the perception.[7] The organization can lower or raise numerical price or add or subtract value to the experience to reshape value in the consumer's mind. However, because value is so drastically subjective in the arts, these processes are less effective (or completely ineffective). Sheth found that in a new marketing paradigm, the focus placed on delivering and creating value by developing and nurturing customer relationships takes precedence over making exchanges satisfactory. In other words, relationships now also mediate the hard cost of price. Defining engagement by the exchange means that we must focus on factors that expand beyond simple cost and profit and the associated pricing components. Because this new marketing paradigm is relationship-focused, price becomes a very small facet in the exchange, which we refer to as ease of access.

Kolb found that 43% of consumers note they would not attend the arts due to reasons having to do with ease of access other than price, and only 31% found that price was the primary barrier to attendance.[8] What were those barriers to ease of access that preclude people from attending? First, they noted they had difficulty finding enough information about the art they would be viewing to feel informed enough to attend. Certainly, this is a commentary on lack of education and not a desire for more promotional materials. Second, even if they found the information they thought was necessary, it did not supply the right or appropriate information or was not thorough enough to help them understand the experience they would be enjoying. Again, this is directly related to education and not promotion. Third, they found it difficult to find peer support for their decision to want to attend. Again, we see this as a failing of education. If the person who is interested in attending feels educated enough to do so, but they have difficulty in educating or supplying appropriate educational materials to their peers to gain companionship or support for their choice, this clearly demonstrates an interplay between education and ease of access. Although we have not suggested all the ways in which an arts organization might ease access for consumers, in Kolb's study, 69% of respondents felt access to the arts experience would be eased substantially if food was readily available either before or after the offering. Because the process of attending the arts is time-consuming, and often intersects with lunch or dinner hours, providing food is another way to ease access to the art.

Pricing Factors

Chapter 12 discussed four pricing factors that contribute to the decision-making process in determining price: cost, demand, competition, and the purchasing power of the consumer. The following reveals how they relate to the nonprofit arts:

Cost is a main factor for determining price. As we have seen with cost-based pricing, the cost is the amount of money required by the consumer to pay to recoup all money invested into the creation of the product, including a portion of general and administrative expenses relative to the product or service. In order to ascertain the average per sale cost, we must make an accurate projection of the total number of units we expect to sell. Suppose an arts organization can expect to sell 2,000 tickets to an event and the total cost to produce the event was $200,000. The average cost per ticket is $100. On top of this amount, a business will add a margin for profit. Because the nonprofit arts organization is not concerned with profit, this final piece is unnecessary. If the organization only sells 1,500 tickets, however, the art will have been created at a loss.

Additionally, $100 may be too expensive for enough community members to purchase tickets, so sales could drop even lower, so the organization may choose to set the price at a more palatable $50 and sell 4,000 tickets to break even. As we mentioned, donations offset some of the gross income necessary to offset the total cost. The cost factor may be part of pricing in a for-profit corporation, but it bears little resemblance to the actual operations of a nonprofit arts organization.

Demand is a construct that does work for arts organizations, though time is a limiting factor. If a toothpaste manufacturer creates 2,000 tubes of toothpaste and the tubes do not sell as quickly as anticipated, then time will allow for the slow demand to make up for it. The tubes of toothpaste may sell more slowly than expected, but they will eventually be sold, possibly at a slightly higher cost due to the slow sales since the stock may incur storage costs. For the nonprofit arts, if demand is slow, there simply will not be enough tickets sold, as the art ceases to exist after its final presentation. Certainly, the art could be presented over more time to ensure enough sales to meet costs.

Because costs are higher than the demand for a single ticket, however, by extending the duration of the presentation, the arts organization would increase the total cost at a pace higher than the revenue generated, so the longer the art is presented in this scenario, the greater the loss.

Competition is another important pricing factor. The nonprofit arts struggle to determine who the competition is. Certainly, we can identify other arts organizations as competing for the same (or similar) community members. Hollywood might also be seen as competition, including streaming services, video-on-demand, home role-playing games, and other forms of purchasable entertainment options. Theme parks, bowling alleys, miniature golf courses, and the like may also be considered competition. Restaurants provide a social experience similar to the nonprofit arts but have fewer restrictive requirements such as a set time at which patrons may enjoy their experience. Anywhere discretionary income is spent might be considered competition for a nonprofit arts organization, depending on the consumer. Because the spending is discretionary, each consumer will have, in their mind, what competes for that money and what does not, and every consumer may have a different perspective on this issue.

Variable Pricing

One type of pricing strategy that we have not addressed is *variable pricing*, sometimes known as *dynamic pricing*.[9] Bernard Jacobs of the Shubert Organization once said that Broadway will always struggle with pricing issues until they establish a variable pricing scheme. Variable pricing is a strategy that allows the organization to charge different prices at different purchase points as the market demands. Auctions are a sort of variable pricing, as are stock markets and electricity purchases. A closely related form of variable pricing that has been used minimally in the arts is *real-time pricing*, which is akin to airline pricing. In this scheme, prices are adjusted in real-time (or close to real-time) based on immediate demand. In the case of an arts organization, this would mean evaluating demand constantly and then adjusting prices based on those evaluations. Airlines have the volume, prices, technology, and demand to warrant the intensive and constant research that real-time pricing requires. Arts organizations may capture a margin of additional revenue from real-time pricing, but the trade-off in terms of expenses appears to not be worthwhile—even in the for-profit structure of Broadway.

Objective Setting

Chapter 12 addressed objective-setting for determining pricing strategy, stating that the organization must determine the appropriate objective for their strategy. A company that wishes to expand its reach may set price points lower to realize greater sales volume, while higher prices are likely warranted if the objective is to generate the greatest profit per unit of product. For nonprofit arts organizations, although a goal may be to generate revenue above the amount of total product cost (what would traditionally be considered the profit), if the product cost is already higher than the market can bear and has been offset by donations, the higher price strategy will not work for a high-revenue objective. Arts organizations already typically function by setting prices lower than are sustainable for an organization, with the objective being sustainability.[10] Those two concepts are at odds with one another, and yet they are the reality of the situation for most nonprofit arts organizations. Marketers might say that this situation is a precursor to bankruptcy and closing.

Although we noted that to set price points, one must determine the pricing objectives, without profit as one objective, survival seems to become the dominant factor in pricing. Maximize income as much as possible, and hope that donations offset the total amount of loss relative to cost.

Pricing Strategies

We have addressed the *cost-based* or *cost-plus* strategies whereby an organization determines the total cost per product to create the product and then adds on an amount equal to the net profit for the sale. Because nonprofit arts organizations struggle to reach break-even, this strategy appears largely useless. Even if an arts organization happens to be able to charge a *cost-plus* price, it is not adding on a profit, but a buffer, as the notion of profits is directly related to ownership. Furthermore, because nonprofits are for the public good, they have no owners except the public to whom the benefits of any "profit" would flow via the organization's services.

Value-based pricing occurs when the organization sets a price lower than the product or service is worth to generate sales. This strategy sounds most closely related to nonprofit arts organizations, and in fact, pay-what-you-can is a variant of value-based pricing. The concept works only when we know the actual value of our product or service to the consumer, as well as the actual cost for each product or service sold. In the arts, the value is intrinsic and variable to each audience member, and the range of value is so broad that we cannot use average value among consumers. Hence, pay-what-you-can allows consumers to make that value determination and trusts them to pay accordingly.

Sadly, because price also influences the perception of quality, the idea of running an entire organization based on pay-what-you-can would not be favorable, nor would it provide a structure to create sustainability.

We might consider a competitive pricing strategy, wherein we look to the value and price of the competition and set our prices relative to the offerings they provide. Because the value of the nonprofit arts is subjective and varies so greatly from consumer to consumer, competitive pricing is a bit like comparing the price of a zebra to the price of a giraffe.

Because nonprofit arts organizations already struggle with setting prices below the total cost of creating the art and then backfilling revenue with donations, the idea of *price skimming*, where the organization launches a product with a significantly high price that lowers as demand recedes, is untenable. The same can be said for premium pricing, where the price is intentionally set high to make the product or service appear luxurious and exclusive. One could argue that nonprofit arts organizations may already fall into this category while still not generating enough income from sales to offset costs. Consider that tickets to the Metropolitan Opera in New York City, a nonprofit arts organization, can be almost $1000.

Of all the pricing strategies available to us, optional pricing may be the best fit for nonprofit arts organizations. **Because optional pricing allows us to customize a product or service by adding or deleting value-added pieces, we can tailor how each individual can access the experience.** Optional pricing is what auto dealerships use, where the total value of the purchase includes different options as selected by the consumer. This method provides the easiest access to the perfect car at the right value to the consumer while not diminishing the net revenue or altering the consumer's appreciation of value.

14
Ease of Access and the Arts

Chapter 12 defined widely held perspectives about the words ease and access. This chapter applies many of those ideas to a framework for the nonprofit arts. When you read "access" in this chapter, imagine a line which moves from left to right, ultimately leading to inevitable access to the arts experience. As you look from left to right, (currently unnamed) obstacles of multiple sizes exist. Ease of access is a point in which a potential audience member enters the line to move toward the arts experience. To access the arts organization and its offerings, the audience member must move from left to right through the obstacles until access is inevitable. In considering ease of access, arts organizations explore how they can reduce the obstacles that exist between patrons and the access to the arts experience being inevitable. The farther to the right on the line the community member enters, the easier the access to the arts experience.

This chapter identifies some common obstacles. These broad obstacles, however, are merely categories for the arts organization to consider as every specific obstacle a potential audience member faces is unique. These broad obstacles are an oversimplification for the sake of communication, and should not create the impression that obstacles are always easily definable and solvable. Categorizing these obstacles may make them appear independent of each other, however, multiple obstacles often compound each other further, reducing the ease of access. We examine these obstacles individually for clarity, but arts organizations must recognize that in practice, these obstacles impact each other in a complex system. Arts organizations may never achieve absolute ease of access for every community member, but they should work to reduce the impact of obstacles.

Discussions of accessibility most often center on providing equitable access to a physical place, knowledge, education, work opportunities, property ownership, or economic generation.[1] The word *equitable* is key in the way we frequently use the word *access*. After centuries of systemic discrimination, creating equitable access for underserved and underrepresented groups in all facets of life is vital. This component of accessibility is essential for arts organizations in considering their community, but it is only part of the picture when considering ease of access.

Price, time, location, accessibility in venues, and self-efficacy sometimes create obstacles for the consumer. Obstacles can manifest themselves at any artistic offering at nonprofit arts organizations. Ticket prices may be set at $25, a concert may run for two hours, or the location may have limited parking. These common facts are related to obstacles that frequently impact audience members in some way. Easily identifiable, these examples might be some of the first things that come to mind as ease of access is discussed in terms of the broad definition within the engagement edge. They are a starting place but do not constitute the impact of the obstacle in and of themselves.

The obstacle's impact can be broken into two components: actual impact and how the obstacle occurs in the audience member's mind. Every patron will have a unique way that the obstacles in the way of attendance impact them. In part I, we discussed that since each individual is different, an arts organization could create a unique engagement plan for each community member. Likewise, an arts organization could theoretically create an ease of access plan for every patron and potential patron based upon how obstacles impact them. Few (if any) arts organizations have the resources to undertake such a project. Instead, by knowing the community, an arts organization can segment demographics to help eliminate key obstacles that each group may face. To identify obstacles and demographic groups beyond our own lived experience, we must conduct research. Much of this research can be concurrent with research related to engaging community members through education.

The practical effects are specific to each audience member because the same obstacle does not impact all people equally. The impact varies based on a person's resources, location, and past experiences. Some obstacles exist for some, but not for others. Some obstacles may exist for two different people, but the effects can differ in size and scope.

The same obstacle with the same size and scope may exist for two different people but may feel different for each individual depending on how the obstacle is perceived. Zaffron and Logan proposed that people's behavior "correlates to how situations occur to them."[2] How an obstacle appears to a person has a great impact on their potential participation in the arts.

When thinking about ease of access, we consider everyone in the community. We think of the employed and unemployed, people of all ages, groups who have faced lifetimes of discrimination, people with and without enormous financial resources, those who attend, those who have never attended an event at an arts organization, and more. All people have obstacles to attending arts—but of course, some people enter the line closer to inevitable access than others. Does your organization choose to engage with those with fewer obstacles to access, or do you seek to serve your entire community equitably? Arts organizations must think about obstacles and what steps can be taken to provide greater ease of access to its community by reducing or eliminating these barriers. The following identifies five common obstacles potential audience members face in gaining inevitable access to arts organizations and art experiences.

Price

Although chapter 13 suggested that traditional pricing strategies do not work effectively in the arts, many arts organizations do charge an admission fee for access to artistic offerings. This admission price becomes an obstacle people may face in accessing the arts. In the McCarthy marketing mix, price is the only P that actually generates revenue.[3] Each other P ultimately leads to price where the corporation can earn profit. When an arts organization prices its tickets, this income flows into the organization to help offset costs. As we have read in hundreds of donation appeal letters, "ticket sales cover only a fraction of the cost of the art being produced." Although an uncompelling fundraising phrase, this is true for most arts organizations.[4] As noted, if the arts organization were to divide the organization's costs evenly across the audience members who attend, audience members would see the price skyrocket. Instead, arts organizations request donations, apply for grants, and estimate what their audience will be willing to pay to attend based on their perceived competition and perceived value of the offering.

Suppose the actual price of a ticket is $50. This potential obstacle would be easily identifiable for both the arts organization and the potential audience member. For those with great financial resources, this price of admission to an arts experience may be a very small obstacle relative to other obstacles this demographic faces. For those with fewer expendable financial resources, the cost may be the largest obstacle they face. The $50 ticket price has a very different practical impact for the potential audience member with $1,000 in the bank than the potential audience member with $1,000,000. An arts organization could observe and measure this practical impact, but this information is less available than the publicized price of a ticket.

The way community members think about money is also a factor determining the impact of the admission price. If two audience members each have $1,000 in the bank, and the ticket price is $50, the price for each ticket is 5% of their available cash on hand. For some people, spending 5% of their available cash may be frightening, while for others, it may not be a concern at all. Although the practical impact of the obstacle may be equal, the way the price occurs to each person is vastly different. The potential audience member who has $1,000,000 in the bank may be averse to spending and be equally concerned about spending 0.005% of their cash on hand as the person who fears spending 5%. Though the practical impacts are vastly different for each individual, this may have little impact on how the obstacle occurs to each person.

The arts organization can only control part of this obstacle: the actual price. To determine the price (if any), the arts organization can conduct research to determine resources within the community. They can determine demographics for whom the practical impact of the price is more likely to create a greater obstacle and provide ticket vouchers or discounts to reduce the size of the obstacle. Although an arts organization could theoretically attempt to alter the way the price occurs to a potential audience member, this is not advisable. Many for-profit promotional campaigns rely on such tactics. Advertisements sometimes use phrases like "for the price of two cups of coffee" as a way to reframe how a person considers the potential expense. Attempting to change the way price occurs to potential audience members may lean too far into persuasion to be appropriate for a nonprofit arts organization.

Time

If we consider time a finite resource that we lose consistently throughout our lives, the use of time becomes a large obstacle to those who feel they do not have enough of it. Yet, those who have used more of this resource tend to be our primary audience base.[5] Of course, this is because younger people often have more factors competing for their time: formal education, a job, raising children, or any number of other competing interests. People who are not engaged in formal education, are retired (or never worked), and are not engaged in raising children may be more inclined to see the arts as a valuable use for their time. Although time remains a constant for all people, the practical impact of time varies greatly. The greater the amount of flexibility a person has with their time, the smaller the obstacle time becomes.

In the performing arts, time becomes a greater obstacle than in many other art forms. The audience must all arrive at approximately the same time. This restriction is rare in nearly every other product offered by both non-profit and for-profit organizations. There are certain services offered that begin at a specific time, a massage, for example, but the consumer is involved in determining when they will specifically attend. Movie theaters have set times, but they tend to offer the same film many times each day. If the audience member cannot make the movie at 5:10, they can usually find a new start time within an hour or two. Sporting events are an exception. Sporting events have specific start times and usually occur no more than once per day. The start time at sporting events is still less of an obstacle, however, because, if late to a sporting event, they do not bar people from entry. In contrast, many arts organizations do not permit someone to enter a performing arts event after it has begun.

Note that the time it takes for the art experience is only part of the picture. If it takes an hour and forty minutes to explore a museum exhibit, it is easy for the engagement manager to think, "it's just over an hour and a half to have this experience. Why are they so concerned with that much time?" In thinking this way, the person fails to recognize the time in researching the exhibit, making a reservation, preparing to go out, traveling to the location, traveling home, and all the time-taking moments along the way. An hour-and-forty-minute arts experience can easily add up to four hours or more.

Determining the duration of an arts experience is often beyond the immediate control of an engagement manager at a nonprofit arts organization. In selecting what offerings the organization will provide, however, the duration of the event should be included as a determining factor. This suggestion does not mean that shorter durations are superior. Rather, an organization could conduct research to determine ideal durations and work to ensure that multiple offerings are provided that meet the needs of many demographics. For some community members, a short duration may not feel valuable enough to overcome the obstacle of the ticket price or that of traveling to the location.

Location

Location is about a geographic place and the effort associated with travel to and from the location where the audience will experience the art. The specific length of time and effort it takes for a potential audience member to travel to the location is the practical impact of the obstacle. For some people in the community, a venue might be across the street. For others, the venue might require a forty-five-minute journey.

For some, the concept of leaving the house may be the largest obstacle to attending an offering from an arts organization. Consider the movie theater industry over the last twenty years. Because of cable television and streaming services, movie theaters have experienced a decrease in attendance.[6] Other companies have succeeded in providing similar value while reducing obstacles associated with location, which increased the ease of access. By making the location easier to access (since a viewer could stay home), these services captured customers for whom the location provided an obstacle. Yet, movie theaters remain in business because, for some, going to the location is not an obstacle—it is part of the experience. In this for-profit example, the view-from-home attribute is a component of the product, but it presents a good example of how location can be an obstacle for some community members.

The distance a person must travel is only one element of the obstacle of location. Traveling requires some mode of transportation (e.g., walking, public transportation, a car), which may add to the financial cost and time obstacles. These added components of cost and time are practical impacts to the obstacle of location. How people think about time and travel has also had an effect. Before Jay and Anthony each moved to Tallahassee, they lived near large cities (Boston and Detroit), and it was common to spend forty-five minutes or more driving from one location to another. Within a year of moving to Tallahassee, the thought of driving more than twenty minutes to a destination in town feels far to them. A twenty-minute drive in Tallahassee can be more of an obstacle than a forty-five-minute drive in a different city—even to the same person, because the way an obstacle occurs in their mind changes based on their lived experience.

Weather changes the feeling of effort in traveling to a location: The more pleasant the weather, the more pleasant the travel experience. If surveyed in the spring, people may feel that a twenty-minute walk is reasonable, yet, in the cold winter, the same people may respond differently. Like the weather, darkness has an effect. Anecdotally, we recognize that many people over seventy-five prefer not to drive after dark. This obstacle is heightened for this demographic in winter since the sun may set close to 4:00 p.m. in the United States. For some, an event starting earlier in the day is an obstacle, while for others, an event starting in the evening is an obstacle.

Some arts organizations rarely consider location because they have presented their artistic offering in the same venue for decades. These organizations should consider an analysis of perceptions in their community about their location and seek to reach people who do not attend to understand if the location is prohibitive to their participation. As we describe in the case of the Public Theater's Mobile Theater, some arts organizations bring art directly to communities for whom the typical location provides too significant an obstacle.

The Case of The Public Theater's Mobile Theater

The Public Theater (the Public) in New York City is one of the most highly regarded nonprofit theater companies in the United States. The Public has transferred more than fifty productions to Broadway.[7] These productions include *A Chorus Line, For Colored Girls Who Have Considered Suicide/ When the Rainbow is Enuf, Hair, Caroline or Change, Fun Home,* and perhaps the most recognized, *Hamilton.* Since its inception, in addition to developing new art, the Public has sought to enhance access to theater arts for people across New York City. Every summer, the Public produces their program Shakespeare in the Park. Performances take place at the Delacorte Theater in New York City's Central Park, an open-air performance space built in part through the efforts of the Public in the 1960s.[8] Tickets to the plays are distributed for free on the day of each performance. The theater's focus on easing access to the arts goes back to the 1950s when Joseph Papp developed the Mobile Theater.[9]

Papp was a driving force behind creating accessible theater in New York City. His Mobile Theater provided ease of access in every broad area identified in this chapter and stands as a model for arts organizations around providing accessible arts experiences. Papp passed away in 1991, so Shareeza Bhola of the Public provided information and resources about the history of the Mobile Theater and the development of new programs at the Public.

Rehearsals for the productions occurred in Manhattan, but the Mobile Theater (as implied) would travel to various locations around the city. The Mobile Theater used trucks to transport scenery, props, costumes, and theatrical equipment to parks where the performances would occur. The Mobile Theater program partnered with city officials to establish locations and move and construct risers for seating. The partnership was so strong that the city provided the trucks and other vehicles to assist in the endeavor. Various sources provided funding, including the New York Foundation for the first iteration of the Mobile Theatre.[10]

Papp was driven by excellence and saw this level of community engagement as equally, if not more valuable, than the commercial work produced on Broadway. He aggressively fought the notion that great art could not be community-centered. On the contrary, Papp believed that art was for everyone and that great art can exist anywhere. He sought to break down elitist notions of fine art while simultaneously insisting upon what he saw as artistic excellence in productions.

Papp's approach focused on social engagement and service before the United States recognized nonprofit organizations as they are known today. The first touring production by the Mobile Theatre (*Romeo and Juliet*) launched in 1957, more than ten years before the current version of 501(c)(3) nonprofit status existed in the United States tax code. The spirit of community service exhibited by Papp and the Mobile Theatre exceeds many nonprofit arts organizations today.

A core element of the Mobile Theater was a commitment to reduce the obstacle of ticket price for access to theater performances. The performances were offered to community members for free. The productions could often accommodate more than seven hundred people at a single performance. By eliminating the ticket price, Papp helped to reduce some socio-economic factors that could hinder participation. Although the Mobile Theater greatly reduced an obstacle by having no price, they could not eliminate the obstacle of cost completely, since some audience members may have had to take time off from work to attend performances or experience expenses other than admission costs relating to their attendance. Since the Mobile Theater had no admission price associated with attendance, it provides a great example of how McCarthy's pricing strategies as a framework are not suitable for the arts. If there is no price, traditional pricing strategies serve no use, and the marketing mix loses its balance.

Papp designed the Mobile Theater program to reach community members who were unacquainted and inexperienced with theater performances by making the location less of an obstacle. Although population density is high across all five boroughs of New York City, the overwhelming majority of cultural institutions are located in Manhattan. By traveling into communities with the Mobile Theatre, Papp reduced the amount of effort community members had to expend to travel to a performance. In addition to reducing effort, moving the location reduced the expense for audience members associated with travel, helping to reduce the overall cost. Likewise, the amount of time the overall arts experience takes was reduced because travel time was greatly reduced. By moving the location to be nested within communities, Papp reduced elements of several broad obstacles. Many arts organizations would say they do not have the resources to both produce great art and transport it directly into communities. For Papp, doing both was a central objective.

Through our research and in our exchange with Bhola, there was no clear indication about the level of accessibility that existed within the many outdoor venues in the 1950s and beyond. We can presume that the performances were not fully ADA compliant with today's standards. Since the venues were set up in open-air spaces, however, it can also be assumed that the flexibility provided ample accessibility relative to stairs and aisles. From available photos, it appears that some of the audience was seated in risers, and other audience members were seated in chairs directly on the ground—requiring no climbing. Restrooms were a component that limited accessibility in the venues relative to traditional venues. Permanent venues can provide indoor plumbing and are designed with an audience's needs in mind.

Through promoting the idea that theater is for everyone, Papp increased attendance by helping communities recognize that these performances were for them. People who may have perceived that theater attendance was an elite activity were encouraged to attend because the Mobile Theater brought the experience directly to their neighborhood. Many old theaters functioned for the audience to see a performance and audience members to be seen by other audience members. Some still see the attendance of the arts as a status symbol. By bringing the art out of old, traditional venues, they reduced the hierarchical perception created by some theaters, making the experience more welcoming and organic. The Mobile Theater collaborated with potential attendees and leaders in each community to create a level of engagement that enhanced the community members' self-efficacy for participation because they saw themselves and their community reflected in the audience and overall experience.

Papp committed himself to continue with the Mobile Theater after that first season. At times, however, the Mobile Theater failed to maintain its programming. For many years, the Mobile Theater struggled with sustainability and consistently producing productions. In the mid-1960s, there were multiple back-to-back summers with no performances. In the 1970s, the Mobile Theater gained a greater financial foothold and produced more frequently and to larger audiences. The Mobile Theater brought plays to all five boroughs consistently and continued to have support from the New York City government.

Throughout this time, Papp had developed and continued to grow the Shakespeare in the Park performances at the Delacorte Theater in Central Park. In the late 1970s, after two decades of performances, he closed the Mobile Theater to focus solely on developing a physical location and the Shakespeare in the Park events. By running the Mobile Theater, Papp helped welcome tens of thousands of people who, otherwise, may not have attended theatre events. By increasing the ease of access, audience members had to overcome fewer obstacles (or the obstacles were reduced in size) in order to engage with the Mobile Theater.

The legacy of the Mobile Theater continues today at the Public, even beyond the Shakespeare in the Park performances. In 2010, over three decades since the final production of the Mobile Theater closed, the Public launched the Mobile Unit. The Mobile Unit is a pared-down version of the Mobile Theater. They travel with props, costumes, and simple set pieces to perform in community spaces and engage with underserved communities in New York City. Although they may not travel with a stage and significant production elements, they have a great impact on communities around New York City. Thousands of people across New York City have experienced theater through the Mobile Unit. They have toured to community centers, educational institutions, shelters, and prisons. An article in American Theatre Magazine by Ciara Murphy and Kevin Landis chronicles a visit to a performance at Rikers Island Correctional Facility in 2017 where nearly one hundred people engaged around a theater performance of *Romeo and Juliet*.[11] The Public currently produces two tours with the Mobile Unit annually. The Mobile Unit's productions each run for six weeks. They perform for three weeks touring to different communities and another three weeks at the Public's primary space near Washington Square in Manhattan. True to Papp's vision, and though centered in community engagement, the performances are driven by artistic excellence and are reviewed by critics, just like the productions the Public moves to Broadway.

We recognize that not all arts organizations are centered on serving underserved populations and that the nature of serving underserved populations is directly tied to creating ease of access. We do suggest, however, that all arts organizations develop programming to eliminate elitism and welcome all community members by reducing obstacles that stand in their way of participation. As noted, all people have obstacles that stand in their way. By identifying and minimizing, or eliminating them, arts organizations can better serve more people within their community.

Accessibility in Venues

Once the audience has overcome the obstacles they face before arriving at the location where the art will be experienced, they face new obstacles. If an audience member drives to the venue, where will they park? Is the parking lot well lit? Does the parking lot feel safe? This question of *feeling* safe is, of course, subjective. What feels safe to someone who frequents the area may not feel safe to someone who has never been there. From the moment potential audience members arrive on the premises, obstacles to the arts experience abound.

Depending on the venue, there may be physical obstacles providing practical impacts to participation. Many older buildings are still not fully ADA compliant.[12] Some venues are only accessible by using stairs. Stairs can be an obstacle for people with ADA-recognized physical disabilities and those who are uncomfortable using stairs. For some, stairs provide a complete barrier to access, while for others, stairs are an obstacle they must overcome. Suitable access to restrooms is another key factor ensuring a space is ADA accessible.

Even having complete ADA accessibility is not sufficient to fully reduce the obstacle of physical accessibility within a venue. Potential audience members who have never been to the venue may presume that they would be required to use stairs or that the restrooms may be inaccessible to them (again, especially in the case of older buildings). Arts organizations often leave audience members with disabilities to conduct their own research to determine accessibility in the venue. Even the presumption and the process of calling the arts organization to inquire about accessibility may be an obstacle depending how that call strikes the potential audience member.

As a start, nonprofit arts organizations can strive to ensure that all ADA requirements are met in their venues. Additionally, active education about what to expect in the venues is essential. Some arts organizations provide virtual walkthroughs of their venue so that audience members can see the parking lot, lobby, restrooms, and gallery or performance space in advance to be well prepared, and the prospect of walking into an unknown space is less of an obstacle.

Self-efficacy

Part I noted that regardless of a person's level of arts expertise, everyone can experience and appreciate what the arts have to offer. Creating educational programs to help community members discover the value of the arts experience is vital; however, simply understanding the value is not enough for a person to commit to attending. A person's perspective about their capabilities of participating in an arts experience can be a significant obstacle. Self-efficacy refers to a person's belief about their ability to participate in a subject at accepted levels.[13] The social factors and fear of not fitting in can stand in the way of a community member attending. An obstacle related to self-efficacy is unlike the other broad obstacles identified in this chapter as it exists as an obstacle only in the way it occurs to the potential audience member. This obstacle exists only if the potential audience member does not believe they *are capable* of what others might deem socially acceptable participation.

When children attend arts organizations on school field trips, many are taught forms of acceptable behavior (which is largely determined by their teacher). As people age and socialize, they develop new behaviors based upon their lived experiences. Those who do not practice attending the arts may fear breaking social constructs that they believe are expected in an arts venue. For some, these expectations may be ingrained from school. This feeling of "not belonging there" and "not knowing what to do" can be a substantial obstacle for members in your community who do not currently attend.

Arts organizations must actively break down perceived exclusivity which may exist in the community. **Many nonprofit arts organizations say that the arts are for everyone but continue to promote unspoken rules and expected** behaviors that create an elitist environment. Rather than seeking to teach community members to "be good audience members," arts organizations should closely examine potentially elitist underpinnings of their expectations and seek to actively welcome community members exactly as they are without any implications that they must change in order to participate.

Final Notes on Ease of Access

Each of the points discussed above presents multiple obstacles. These obstacles will not apply to all people, and in some circumstances, what is an obstacle for some is a key part of the experience for others. Ease of access is not about eliminating all obstacles between all community members and the art—because this is impossible. Instead, arts organizations will research and examine obstacles that exist for their community members and how those obstacles occur to them. Arts organizations can then work to reduce obstacles to increase ease of access for all community members. In introducing ease of access, we noted that accessibility is frequently used to refer to equity. Although all people enter the ease of access line and have some obstacles to overcome, we recognize that privilege impacts the size and types of obstacles a person will face. Choosing between spending time working in the flower garden or going to an arts event is different from a person who must work a second job to care for their family or go to an arts event. Both involve an obstacle of time, but the obstacles take on a different significance. As a result of centuries of discrimination in the United States, BIPOC communities are likely to experience more obstacles with greater significance than communities that have not or do not face systemic discrimination.[14] Although these obstacles will vary, arts organizations should be purposeful in their approach to create ease of access and seek to serve the community's demographic most in need first.

In McCarthy's marketing mix, price is a key component because earning profits is a for-profit corporation's primary purpose.[15] The greater the value provided to the consumer, the greater the opportunity for profit. Think about ease of access as the chapter described it. Nonprofit arts organizations are not in the business of obstacles. **The aim is not to create an artistic product so stunning that everyone in the community will overcome a plethora of obstacles to experience it; the aim is to reduce as many obstacles as possible to make that stunning artistic product more accessible.**

Conclusion

Piecing Everything Together

Introduction

Parts II through V explored definitions of the four Ps and the four Es, explored what they each mean in the context of the arts, and presented how the Ps fail to fit neatly into the arts and, in many cases, simply do not apply. The parts described how the conceptual framework of each of the four Es is a tighter fit for the nonprofit arts. This final component of the book looks at how these pieces work together. Chapter 1 proposed the notion of the engagement edge.

In considering the shifting paradigms, changing approaches, and fast-paced scholarly explorations of arts marketing in relation to the concept of engagement, one may see a vast list of concepts that seem to have little resemblance to one another. In fact, the marketing mix, the arts as value-consideration for the consumer, and the changing ways we as human beings interact have contributed to a new approach to examining, disseminating, and incorporating the arts into our society. This process that is the primary function of arts management is not simply an instruction to be followed. Rather it is a cutting-*edge* approach where four conceptual frames meet. Each frame requires different levels of input based on the individual needs and characteristics of the art, community, artists, organization, and consumer.

The engagement edge maintains the simplicity of the McCarthy model, has its foundations in consumer-centric marketing and takes a managerial approach to problem-solving.

In order to describe the way the four Es serve communities, we have developed a model. The hope is that this model can be used, dismantled, reassessed, built upon, and ultimately proven as a foundation upon which the next era of arts engagement can begin. We invite improvements and strengthening of the conceptual structure.

244   CONCLUSION

At the base of the model is the engagement zone, a place where people within a community are engaged with a nonprofit arts organization. As seen throughout this book, engagement can take many forms as long as both the arts organization and the community members are actively engaged in something. Sometimes this occurs through an arts experience, but it may also occur through other facets while an audience member is not having an arts experience (see figure C.1).

At the center of nonprofit arts organizations are the shared and individual arts experiences community members have in partnership with the organization. Sometimes these partnerships are intentional, like when someone purchases a ticket to an event, and sometimes they are unintentional, such as when a person walks down the street and has an arts experience interacting with a piece of art in public. The experience may be a culminating moment as an audience member experiences designed offerings through their senses, as in the case of Sally Taylor and *Consenses* which built an arts experience based on artists' perceptions of each other's work. It may also occur through direct interaction and co-creation as seen in the case of Moletedi One Ntseme's theater in Botswana. Experience may occur directly through an arts offering, or may begin with an engaged conversation with a ticket agent that provides a spark of inspiration about a piece of art. In any case, arts experiences are the core of what

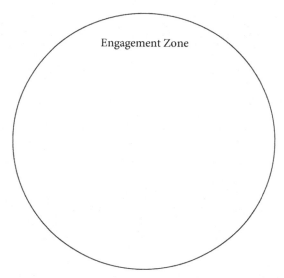

Figure C.1 The engagement zone, a space where both audience and organization are engaged in activity together.

nonprofit arts organizations provide to their community, and as we have shown, are clearly distinct from product, as proposed by McCarthy. To represent this primary function of nonprofit arts organizations, we have placed experiences at the center of the model (see figure C.2). The total experience is often more than the arts offering provided because it occurs within a community member.

All experiences are nested within an environment of some type. Sometimes these environments are incredibly controlled as we saw in the case of Felix Barrett and *Sleep No More*, the theater experience that occurs across five floors of a former New York City hotel.

Sometimes these environments are carefully selected and even altered through the art, as presented in the Sing for Hope Pianos case where pianos are installed in public spaces for community members to play. Although environment is an important factor for how education is delivered to the community, the environmental consideration central to this paradigm is focused on the space in which community members have the overall arts experience. Environments impact arts experiences, but they do not transport, warehouse, or distribute arts experiences as place does with product under McCarthy's marketing mix—a framework that, as we have shown, is inappropriate for the arts. Whether the environment is physical or not, audience members have the experience in an environment which inevitably affects the experience itself.

Figure C.2 The actual arts experience occurs at the center of the engagement zone.

Experience occurs within environments (controlled or otherwise) and for the engaged community member, both occur within the engagement zone (see figure C.3).

Nonprofit arts organizations have two primary vehicles to enhance engagement with community members which lead members to have the arts experiences. First, we will discuss education. To help community members discover what arts experiences may or may not be for them, we have suggested education. As presented in the Aubrey Bergauer and California Symphony case, through education, arts organizations can serve their community before a purchase even occurs. In the case of *Prospero*, Jennifer Glech used games and activities to engage her existing audiences through education to help them discover and rediscover Shakespeare. Through a constructivist approach and a learner-centered lens, education empowers community members to make decisions and discoveries and to build the self-efficacy to participate. Promotion under McCarthy's marketing mix persuades people to make purchases often for the sake of profit; education for arts organizations helps community members make new discoveries relative to art and empowers them to opt-in or opt-out without elements designed to persuade.

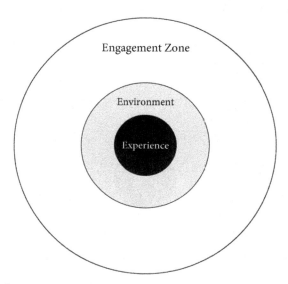

Figure C.3 The experience of audience members occurs within an environment, and the audience must move through multiple environments on the path to accessing the experience. Both experience and environment occur within the engagement zone.

CONCLUSION 247

Ease of access is the process by which a nonprofit arts organization reduces barriers to engagement and arts experiences. Some of these obstacles are within a nonprofit arts organization's control, but the organization cannot control how each community member considers the obstacles—they can only work to reduce the practical effect. Chapter 14 identified broad obstacles including price, time, location, accessibility in venues, and self-efficacy. It presented how Joseph Papp eased most of these obstacles with his mobile theater in the 1950s which traveled to underserved communities to create arts experiences. McCarthy's framework of price serves the purpose to ultimately extract the greatest profit from consumers possible; ease of access serves to reduce barriers to serve the community. Elements of ease of access influence and are influenced by environment and education. It exists as its own entity in the model, wholly separate, because the entire concept of ease of access is vital to the engagement manager to consider in increasing engagement. Paths to ease access continue to develop. As seen in the Commonwealth Shakespeare Company case, where they are developing virtual reality theater experiences, some arts organizations are already looking to the future at how new technology might transform ease of access to arts experiences (see figure C.4.).

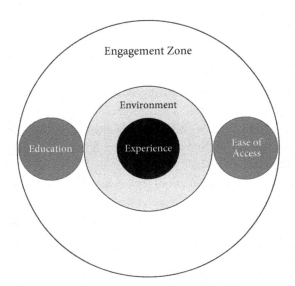

Figure C.4 Elements of ease of access and education work in tandem to heighten and create access to the space where community members and arts organizations engage.

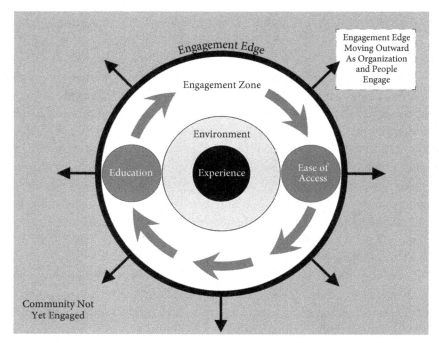

Figure C.5 Education and ease of access move along the engagement edge pushing it out into the community as people enter the engagement zone and move through environment to have life enriching, engaged experiences.

So, how does this model function, and where is the engagement edge? Ease of access circles around, reducing obstacles for the community to the engagement zone, environment, and ultimately experience. Education works in tandem with ease of access and also orbits the model to engage with community members, who so desire, to help them discover for themselves what arts experiences can be.

Together, their rotation pushes out the engagement edge into the community through which people enter the engagement zone and move through environment to have life enriching, engaged experiences. As the rotation of education and ease of access pushes the engagement edge out, the engagement zone grows and becomes larger as more people from the community become engaged with the arts organization and access arts experiences (see figure C.5).

The Extra Es

In the engagement edge, certainly external influences still exist and exert pressure on the organization. An additional set of Es has great bearing on the nonprofit arts and works with the engagement edge in unexplored and untested ways.

Echoing and Encouragement

In the process of *echoing*, the messaging and education we share about our art is repeated throughout the community as part of the engagement process. This seasoned manner of oral communication, a heightened form of word-of-mouth, is more testimony and affirmation of the art and the entire experience that participants echo as engagement takes hold. When accompanied by *encouragement* to participate and engage, we see the process of echoing and encouragement as expanding our reach into the pools of non-attenders and helping them become arts lovers.

Effectiveness

In terms of *effectiveness*, there is value in measuring the results of the ongoing use of the engagement edge. The standard measures for any approach aimed at increasing participation in the arts is to document changes in ticket sales and donations. Instead, nonprofit arts organizations should create plans to measure engagement. The engagement edge may encourage a new focus on the nonprofit arts organization's mission, requiring an evaluation and realignment of guiding principles. Engagement levels can be measured in terms of quantity of engagement but also by asking participants about the quality of the engagement.

Evolution, the Final E

We have mentioned that art forms can and do disappear from active creation in our society. Vaudeville is a good example of an art form that has essentially disappeared. Though some mutated forms of that old art form do exist, the traditional Vaudeville has gone into the history books. Although this may suggest that certain forms may be subject to *extinction*, we see a different fate for those that follow the engagement edge.

By following the approach provided in this book, a nonprofit organization can fend off possible extinction through constant and ongoing change that keeps the arts organization relevant for the artist, the community, and for the audience. That process of change is, of course, *evolution*, and the engagement edge allows for the evolution of an arts organization to be embedded in its culture and way of approaching the world. By incorporating the engagement edge into the daily operations of a nonprofit organization, the risk of extinction is replaced by guided evolution. Change is inevitable, but we can guide and embrace it if we have the right approach.

Notes

Chapter 1

1. Ben Walmsley, "The Death of Arts Marketing: A Paradigm Shift from Consumption to Enrichment," *Arts and the Market* (2019): 32. ISSN 2056-4945.
2. *The Arts and Civic Engagement: Involved in Arts, Involved in Life* (2006), National Endowment for the Arts.
3. Grace McQuilten and Anthony White, *Art as Enterprise: Social and Economic Engagement in Contemporary Art* (London: IB Tauris, 2019).
4. Daniel Wheatley and Craig Bickerton, "Measuring Changes in Subjective Well-Being from Engagement in the Arts, Culture and Sport," *Journal of Cultural Economics* 43, no. 3 (2019): 421–442. Retrieved from https://doi.org/10.1007/s10824-019-09342-7.
5. Lynne Conner, *Audience Engagement and the Role of Arts Talk in the Digital Era* (New York: Springer, 2013).
6. Doug Borwick, *Building Communities, Not Audiences: The Future of the Arts in the United States* (Winston-Salem, NC: ArtsEngaged, 2012).
7. Shelley Boulianne, "Does Internet Use Affect Engagement? A Meta-Analysis of Research," *Political communication* 26, no. 2 (2009): 193–211. doi: 10.1080/10584600902854363.
8. Alan Peacock, "The Arts and Economic Policy," *Handbook of the Economics of Art and Culture* 1 (2006): 1123–1140.
9. Borwick, *Building Communities, Not Audiences*.
10. Yerin Shim, Louis Tay, Michaela Ward, and James O. Pawelski, "Arts and Humanities Engagement: An Integrative Conceptual Framework for Psychological Research," *Review of General Psychology* 23, no. 2 (2019): 159–176.
11. Walmsley, "The Death of Arts Marketing."
12. J. Dewey, *Art as Experience* (New York: Minton, Balch, and Company, 1934).
13. Walmsley, "The Death of Arts Marketing."
14. F. Colbert, *Marketing Culture and the Arts* (Montreal: HEC Montreal, 2007).
15. Ibid.
16. Philip Kotler and Joanne Scheff, *Standing Room Only: Strategies for Marketing the Performing Arts* (Brighton, MA: Harvard Business School Press, 1997).
17. Neil H. Borden, "The Concept of the Marketing Mix," *Journal of Advertising Research* 4, no. 2 (1964): 2–7.
18. Neil H. Borden, "Findings of the Harvard Study on the Economic Effects of Advertising," *Journal of Marketing* 6, no. 4_part_2 (1942): 89–99.
19. Borden, "The Concept of the Marketing Mix," 2–7.
20. Ibid.

21. Jagdish N. Sheth, David M. Gardner, and Dennis E. Garrett, *Marketing Theory: Evolution and Evaluation*, vol. 12 (Hoboken, NJ: John Wiley & Sons, 1988).
22. Barton A. Weitz and Robin Wensley, eds., *Handbook of Marketing* (Thousand Oaks, CA: Sage, 2002).
23. L. O'Malley and M. Lichrou, "Marketing Theory," in *The Marketing Book*, 7th ed., ed. M. J. Baker and S. Hart (Oxon, UK: Routledge, 2016), 37–52; and Shelby D. Hunt and Jerry Goolsby, "The Rise and Fall of the Functional Approach to Marketing: A Paradigm Displacement Perspective," in Kassarjian, Harold H., and Thomas S. Robertson. "Perspectives in consumer behavior." (1968). Stanley Hollander, Terence Nevett and Ronald Fullerton (Eds), (Lexington, MA: Lexington Books), 35–37.
24. Oxford Dictionary of Marketing, "Edmund Jerome McCarthy," *Oxford Reference, Oxford University Press.*
25. John A. Quelch and Katherine E. Jocz, "Milestones in Marketing," *The Business History Review* 82, no. 4 (2008): 827–838. doi: https://doi.org/10.1017/S0007680500063236; and Pundrik Mishra, *Sales Management: Keys to Effective Sales* (New Delhi: Global India Publications, 2009), 34–35.
26. "News Briefs" (PDF), *The Scholastic*, Notre Dame University, 100(18): 29, March 29, 1959.
27. Efthymios Constantinides, "The Marketing Mix Revisited: Towards the 21st Century Marketing," *Journal of Marketing Management* 22, nos. 3–4 (2006): 407–438.
28. Gandolfo Dominici, "From Marketing Mix to E-Marketing Mix: A Literature Overview and Classification," *International Journal of Business and Management* 4, no. 9 (2009): 17–24.
29. Borden, "The Concept of the Marketing Mix," 2–7.
30. Dominici, "From Marketing Mix to E-Marketing Mix," 17–24.
31. Stacey Marien, "Everyday Finance: Economics, Personal Money Management, and Entrepreneurship," *Reference & User Services Quarterly* 48, no. 3 (2009): 310.
32. Stephen Dann, "Redefining Social Marketing with Contemporary Commercial Marketing Definitions," *Journal of Business Research* 63, no. 2 (2010): 147–153.
33. Dewey, *Art as Experience.*
34. Dewey, *Art as Experience.*
35. Varsha Verma, Dheeraj Sharma, and Jagdish Sheth, "Does Relationship Marketing Matter in Online Retailing? A Meta-Analytic Approach," *Journal of the Academy of Marketing Science* 44, no. 2 (2016): 206–217.
36. Dewey, *Art as Experience.*
37. Miguel Ángel López-Lomelí, María-del-Carmen Alarcón-del-Amo, and Joan Llonch-Andreu, "Segmenting Consumers Based on Their Evaluation of Local, Global and Glocal Brands," *Journal of International Consumer Marketing* 31, no. 5 (2019): 395–407.
38. Dewey, *Art as Experience.*
39. Geah Pressgrove and Richard D. Waters, "Defining the Concepts: What Is the Nonprofit Sector?," *Public Relations Theory: Application and Understanding* (2019): 113.

40. Jennifer Kuan, "The Phantom Profits of the Opera: Nonprofit Ownership in the Arts as a Make-Buy Decision," *Journal of Law, Economics, and Organization* 17, no. 2 (2001): 507–520.
41. Anonymous, National Guild for Community Arts Education, 2019, https://www.nationalguild.org/resources.
42. D. Crane, N. Kawashima, and K. I. Kawasaki, eds., *Global Culture: Media, Arts, Policy, and Globalization* (New York: Routledge, 2016).
43. Kotler and Scheff, *Standing Room Only*.

Chapter 2

1. Donald Getz and Stephen J. Page, *Event Studies: Theory, Research and Policy for Planned Events* (London: Routledge, 2016); Rachael E. Nicholson and Douglas G. Pearce, "Why Do People Attend Events: A Comparative Analysis of Visitor Motivations at Four South Island Events," *Journal of Travel Research* 39, no. 4 (2001): 449–460; and Ben Walmsley, "Why People Go to the Theatre: A Qualitative Study of Audience Motivation," *Journal of Customer Behaviour* 10, no. 4 (2011): 335–351.
2. Lara B. Aknin et al., "Does Social Connection Turn Good Deeds into Good Feelings?: On the Value of Putting the 'Social' in Prosocial Spending," *International Journal of Happiness and Development* 1, no. 2 (2013): 155–171.
3. Barbara Brown Wilson, "Learning to Listen: Designing Architectural Education through University-Community Partnerships," *NEW SOLUTIONS: A Journal of Environmental and Occupational Health Policy* 18, no. 2 (2008): 177–192.
4. Larry Ferlazzo and Lorie A. Hammond, *Building Parent Engagement in Schools* (Santa Barbara, CA: ABC-CLIO, 2009).
5. Geni Cowan et al., "Evaluation Report: The Home Visit Project," (2002).
6. Ibid.
7. Lyda J. Hanifan, "The Rural School Community Center," *The Annals of the American Academy of Political and Social Science* 67, no. 1 (1916): 130–138.
8. A. Maslow, "A Theory of Human Motivation," *Psychological Review* 50, no. 4 (1943): 370–396.
9. Collins, Jim, *Good to Great* (London: Random House Business Books, 2001); Lee G. Bolman and Terrence E. Deal, "Reframing Organizations Artistry, Choice, and Leadership. San Francisco," *CA: Josey-Bass* (2008); and Steve Zaffron and Dave Logan, *The Three Laws of Performance: Rewriting the Future of Your Organization and Your Life*, vol. 170 (John Wiley & Sons, 2011).
10. Jim Collins, "Good to Great."
11. Bolman and Deal, "Reframing Organizations Artistry, Choice, and Leadership. San Francisco."
12. Jung Yuha and Neville Vakharia, "Open Systems Theory for Arts and Cultural Organizations: Linking Structure and Performance," *The Journal of Arts Management, Law, and Society* 49, no. 4 (2019): 257–273.

13. John Dewey, *Art as Experience* (New York: Minton, Balch and Co, 1934).
14. Michela Addis, *Engaging Brands: A Customer-Centric Approach for Superior Experiences* (New York: Routledge, 2020).
15. Collins, "Good to Great."
16. Jeremy Pincus, "The Consequences of Unmet Needs: The Evolving Role of Motivation in Consumer Research," *Journal of Consumer Behaviour: An International Research Review* 3, no. 4 (2004): 375–387.
17. Alan S. Brown, Shelly Gilbride, and Jennifer Novak, *Getting In on the Act: How Arts Groups Are Creating Opportunities for Active Participation* (San Francisco, CA: The James Irvine Foundation, 2011).
18. Ibid.
19. Ibid.
20. Ibid.
21. Michelle Bergadaà and Simon Nyeck, "Quel marketing pour les activités artistiques: une analyse qualitative comparée des motivations des consommateurs et producteurs de théâtre," *Recherche et Applications en Marketing (French Edition)* 10, no. 4 (1995): 27–45.
22. Walmsley, Ben, "Why People Go to the Theatre: A Qualitative Study of Audience Motivation," *Journal of Customer Behaviour* 10, no. 4 (2011): 335–351.
23. Walmsley, "Why People Go to the Theatre," 335–351.
24. J. Carnwath, *Triple Play Audience Perceptions of New Plays* (San Francisco: WolfBrown, 2017).
25. Suzanne Meeks, Sarah Kelly Shryock, and Russell J. Vandenbroucke, "Theatre Involvement and Well-Being, Age Differences, and Lessons from Long-Time Subscribers," *The Gerontologist* 58, no. 2 (2018): 278–289.
26. Ben Walmsley, "Co-Creating Theatre: Authentic Engagement or Inter-Legitimation?," *Cultural Trends* 22, no. 2 (2013): 108–118.
27. Eugene Carr and Michelle Paul, *Breaking the Fifth Wall: Rethinking Arts Marketing for the 21st Century* (New York: Patron Publishing, 2011).

Chapter 3

1. "Tick, Tick, Tick . . . California Symphony's New Composer about to Unveil a Timely New Work," *The Mercury News*, May 2, 2018, retrieved June 20, 2019.
1. L. Boone and D. Kurtz, *Contemporary Marketing* (Hinsdale, IL: Dryden Press, 1974).
2. W. Stanton, *Fundamentals of Marketing* (New York: McGraw-Hill, 1984).
3. Maurits Kaptein and Aart Van Halteren, "Adaptive Persuasive Messaging to Increase Service Retention: Using Persuasion Profiles to Increase the Effectiveness of Email Reminders," *Personal and Ubiquitous Computing* 17, no. 6 (2013): 1173–1185.
4. N. Jay, C. Salmon, and S. Chang, "The Hidden History of Product Placement," *Journal of Broadcasting & Electronic Media* 50, no. 4 (2006): 575–594.

5. Sunita Kumar, "Influence of Product Placements in Films and Television on Consumers Brand Awareness," *Archives of Business Research* 5, no. 2 (2017): 163–179.
6. Leo Kivijarv and Patrick Quinn, "U.S. Product Placement Market Grew 13.7% in 2017, Pacing for Faster Gr," *PRWeb*, Cision, June 13, 2018, www.prweb.com/releases/2018/06/prweb15558424.htm.
7. Jay, Salmon, and Chang, "The Hidden History of Product Placement.".
8. G. Cătălina and S. Ranchordás, *The Regulation of Social Media Influencers*, Elgar Law, Technology and Society Series (Cheltenham, UK: Edward Elgar Publishing, 2020).
9. Arzu Sener, Ayfer Aydiner Boylu, and Seval Guven, *Children and Advertising: What Do They Think about Advertisements, How Are They Affected by Advertisements?* (New York: Nova Science, 2010).
10. Elizabeth L. Eisenstein, *The Printing Press as an Agent of Change*, vol. 1 (Cambridge: Cambridge University Press, 1980).
11. P. Freire, M. B. Ramos, and D. P. Macedo, *Pedagogy of the Oppressed*. 30th anniversary ed. (London: Bloomsbury, 2012).
12. Susan Pass, *Parallel Paths to Constructivism: Jean Piaget and Lev Vygotsky* (Greenwich, CT: Information Age Publishing, 2004).
13. L. S. Vygotsky and Michael Cole, *Mind in Society: The Development of Higher Psychological Processes* (Cambridge, MA: Harvard University Press, 1978).
14. Pass, *Parallel Paths to Constructivism*.
15. Nadine M. Lambert and Barbara L. McCombs, *How Students Learn: Reforming Schools through Learner-Centered Education* (Washington, DC: American Psychological Association, 1998).
16. T. Doyle, *Learner-Centered Teaching: Putting the Research on Learning into Practice* (Sterling, VA: Stylus, 2011).
17. Richard E. Mayer, "Rote versus Meaningful Learning," *Theory into Practice* 41, no. 4 (2002): 226–232.
18. Ibid.
19. Ben Cameron, "Theatre Communications Group Opening Keynote Address," Dance/USA Winter Council Meeting, January 2003.
20. Grant H. Kester, *Conversation Pieces: Community and Communication in Modern Art* (Oakland, CA: University of California Press, 2004).

Chapter 4

1. Alison Morrison, John Breen, and Shameem Ali, "Small Business Growth: Intention, Ability, and Opportunity," *Journal of Small Business Management* 41, no. 4 (2003): 417–425.
2. Bruce D. Thibodeau and Charles-Clemens Rüling, "Nonprofit Organizations, Community, and Shared Urgency: Lessons from the Arts and Culture Sector," *The Journal of Arts Management, Law, and Society* 45, no. 3 (2015): 156–177.

3. George E. Belch and Michael A. Belch, *Advertising and Promotion: An Integrated Marketing Communications Perspective* (New York: McGraw-Hill, 2003).
4. Albert Bandura, "The Evolution of Social Cognitive Theory," in *Great Minds in Management*, ed. K. G. Smith and M. A. Hitt (Oxford: Oxford University Press, 2005), 9–35.
5. Owen A. Bevan, "Marketing Tactics," in *Marketing and Property People* (London: Palgrave, 1991), 156–213.
6. Rajkumar Venkatesan and Paul W. Farris, "Measuring and Managing Returns from Retailer-Customized Coupon Campaigns," *Journal of marketing* 76, no. 1 (2012): 76–94.
7. Thomas O'guinn et al., *Advertising and Integrated Brand Promotion* (Nashville, TN: Nelson Education, 2014).
8. Leonard L. Berry, "Relationship Marketing of Services Perspectives from 1983 and 2000," *Journal of Relationship Marketing* 1, no. 1(2002): 59–77.
9. R. Rentschler, J. Radbourne, R. Carr, and J. Rickard, "Relationship Marketing, Audience Retention and Performing Arts Organisation Viability," *International Journal of Nonprofit and Voluntary Sector Marketing* 7, no. 2 (2002): 118–130.
10. Leonard Berry, "Relationship Marketing of Services Perspectives from 1983 and 2000."
11. Linda D. Molm, Jessica L. Collett, and David R. Schaefer, "Building Solidarity through Generalized Exchange: A Theory of Reciprocity," *American Journal of Sociology* 113, no. 1 (2007): 205–242.
12. John M. T. Balmer et al., "Strong Brands and Corporate Brands," *European Journal of Marketing* 40, no. 7/8 (2006): 742–760.
13. Daniel H. Fine, "Listerine: Past, Present and Future—A Test of Thyme," *Journal of Dentistry* 38 (2010): S2–S5.
14. Nancy R. Lee, "How and Why Segmentation Improves ROI," in *Segmentation in Social Marketing*, ed. T. Dietrich, S. Rundle-Thiele, and K. Kubacki (Singapore: Springer, 2017), 61–74.
15. Ana Roncha and Natascha Radclyffe-Thomas, "How TOMS' 'one day without shoes' Campaign Brings Stakeholders Together and Co-Creates Value for the Brand Using Instagram as a Platform," *Journal of Fashion Marketing and Management* 20, no. 3 (2016): 300–321.

Chapter 5

1. Liz Hill et al., *Creative Arts Marketing* (New York: Routledge, 2017).
2. Richard E. Mayer, "Rote versus Meaningful Learning," *Theory into Practice* 41, no. 4 (2002): 226–232.
3. T. Doyle, *Learner-Centered Teaching: Putting the Research on Learning into Practice* (Sterling, VA: Stylus, 2011).

4. Alan H. Goldman, "Aesthetic Qualities and Aesthetic Value," *The Journal of Philosophy* 87, no. 1 (1990): 23–37.
5. Alex C. Michalos, ed., *Encyclopedia of Quality of Life and Well-Being Research* (Dordrecht: Springer Netherlands, 2014).
6. J. O. Young, "Art and the Educated Audience," *Journal of Aesthetic Education* 44, no. 3 (2010): 29–42.
7. Albert Bandura, "The Evolution of Social Cognitive Theory," in *Great Minds in Management*, ed. K. G. Smith and M. A. Hitt (Oxford: Oxford University Press, 2005): 9–35.
8. Alice Y. Kolb and David A. Kolb, "Experiential Learning Theory: A Dynamic, Holistic Approach to Management Learning, Education and Development," *The SAGE Handbook of Management Learning, Education and Development* 42 (2009): 68.
9. Rosemary Polegato and Rune Bjerke, "Looking Forward: Anticipation Enhances Service Experiences," *Journal of Services Marketing* 33, no. 2 (2019): 148–159.
10. Eleanor L. Brilliant, *The United Way* (New York: Columbia University Press, 1990).
11. Young, "Art and the Educated Audience."

Chapter 6

1. John Dewey, *Art as Experience* (New York: Penguin, 2005).
2. Simon Sinek, *Start with Why: How Great Leaders Inspire Everyone to Take Action* (New York: Penguin, 2009).
3. E. Jerome McCarthy and William D. Perreault, *Basic Marketing*, 15th ed. (Burr Ridge, IL: McGraw Hill Publishing, 2004), 228.
4. Dewey, *Art as Experience*.
5. Philip Kotler and Gary Armstrong, *Principles of Marketing* (New York: Pearson Education, 2010).
6. Ben Cameron, "Ben Cameron at Arts Learning Exchange," Arts Midwest, August 12, 2012, https://transcriptvids.com/v/B7DoJIwrchM.html.
7. Gary Armstrong et al., *Principles of Marketing* (Melbourne, VI: Pearson Australia, 2014).
8. Kant Immanuel, *Critique of Pure Reason* (Cambridge, MA: Charles River Editors, 2018).
9. Martin Zwilling, "Customer Experience Is Today's Business Benchmark," *Forbes* (March 10, 2014): 2014.
10. Pine and Gilmore, *The Experience Economy*.
11. Ibid.
12. Ibid.
13. A. S. Brown and J. L. Novak, *Getting In on the Act: How Arts Groups Are Creating Opportunities for Active Participation* (San Francisco: Wolf Brown, 2011).
14. Dewey, *Art as Experience*.
15. Ibid.

16. Ibid.
17. B. Joseph Pine and James H. Gilmore, *The Experience Economy: Work Is Theatre & Every Business a Stage* (Boston: Harvard Business Press, 1999).
18. Dewey, *Art as Experience*.
19. Pine and Gilmore, *The Experience Economy*.
20. Dewey, *Art as Experience*.
21. Pine and Gilmore, *The Experience Economy*.
22. Dewey, *Art as Experience*.
23. Pine and Gilmore, *The Experience Economy*.
24. Dewey, *Art as Experience*.
25. Ibid.
26. Pine and Gilmore, *The Experience Economy*.
27. Dewey, *Art as Experience*.

Chapter 7

1. John Dewey, *Art as Experience* (New York: Minton, Balch and Co, 1934).
2. Ramond Hendry Williams, "Science: The Mainspring of Art," *Design* 39, no. 4 (1937): 4–6.
3. Simon Sinek, *Start with Why: How Great Leaders Inspire Everyone to Take Action* (New York: Penguin, 2009).
4. E. Jerome McCarthy and William D. Perreault, *Basic Marketing*, 15th ed. (Burr Ridge, IL: McGraw Hill Publishing, 2004).
5. B. Joseph Pine and James H. Gilmore, *The Experience Economy* (Boston: Harvard Business Press, 2011).
6. Henri Neuendorf, "Art Demystified: What Determines an Artwork's Value?" *Artnet*, September 1, 2016, retrieved March 28, 2021, https://news.artnet.com/art-world/art-demystified-non-profits-role-629618.
7. Ben Cameron, "Epilogue: A Speech by Ben Cameron," *Youth Theatre Journal* 13 (1999): 93–104.

Chapter 8

1. John Dewey, *Art as Experience* (New York: Penguin, 2005).
2. Jeffrey Nytch, *The Entrepreneurial Muse: Inspiring Your Career in Classical Music* (New York: Oxford University Press, 2018).
3. Jennifer Radbourne, Hilary Glow, and Katya Johanson, *The Audience Experience: A Critical Analysis of Audiences in the Performing Arts* (Bristol, UK: Intellect Books, 2013).
4. Mark Dietrich Tschaepe, "The Creative Moment of Scientific Apprehension. Understanding the Consummation of Scientific Explanation through Dewey and Peirce," *European Journal of Pragmatism and American Philosophy* 1 (2013): 35.

5. B. Joseph Pine and James H. Gilmore, *The Experience Economy* (Boston: Harvard Business Press, 2011).
6. John Dewey, *Art as Experience* (New York, Capricorn Books, 1939): 35–57.
7. Frazer Ward, *No Innocent Bystanders: Performance Art and Audience* (Hanover: Dartmouth College Press, 2012).
8. Joseph Pine and James H. Gilmore, *The Experience Economy: Work Is Theatre & Every Business a Stage* (Harvard Business Press, 1999).
9. Dewey, *Art as Experience*.
10. Ed Petkus Jr, "Enhancing the Application of Experiential Marketing in the Arts," *International Journal of Nonprofit and Voluntary Sector Marketing* 9, no. 1 (2004): 49–56.
11. T. L. Taylor, "Playing Disney: Experience and Expression in the Land of Curation," Proceedings of DiGRA (2020).
12. Edmund Jerome McCarthy, Stanley J. Shapiro, and William D. Perreault, *Basic Marketing* (Ontario: Irwin-Dorsey, 1979).

Chapter 9

1. L. Motley, "Worth Reviewing: The Four P's: The Internet Has Changed Some of the Ways Companies Approach the Four P's, but the Basics Are Still There. (Customer Satisfaction)," *ABA Banking Journal* 34, no. 3 (2002): 48.
2. Mohammed T. Nuseir and Hilda Madanat, "4Ps: A Strategy to Secure Customers' Loyalty via Customer Satisfaction," *International Journal of Marketing Studies* 7, no. 4 (2015): 78.
3. Kevin L. Webb and C. Jay Lambe, "Internal Multi-Channel Conflict: An Exploratory Investigation and Conceptual Framework," *Industrial Marketing Management* 36, no. 1 (2007): 29–43.
4. Anthony J. Tortorici, "Maximizing Marketing Communications through Horizontal and Vertical Orchestration," *Public Relations Quarterly* 36, no. 1 (1991): 20.
5. The alliance between particular airline companies allows each to book seats on flights operated by the other company or companies.
6. Minhwan Park et al., "Modeling of Purchase and Sales Contracts in Supply Chain Optimization," *Industrial & Engineering Chemistry Research* 45, no. 14 (2006): 5013–5026.
7. Clive Wynne et al., "The Impact of the Internet on the Distribution Value Chain: The Case of the South African Tourism Industry," *International Marketing Review* 18, no. 4 (2001): 420–431.
8. Terry L. Esper et al., "Everything Old Is New Again: The Age of Consumer-Centric Supply Chain Management," *Journal of Business Logistics* 41, no. 4 (2020): 286–293.
9. V. Muthu Krishna, Swathipriya Dhavala, and A. Siddharth, "Operations as Management Science: A Journey towards Building Strategic Customer Centricity," *IIMS Journal of Management Science* 5, no. 1 (2014): 50–66.

10. J. Swartz, "The Doctor's Office: Poor Design May Cost You Patients," *Canadian Medical Association Journal* 140, no. 3 (February 1, 1989): 320–321.
11. Joshua D. Evans, Valorie A. Crooks, and Paul T. Kingsbury, "Theoretical Injections: On the Therapeutic Aesthetics of Medical Spaces," *Social Science & Medicine* 69, no. 5 (2009): 716–721. doi:10.1016/j.socscimed.2009.06.040.
12. Swartz, "The Doctor's Office: Poor Design May Cost You Patients."
13. Jaishikha Nautiyal, "Aesthetic and Affective Experiences in Coffee Shops: A Deweyan Engagement with Ordinary Affects in Ordinary Spaces," *Education and Culture* 32, no. 2 (2016): 99–118. doi:10.5703/educationculture.32.2.0099.
14. Ibid.
15. Ibid.
16. Catherine M. Tucker, *Coffee Culture: Local Experiences, Global Connections*, 1st ed. (New York: Routledge, 2011), 7.
17. Jill H. Casid, "Queer(y)ing Georgic: Utility, Pleasure, and Marie-Antoinette's Ornamented Farm," *Eighteenth-Century Studies* 30, no. 3 (1997): 304–318. doi:10.1353/ecs.1997.0015.
18. Christian Duvernois and François Halard, *Marie-Antoinette and the Last Garden at Versailles* (New York: Rizzoli, 2008).

Chapter 10

1. John Dewey, *Art as Experience* (New York: Penguin, 2005).
2. Karin Botha, Pierre-Andre Viviers, and Elmarie Slabbert, "What Really Matters to the Audience: Analysing the Key Factors Contributing to Arts Festival Ticket Purchases," *South African Theatre Journal* 26, no. 1 (2012): 22–44.
3. Danny Newman, *Subscribe Now! Building Arts Audiences through Dynamic Subscription Promotion* (New York: Theatre Communications Grou, 1977).
4. Ibid.
5. Ruth Rentschler et al., "Relationship Marketing, Audience Retention and Performing Arts Organisation Viability," *International Journal of Nonprofit and Voluntary Sector Marketing* 7, no. 2 (2002): 118–130.
6. Julie A. Nelson, "Household Economies of Scale in Consumption: Theory and Evidence," *Econometrica: Journal of the Econometric Society* 56, no. 6 (1988): 1301–1314.
7. Aaron B. Charlton and T. Bettina Cornwell, "Authenticity in Horizontal Marketing Partnerships: A Better Measure of Brand Compatibility," *Journal of Business Research* 100 (2019): 279–298.
8. Ben Cameron, "Ben Cameron's Remarks at the Arts Learning Xchange," Arts Midwest, July 16, 2009, https://www.artsmidwest.org/files/09MinnesotaSpeechfinalPDFforWebsite72209_2.pdf.
9. G. Frank Mathewson and Ralph A. Winter, "The Economics of Franchise Contracts," *The Journal of Law and Economics* 28, no. 3 (1985): 503–526.

10. Sidney G. Winter and Gabriel Szulanski, "Replication as Strategy," *Organization Science* 12, no. 6 (2001): 730-743.
11. Frédéric Jallat and Michael J. Capek, "Disintermediation in Question: New Economy, New Networks, New Middlemen," *Business Horizons* 44, no. 2 (2001): 55-60.
12. B. Joseph Pine II and James H. Gilmore, *The Experience Economy, with a New Preface by the Authors: Competing for Customer Time, Attention, and Money* (Boston: Harvard Business Press, 2019).
13. Clive Wynne et al., "The Impact of the Internet on the Distribution Value Chain," *International Marketing Review* 18, no. 4 (2001): 420-431.
14. Chad Vergine, "Amazon to Make Themselves the New Ticketmast in the U.S.?," *NYS Music*, accessed January 14, 2021, https://nysmusic.com/2016/11/26/amazon-to-make-themselves-the-new-ticketmaster-in-the-u-s/.
15. Lois Foreman-Wernet, "Reflections on Elitism: What Arts Organizations Communicate about Themselves," *Journal of Arts Management, Law & Society* 47, no. 4 (October 2017): 274-289. doi:10.1080/10632921.2017.1366380.

Chapter 11

1. Victoria Newhouse, *Art and the Power of Placement* (New York: Monacelli Press, 2005).
2. Ann Markusen and Anne Gadwa, *Creative Placemaking* (Washington, DC: National Endowment for the Arts, 2010).
3. *Creative Placemaking*, Arts.gov, www.arts.gov/impact/creative-placemaking.
4. Ibid.
5. Hansjörg Hohr, "The Concept of Experience by John Dewey Revisited: Conceiving, Feeling and 'Enliving,'" *Studies in Philosophy and Education* 32, no. 1 (2013): 25-38.
6. Mark Mattern, "John Dewey, Art and Public Life," *The Journal of Politics* 61, no. 1 (1999): 54-75.
7. Laura Schneider, "Sing for Hope Pianos" (2013).
8. Sing for Hope | museworthy, https://artmodel.wordpress.com/2016/06/20/sing-for-hope/.
9. Ylva Dahlman, "Towards a Theory That Links Experience in the Arts with the Acquisition of Knowledge," *International Journal of Art & Design Education* 26, no. 3 (2007): 274-284.
10. John Dewey, *Art as Experience* (New York: Penguin, 2005).
11. Mehmet Mehmetoglu and Marit Engen, "Pine and Gilmore's Concept of Experience Economy and Its Dimensions: An Empirical Examination in Tourism," *Journal of Quality Assurance in Hospitality & Tourism* 12, no. 4 (2011): 237-255.
12. Newhouse, *Art and the Power of Placement*.

Chapter 12

1. Philip Kotler, *Kotler on Marketing* (New York: Simon and Schuster, 2012).
2. Steve Zaffron and Dave Logan, *The Three Laws of Performance: Rewriting the Future of Your Organization and Your Life* (San Francsico: John Wiley & Sons, 2011).
3. Alan Pomering, "Marketing for Sustainability: Extending the Conceptualization of the Marketing Mix to Drive Value for Individuals and Society at Large," *Australasian Marketing Journal (AMJ)* 25, no. 2 (2017): 157–165.
4. Ibid.
5. Birger Wernerfelt, "The Dynamics of Prices and Market Shares over the Product Life Cycle," *Management Science* 31, no. 8 (1985): 928–939.
6. Ibid.
7. Kotler, *Kotler on Marketing*.
8. Ibid.
9. Ibid.
10. Ibid.
11. Robert C. Blattberg and Kenneth J. Wisniewski, "Price-Induced Patterns of Competition," *Marketing Science* 8, no. 4 (1989): 291–309.
12. Ma Huimin and Jose Antonio Hernandez, "Price Skimming on a Successful Marketing Strategy: Study of iPad Launching as Apple's Innovative Product," *Proceedings of the 8th International Conference on Innovation & Management*, Japan, 2011.
13. Chien-Huang Lin and Jyh-Wen Wang, "Distortion of Price Discount Perceptions through the Left-Digit Effect," *Marketing Letters* 28, no. 1 (2017): 99–112.
14. Ibid.
15. Kotler, *Kotler on Marketing*.
16. Asim Ansari, S. Siddarth, and Charles B. Weinberg, "Pricing a Bundle of Products or Services: The Case of Nonprofits," *Journal of Marketing Research* 33, no. 1 (1996): 86–93.
17. Kotler, *Kotler on Marketing*.
18. Michaela Draganska and Dipak C. Jain, "Consumer Preferences and Product-Line Pricing Strategies: An Empirical Analysis," *Marketing Science* 25, no. 2 (2006): 164–174.

Chapter 13

1. Edmund Jerome McCarthy, Stanley J. Shapiro, and William D. Perreault, *Basic Marketing* (Ontario: Irwin-Dorsey, 1979).
2. Ibid.
3. B. Kolb, "Pricing as the Key to Attracting Students to the Performing Arts," *Journal of Cultural Economics* 21, no. 2 (1997): 139–146.
4. Kara Larson, "Pricing Strategies to Attract Audiences and Keep Them Coming Back for More," *National Arts Marketing Project Arts Marketing Blog*, 2011, https://namp.

americansforthearts.org/2019/05/15/pricing-strategies-to-attract-audiences-and-keep-them-coming-back-for-more.
5. Anthony Rhine, *Marketing the Arts: An Introduction* (Washington, DC: Rowman & Littlefield, 2020).
6. Chen, Yuxin, Oded Koenigsberg, and Z. John Zhang, "Pay-as-You-Wish Pricing," *Marketing Science* 36, no. 5 (2017): 780–791.
7. Jagdish N. Sheth and Can Uslay, "Implications of the Revised Definition of Marketing: From Exchange to Value Creation," *Journal of Public Policy & Marketing* 26, no. 2 (2007): 302–307.
8. David A. Kolb, *Experiential Learning: Experience as the Source of Learning and Development* (New Jersey: FT Press, 2014).
9. Michael Rushton, "Pricing the Arts," *Handbook of Cultural Economics*, 3rd ed. (Massachusetts: Edward Elgar Publishing, 2020).
10. Michael Rushton, *Strategic Pricing for the Arts* (UK: Routledge, 2014).

Chapter 14

1. RaJade M. Berry-James, Brandi Blessett, Rachel Emas, Sean McCandless, Ashley E. Nickels, Kristen Norman-Major, and Parisa Vinzant, "Stepping Up to the Plate: Making Social Equity a Priority in Public Administration's Troubled Times," *Journal of Public Affairs Education* 27, no. 1 (2021): 5–15.
2. Steve Zaffron and Dave Logan, *The Three Laws of Performance: Rewriting the Future of Your Organization and Your Life*, vol. 170 (San Francisco: John Wiley & Sons, 2011).
3. Edmund Jerome McCarthy, Stanley J. Shapiro, and William D. Perreault, *Basic Marketing* (Ontario: Irwin-Dorsey, 1979).
4. Laura L. Vedenhaupt, "Analyzing the Relationship between Social Media Usage and Ticket Sales at Small Nonprofit Performing Arts Organizations" (DBA diss., Capella University, 2016).
5. Joanne Bernstein, *Standing Room Only: Marketing Insights for Engaging Performing Arts Audiences* (New York: Springer, 2017).
6. John Savage, "The Effect of Video on Demand Services on the Cinema Industry," Letterkenny Institute of Technology. Dissertation. July 2014.
7. J. Panzera, "9 Shows that Originated at the Public," *TodaysTix.com*, September 6, 2016, accessed April 9, 2021, https://www.todaytix.com/insider/nyc/posts/9-shows-that-originated-at-the-public.
8. "Delacorte Theatre," *CentralPark.com*, accessed April 9, 2021, https://www.centralpark.com/things-to-do/attractions/delacorte-theater/.
9. Helen Epstein, *Joe Papp: An American Life* (Massachusetts: Plunkett Lake Press, 2019).
10. C. Murphy and K. Landis, "The Public Theater's Mobile Unit: Lean and Mean Shakespeare. American Theatre," *Theatre Communications Group*, March 3, 2017, accessed April 9, 2021, www.americantheatre.org/2017/03/29/the-public-theaters-mobile-unit-lean-and-mean-shakespeare.

11. Ibid.
12. Carol Kaufman-Scarborough, "Publicly-Researchable Accessibility Information: Problems, Prospects and Recommendations for Inclusion," *Social Inclusion* 7, no. 1 (2019): 164–172.
13. Albert Bandura, "Self-Efficacy: Toward a Unifying Theory of Behavioral Change," *Psychological Review* 84, no. 2 (1977): 191.
14. Berry-James et al., "Stepping Up to the Plate."
15. Muhammad Tariq Khan, "The Concept of 'Marketing Mix' and Its Elements (A Conceptual Review Paper)," *International journal of information, business and management* 6, no. 2 (2014): 95.

Index

For the benefit of digital users, indexed terms that span two pages (e.g., 52–53) may, on occasion, appear on only one of those pages.

access, 213–14
accessibility, 230–31, 240–41
active learning, 96
advertisement, 54–55
advertising objectives, 52–53
advertising objectives, 75–76
aesthetic experience, 85
aesthetic qualities, 85
aesthetic value, 84–85
aesthetics, 84–85, 187
Ahmadi, Sandra, 200–2
Amazon, 116, 163, 182–83
Amazon Tickets, 182–83
American Cancer Society, 115
American Heart Association, 8
American Red Cross, 8, 115
American Repertory Theater, 154
American Theatre Magazine, 239–40
Amsterdam and Partners, 200–2
Apple, 78–79
Art as Experience, 9, 139
artist process, 86
artists and education, 100–1
audience development, 5–6, 7
audience involvement spectrum, 37–38
audience motivation, 40
audience neglect, 86
audience replacement, 30
audience talk engagement, 7
audience-as-artist, 38–39

Barnum, 150
Barrett, Felix, 154–57, 166–67, 245
Basic Marketing: A Managerial Approach, 13
Bedandbreakfast.com, 181
Bergauer, Aubrey, 45, 46–49, 246

Berry, Leonard, 76–77
Bezos, Jeff, 182–83
Bhola, Shareeza, 236, 238
Borden, Neil, 10–14, 19, 21–22, 25–26
Borwick, Doug, 9, 21–22
Botswana, 104–7
BP, 193
brand, 77–78, 90, 99–100
Broadway tour, 133–34
Bundle pricing, 210
Buy one get one, 209

California Symphony, 45, 46–49, 246
Cameron, Ben, 25, 63, 111–12, 134–35, 179–80
Canadian Medical Association Centre for Practice Productivity, 167
capital items, 114–15
Carr, Eugene, 41–42, 43–44
channel conflict, 161
channel design, 182
channel length, 160, 178–79
channel management, 164
Chateau de Versailles, 169
Cherry Orchard, The, 156
churches, 8
civic engagement, 5–6, 7
co-creation, 38, 43–44
Colbert, Francois, 10
Coleman, Cy, 150
collaborative learning, 96
commercialized art, 24, 86, 100–1
Commonwealth Shakespeare Company, 202–4, 247
communication loop, 80
community engagement, 7, 22, 23
community outreach, 22

community service, 22
competition, 206, 227
competition pricing, 208–11
Concept of the Marketing Mix, The, 11
conformance quality, 116
Conner, Lynne, 34
Consenses, 140–45, 244–45
constructivism, 58–59
consumer-centric logistics, 164–65
contractual system, 161–62, 180–81
control, 188
core customer level, 112
corporate social responsibility, 56
cost, 206, 226
cost-based pricing, 207–8, 226, 228
cost-plus pricing, 207–8, 228
Crash of Elysium, The, 157
created materials, 114–15
Creative Arts Marketing, 83
creative placemaking, 186, 194
credibility, 68–69
critics, 68–69
crowd-sourcing, 38
CTS Eventim, 182
cues, negative, 122–23
cues, positive, 122
customer experience, 118, 145, 152
customer participation, 120–21
customer service, 116

Dale, Jim, 150
Delacorte Theater, 236, 239
demand, 206, 226–27
demographics, 84, 96
determining objectives, 93–94
Dewey, John, 9, 66–67, 103, 109, 121–24, 131, 139, 146, 147–48, 151, 195
direct marketing, 160–61
discounts, 72
disintermediation, 162, 181
Disney, 111–12, 120, 132–34, 147, 149
disruption, 196–97
distribution channels, 160
distribution logistics, 164–65
donations, 20–21, 221–22
downstream distribution channels, 159, 176
Drexel, Judith, 216–21, 224

Dunkin' Donuts, 168
dynamic pricing, 227

E.T., 55
ease, 212–13
ease of exchange, 213
echoing, 249
economic engagement, 7
economies of scale, 178
economy, 206–7
ecosystem, 166
educational elitism, 40
educational objectives, 92–93
effectiveness, 249
employee engagement, 36
encouragement, 249
engagement, 28–29
enhanced product, 140
Enigma Theatre Productions, 106–7
enjoyment for audiences, 98
entertainment, 40
entertainment, 121–22
Entrepreneurial Muse, The, 139–40
environment plan, 188
environmental aesthetics, 187
environmental management, 166
environmental partners, 188–89
environs, 165
equilibrium, 133
equitable, 230–31
escapism, 121–22
evaluation, 95
evolution, 249–50
exchange, 213
exclusive distribution, 182
exclusive intermediaries, 163–64
Experience Economy, The, 134
extinction, 249–50

Faust, 155–56
Ferrari 116
festivals, 104
Fillis, Ian, 15
FLASH Pass, The, 150–51
focus group, 88
Forbes, 118
Ford, 116
Forum Shops at Caesar's Palace, 148

franchise, 180
franchise contract, 161–62
Freire, Paulo, 58
Funerals, 104

Geico, 54–55
Gerontologist, The, 42–43
Gilmore, James H., 103, 119–22, 146, 147–48, 187, 195–96, 213
globalization of commerce, 7
goal setting, 95, 96

Hamlet 360, 202–4
Hard Rock Café, 120
Harvard Business Review, 119
health and well-being engagement, 7
Hershey Company, 55
hook, 68, 71–72
horizontal marketing, 161, 179

I Amsterdam City Card, 181, 200–2
IBM, 120
inbound logistics, 164–65
indirect marketing, 160–61
information-based communication, 67–68, 83–84
informative advertisements, 53
intensive distribution, 182
intensive intermediaries, 163–64
interaction, 176–77
Internal Revenue Service, 8
international brands, 19

Jacobs, Bernard, 227
James Irvine Foundations, 37
Jekowsky, Barry, 46
Juilliard, 105, 189–90

Kant, Immanuel, 118
Kolb, David H., 225–26
Kotler, Philip J., 11, 111–12

Landis, Kevin, 239–40
learner-centered education, 59
learner-centered teaching, 96
learning objectives, 95–96
lease, 224
left-digit-effect, 209

life enrichment, 40
Lin and Wang, 209
Listerine, 79
LiveNation Entertainment, 182
Liverpool John Moores University, 15
location, 235–40
logistics, 164–65
Louis Vuitton, 114, 219–20
luxury pricing, 210

Madison and Vine, 54–55
Maitisong Festival, 105
Maler, Steve, 202–4
Manscott Puppet Club, 171, 172–73, 195
Marie Antoinette, 169
markup pricing, 207–8
Mars Inc., 55
Maslow, 34–35, 42–43, 59–60
Mayer, Richard, 62
McCarthy, Jerome, 10–11, 13, 14, 15, 19, 21–22, 45, 51, 103, 110–17, 133–34, 136, 146, 151–52, 201–2, 205, 215, 222, 237, 243, 244–45, 246
memorabilia, 123, 149
Mercedes-Benz, 223
Metropolitan Museum of Art, 224
Metropolitan Opera, 229
Middle English, 132
Midsummer Night's Dream, 87
Milne, Patricia, 167–68
mission, 20
Mobile Unit, 239–40
Monk, Otis, 172–73, 195
motivation, 34–35
MoviePass, 181
Murphy, Ciara, 239–40
Mycoskie, Blake, 80–81

National Guild for Community Arts Education, 23
Nautiyal, Jaishikha, 168–69
New York Foundation, 237
New York Magazine, 193
Newman, Danny, 86–87, 177
North Shore Music Theatre, 150
Ntseme, Moletedi One, 103, 104–7, 244–45
Nytch, Jeffrey, 139–40

obstacles, 230
optional pricing, 210, 229
outbound logistics, 164–65

Paiget, Jean, 58–59
Papp, Joseph, 236, 237, 238–39, 247
participation economy, 38–39
participatory public art, 38
Paul, Michelle, 41–42, 43–44
pay-what-you-can, 224, 228–29
Pedagogy of the Oppressed, 58
penetration pricing, 208
performance quality, 116
persuasion, 66
persuasive advertisements, 53–54
Pine II, B. Joseph, 103, 119–22, 146, 147–48, 187, 195–96, 213
point of consummation, 146
Pollock, Jackson, 135
Porsche, 116
premium pricing, 210, 229
prestige pricing, 210
price skimming, 209, 229
pricing factors, 226–27
pricing mix, the, 211
pricing strategies, 207–8, 228–29, 232–33
process art, 135–36
product attributes, 115–17
product features, 116
product placement, 55
product quality, 116
product style and design, 116–17
product use, 79
product-line pricing, 210–11
products, actual, 113
products, augmented, 113
products, consumer, 113
products, convenience, 113
products, industrial, 113, 114–15
products, shopping, 114
products, specialty, 114
products, unsought, 114
Progressive, 54–55
promotion mix, 51–52, 75
promotional messaging, 66–75
Prospero, 85, 90–91, 246
psychographics, 84
psychological pricing, 209

public relations, 80–81
Public Theater, The, 202–3, 236, 239–40
purchasing power, 206
push advertisements, 51

Queen's hamlet, The, 169

Rainforest Café, 120
raw materials, 114–15
real-time pricing, 227
Reece's Pieces, 55
relationship marketing, 76–77
religious ceremonies, 8
reminder advertisements, 54, 83–84
renaissance festivals, 120
Renstcheler, Ruth, 15, 76
retail cooperative, 180, 181
retail sponsored system, 161–62
retention advertisements, 54
reverse logistics, 164–65
Riker's Island Correctional Facility, 239–40
Riverside Community College, 86
Romeo and Juliet, 237, 239–40
running cost, 178

sales pitch, 101
Scars Project, 106–7
Scheff, Joanne, 11
schools and engagement, 31–32
selective distribution, 182
selective intermediaries, 163–64
self-efficacy, 241–42
service, 134–35
Shakespeare in the Park, 236, 239–40
Shakespeare, William, 8, 87–89, 90–91, 136
Shelley, Lisa, 216–17, 218, 219–20
Sheth, Jagdish N., 225
Shubert Organization, 227
Sinek, Simon, 109, 133
Sing for Hope Pianos, 189, 190, 192–93, 245
single ticket buyers, 87
Six Flags Magic Mountain, 150–51
Sleep No More, 154–57, 159, 245
social experience, 140–45
social hedonism, 40

social integration, 62–63
social interaction, 35
social marketing, 56
social media influencers, 55
socialization, 62–63
societal marketing, 56
Spas.com, 181
sponsored chain system, 161–62
spontaneity, 151
Standing Room Only, 11
Starbucks, 161, 168, 179
Subscribe Now!, 86–87
subscriptions, 68, 71–72, 87
supply chain management, 164–65
survey, 38
sustainable development, 56
Swartz, J., 167–68
systems analysis, 166

talk backs, 33, 38
tangible, 132
Target, 161, 179
Taylor, Sally, 140–45, 244–45
technological advances, 37
The Tempest, The, 90–91
The Doris Duke Charitable
   Foundations, 41–42
Theatre Bay Area, 41–42
Theatre Development Fund, 41–42
theme, 122
TicketMaster, 160–61, 182
Tiffany & Co., 114
time, 233–34
timeshares, 99

Toms Shoes, 80–81
Tosca, 128
Toyota, 116
trade shows, 120
triple bottom line, 56
Triple Play, 41–42
Tucker, Catherina, 168

United Way, 99
University of Leeds, 7
upselling, 79–80
upstream distribution channels,
   159, 176–77
utilitarian products, 66–67

Valencia Dance Ensemble, 69
value exchange, 42
value-based pricing, 208, 228–29
values, 20
variable pricing, 227
vertical marketing, 161
vision, 20
Vygotsky, Lev, 58–59

Walmart, 163, 219–20, 223
Walmsley, Ben, 7, 9–11, 23, 40–41, 43
weddings, 104
Whole Foods, 111–12
wholesaler system, 161–62
Woetzel, Damian, 194

Yunus, Monica, 189–91, 192–93

Zamora, Camille, 189–91, 192